SERMON HEARTS

SERMON HEARTS

By

WILLIAM H. LEACH

Editor of *Church Management*

Author of "Church Administration," "Church Finance,"
"Church Publicity," etc.

THE AUTHOR PLACES WITHIN THIS VOLUME THE CONDENSED OUTLINES
OF ONE HUNDRED AND FIFTY GREAT SERMONS BY MANY PREACHERS

COKESBURY PRESS
NASHVILLE

SET UP, ELECTROTYPED, PRINTED, AND
BOUND AT NASHVILLE, TENNESSEE
UNITED STATES OF AMERICA

R

INTERPRETING THIS BOOK

THE work of the author of this book has been largely that of an editor and copy writer. He has sought to be fair to the writer of each sermon and has endeavored to present in a few words the outline and heart of each sermon studied. Where he has disagreed with the theology of the preacher his personal views have been subordinated to the desire to present the view of the author of the sermon. In some instances he has felt that a few touches could improve the plan of sermon development, but here again he has kept to the idea of being loyal to the original text.

It is a difficult task to crowd even the heart of a great sermon into six hundred words. Typography has been asked to help the typewriter. Thus the Bible texts appear in *italics*. All division headings are set off clearly by themselves. All material directly quoted appears in solid type (no white space between the lines). When quotation marks appear around these insertions the quotation is from some author other than the writer of the sermon. When the quotation is from the author of the sermon the solid material appears without any quotes. The source is given where it appears in the original sermon.

The sermons appear in Biblical order. In this way any text can be instantly located and the volume used as a Bible commentary. Several sermons which have no Bible texts appear in the last pages of the volume. Immediately following this preface is a table listing material for special seasons. A complete subject index and author's index will be found in the last pages.

I want to extend my appreciation for the coöperation I have had from the various publishing houses which have permitted the study of their published material. In each instance you will find the source of each sermon given. I hope that many will be sufficiently interested in the material given to read the complete text of the original sermons which have formed the basis of this study.   WILLIAM H. LEACH.

CLEVELAND, OHIO.

SERMONS ADAPTED TO SPECIAL DAYS

(Number of Sermon given, not page)

CONTENTS

CONTENTS

CONTENTS

CUI BONO?[1]

And the gold of that land is good. Genesis 2: 12.

In the bulk window of a Philadelphia bookstore, somebody, some time ago, piled up twenty books, and on the topmost volume placed the skull of a human skeleton and at the bottom of the pile on a neatly printed placard these two Latin words, "Cui bono?" The books were the production of an author, long dead, and the skull the author's skull. Once it had furnished residence for a mighty brain: now it grinned at the top of the author's life output, as if in appreciation of the post-mortem joke suggested by the Latin words at the bottom. Brusquely translated, "Cui bono" cynically asks the question, "What's the use?"

This does not tell the whole story. There is more to it. Culture is worth while. But it has a threefold advantage and a single obligation.

I. SELF-DISCOVERY

THE man of culture is a man of ideas. Failure nine times out of ten is ignorance. But culture is not alone a matter of ideas but also of ideals. The mark of growth is interrogation. When a man stops asking questions he stops growing. This is the age of the specialist, and everywhere training counts. The trained eye, the trained hand, the trained head will succeed in the long run.

II. CULTURE HAS THE ADVANTAGE OF SELF-RESPECT

The foundation of self-respect goes back into the very origin of a person's being. Heredity has something to do with it, and environment has something to do with it; but neither has everything to do with it. Heredity is not fatality. The man who is not well-born still has left open to him the whole field of opportunity.

[1] By John Snape in "Soul Trapping." Judson Press.

Then self-respect has a great deal to do with the matter of belief. Every man ought to ask himself, "What opinions do I hold concerning God, faith, and Christian experience?" For what a man believes has much to do with the quality of his character.

III. THE THIRD ADVANTAGE OF CULTURE IS SELF-CONTROL

Self-control is concreted gentleness. Jesus Christ was the most perfect gentleman the world ever knew. He was a gentle man. Think of his standing with calmness and poise before those who persecuted him.

Self-control is character in a sovereign way. It does not mean stoicism and stagnation.

IV. THE OBLIGATION OF CULTURE IS SELF-INVESTMENT

This is a universal obligation. No one is freed from the obligation of self-investment. No man is too low nor too high to be excused from social responsibilities, and social responsibilities mean self-investment.

Then this is an altruistic obligation. The commercial spirit is not the dominating spirit in the world after all. If it were, half the preachers in America would resign their jobs.

"How beautiful it is to be alive!
To wake each morn as if the Maker's grace
Did us afresh from nothingness derive,
That we might sing, 'How happy is our case!
How beautiful it is to be alive.'"
(Henry Septimus Sutton.)

THE FLAMING SWORD [1]

So he drove out the man; and he placed at the east of the gar-den of Eden Cherubims, and a flaming sword which turned every way, to keep the way of the tree of life. Genesis 3: 24.

TAKEN literally, these words baffle our understanding. But as symbols of great historic facts they are overpowering in their conception.

I. EDEN

Perhaps for most of us the word Eden has a meaning similar to the Kingdom of God. We picture some time in the distant past when God was really in the hearts of his people. Humanity was happy. We dream that again some day we may find the world in that condition. In the darkest hours mankind has dreamed of Eden. In some respects it seems farther away than ever before, but there has never been a time when so many people have been working, praying, and hoping for Eden as at the present time.

II. EDEN LOST

We may question the historical accuracy of this Bible story. None can question its Divine significance.

We all have lost in our own lives our little garden. We lived in it for a while. We look back to it sometimes with longing. "Heaven lies about us in our infancy."

Simplicity has been lost out of life with the coming of the complex age. Machinery is driving out personality. Education has advanced, but with it have come pride, doubts, unbelief. The things which should make people grateful seem to

[1] By John Edward Bushnell in "Best Sermons, 1924." Harcourt, Brace.

make them unthankful. Vanity and pride keep producing wars. And yet there is Eden. It may be in the distance, but the heart knows that it is there.

III. THE FLAMING SWORD

The sword is that which keeps men out of the Garden of Eden. One must have the secret of entrance. Men are not happy because they have violated certain fundamental laws of life. Right obeyed is the secret of wisdom. In physical life, in social life, in business life, we find this thing true. But the flaming sword not alone keeps us out of Eden. As well, it lights the way to entrance. It shows us how to get in.

IV. THE SHEATHING DAY

Let us make no mistake about it. Happiness is found only when the eternal truths are held in reverence and the everlasting laws obeyed. We may think that we can suspend that what one sows that shall he reap. But the sword is at the gate. The farmer must obey the laws that govern the land or accept an empty granary.

There is coming the day. There is the gate lightened by the flaming sword. It lies beyond the unrest, the loss of faith, the widespread despair, the prevalence of evil. To that day Christ pledged his life.

Yet there may be no sheathing day for Eden's sword. Rather by faith we see it now delivered into the wounded hand of one returning from great wars, victorious. No longer does it tell of the exile from true life, but it beckons homeward where, through the gate, Christ marshals back his own.

CONVICT NUMBER ONE [1]

Where is thy brother? Genesis 4: 9.

THIS was God's second question. The first was, "Where art thou?" That is not selfish. A man must know the way to the light before he brings his brother there.

I. CAIN IS A BROTHER TO OURSELVES

It is hard to believe that, you say. You think of Cain the murderer. But look at Cain as a baby in the home and as a child. When he was born his mother held him fast and said, "I have gotten a man from the Lord." So she named him that—Cain. His mother never dreamed that he would become a murderer. Instead she thought that he was the Christ child.

II. THE TROUBLE WITH CAIN WAS THAT THERE WAS NO VITAL CON-NECTION BETWEEN HIS RELIGION AND MORALITY

The first view of wrongdoing we have with Cain is at the religious altar of sacrifice. That is one of the tragedies of religion. Cain was religious—every man is. But he lacked that vital spark which makes religion so vital in the experience of man.

Cain is not alone in this. A woman who has been traveling in Italy tells me that she saw indulgences hanging up beside onions in the villages. It is said of Louis XI that he never sinned quite as gleefully as when he was praying or just after he prayed.

Believe me, there is but one way to get our offerings accepted before the Lord. That is to come in a spirit of repentance, to come really desiring to get rid of our sins.

[1] By Clovis G. Chappell in "The Village Tragedy and Other Sermons." Cokesbury Press.

There is no more utter mockery in the sight of God than bringing to God an offering of prayer—for instance, a prayer for pardon—when we expect to commit the same old sin the next day.

III. CAIN'S REAL SIN WAS ENVY

Murder was the consequence of his real sin, which was envy born in selfishness. Envy has always been a murderer. It comes upon the first page of human history. And it has been a murderer from then to now. It was envy that made Saul seek to kill David. It was envy that cast Daniel into a den of lions. It was envy that prompted Elizabeth to murder Mary Queen of Scots. It was envy that drove the nails into the hands and feet of Christ.

IV. WHERE IS THY BROTHER?

God is asking that question of each person here. Where is your friend, your roommate, your business associate? Where is your own boy? Perhaps you will reply that you will go your way, and your brother can go his. You will answer as Cain did, "Am I my brother's keeper?" The man who first asked that question of God was a murderer. Your evasion of the responsibility of your brother is just where Cain started on his murderous road.

THE CHOKED WELLS [1]

And Isaac digged again the wells of water, which they had digged in the days of Abraham his father. Genesis 26: 18.

ISAAC was a rich and prosperous man when he pitched his tent in the valley of Gerar. And it was in the valley of Gerar, where he dwelt, that he digged again the wells of his father Abraham. I want to spiritualize the text; raise it to the standard of Christ.

I. THE WELLS OF OUR FATHERS MAY GET CHOKED

They *may* get choked, not *must*. Not every well gets choked. There is the well of Jacob, for instance. For centuries it had been used, and Jesus drank from it when he wearied. Such wells are those kept open by the grace of God.

But the more common experience is that the wells which refresh the fathers become choked and cannot serve the children. They thirst, but the old wells are closed. Symbolically one of the most striking instances is that of the law of Moses in the time of Christ. Originally the law was a well of living water, but under the interpretations of the Pharisees and rabbis it had been choked.

The same thing is true of the Gospels. Take the central doctrine of the sacrifice on Calvary. It was sweet and fresh until it became choked by stilted theological interpretation. So the children go away thirsty from the place where the fathers drank.

The same is true of the sacraments and of the Bible.

II. WE MUST DIG FOR OURSELVES TO REACH THE WATER

One great blight upon the Church to-day is that men and

---

[1] By G. H. Morrison in "Flood-Tide." Hodder and Stoughton.

women will not dig. One of the most impressive parables Jesus gave was that of the man who built his house upon the rock. There is one fine touch in that parable which is almost lost in our English version. We are told that the man digged deep. But it is more than that. It is that he digged and kept on deepening. He digs until he is worn out and tired. But then, striking rock, he knows that he has a firm foundation for his house.

You can always tell when a man has been digging for himself by the freshness and individuality of his religion. There are surface-faced Christians who cannot afford to be original. The humblest souls, if they dig for themselves, will find water, and will have a note in their music that never was heard before. They will know that God is their own.

III. OUR REDISCOVERED WELLS HAVE BEEN LONG SINCE NAMED

The neighbors who gathered around Isaac thought that these were all new wells. But when he told them their names they remembered the wells of Abraham from which they drank as children. The man who is in earnest about the spiritual life will be always digging. He will find water. It is a great thrill. God has been good to him. At first he thinks that this well is his alone. But then he finds its name, and he knows that others know of it. A previous generation has received life from it.

They are the very waters that our fathers drank; but the toil and the effort, the struggle and the prayer that it took to reach them, made them so fresh to us that we thought they were a new thing in the world.

WHERE DO YOU LIVE?[1]

This is none other but the house of God. Genesis 28: 17.

THIS is a rather puzzling statement from this young man, Jacob. He is standing on a rather barren hillside. He has spent the night there with a stone for a pillow and the stars for lights. There is no temple, no dwelling, not even a tent, naught but a barren hillside, yet Jacob said it was God's house, a place where divine presence had been manifest.

Where do you live? The question has not to do with your location, but with your faith and vision. Do you live on a mere hillside or in God's house? Do you live in a mere house or a temple? You may live in either and not call for a moving van.

There is the story of the little lad who lived on the hillside and whose favorite pastime was gazing across the valley to the opposite hill at a house with golden windows. When given permission one day he started out to find that house and examine those windows. Down the hill, across the valley, and up the hill he went and found a very old house, with very ordinary windows; after a fruitless search for the house with the golden windows, he asked a little girl if she knew where such a house might be. "O yes," said she, "here, I shall show you"—and she pointed across the valley to yonder hill and designated his own house, all aglow with windows of gold. Where do you live? Regardless of location, you may have bright, shining golden windows, you may have a holy temple, a house which God will be pleased to honor with his presence.

I. OLD HOUSES

Some people I know live in old houses, the houses of yesterday, houses of memories. Older people are proud to dwell in these old houses, but they are not the only ones who thus live in the past. It may be that those days that are gone were filled

[1] By G. Charles Weaver in *Church Management*.

23

with life's greatest joy or with life's greatest sorrow, but they are gone; do not let the joys of yesterday shut you out from the joy of to-day.

II. NEW HOUSES

Some other people I know live in new houses—houses, they say, which have nothing to do with the old or past; no influence from the past has entered their dwelling. But such a house has really never been builded. What I am to-day is the result of influences that have touched my life in days gone by. The past has helped to make the present. And we live our lives to-day as we live them, with their joy, comfort, and success, because of contributions from the past. A father, a mother, a friend, a countless multitude each gave a share, large or small, that helped to make life what it is for us. While the past is not for us to live in, neither is it to be ignored or forgotten.

III. DREAM HOUSES

Then there are still others I have met who seemingly live in dream houses. I suppose we might call these houses air castles. They are really beautiful things, these dream houses. They are built out of the things we would like to do and out of the good we intend to do. They represent what we would like to be and what we hope to accomplish. It is a fine thing to dream thus; we shall never build anything really worth while or beautiful unless we do first build this dream house. But these dream houses or air castles are not to live in; they are merely the ideals, the plans which shall enable us to build real houses in which we may live. These people who live in dream houses are wasting their time with idle wishing and dreaming instead of doing.

Let us take the best of the old, let us take the finest of the new, let us take the most lofty ideals and build for us a house. Let us shut out the discord, let us make love supreme, and you shall see that God shall come into such a house to dwell.

THE VISION SPLENDID [1]

I will turn aside and see this great sight. Exodus 3: 3.

What the burning bush really was no one will ever know. Trees and bushes on a countryside have often a story attached to them, as all readers of Thomas Hardy well know. To another than Moses the fire might have been some trick of the midday sun blazing down on an isolated desert thorn. There are in natural objects gateways or sacraments which lead us straight to God. . . . David Livingstone tells that in a moment of great discouragement he was emboldened to persevere in his great task of exploration by the sudden sight of some flowers at his feet.

I. AT THE BURNING BUSH MOSES RECEIVED HIS BAPTISM OF SPIRITUAL POWER

THERE is a spiritual power which blazes and burns, yet does not exhaust itself. It is a greater passion than that of social zeal and human sympathy. Moses was naturally a sympathetic man. His heart burned within him when a fellow Hebrew was bullied by the oppressor. But it was not that kind of power which was revealed in the burning bush. Then there is a kind of thinking such as is revealed in a recent book entitled "My Hopes and Fears for the Church." Feverish thinking may, itself, be a sign of failure of nerve. Surely to-day we need to seek the burning bush to find the power which does not exhaust or spend itself.

II. WE MUST TURN ASIDE TO SEE THIS GREAT SIGHT

This business of finding God is something which demands concentration. He who starts out to find God everywhere may end by finding him nowhere. Moses was about to receive a revelation, and a revelation is not just information about God.

[1] By R. H. Strachan in the *Scots Observer*.

God was about to say to this man, "I am." That is very different from hearing another say of him, "He is." "I am the bread of life," will feed a hungry soul. "He is the bread of life," may make us feel like a hungry man gazing at food in a shop window. "I am the good shepherd," says Jesus, and then we say, "Thy rod and thy staff they comfort me."

Those who want to hear the "I am" need to turn aside and concentrate for the personal experience.

III. TURN ASIDE IN REVERENCE

"The place whereon thou standest is holy ground." We need to learn anew to-day what holy ground really is. Calvary is the most holy spot on earth. The burning bush was a holy place in the dim distant history of Israel, and its fire is an eternal fact. To the superstitious holy ground may be a dangerous place. The careless comer may receive hurt if he treads lightly. To the serious worshiper Calvary is both a blessed and a hurtful place—even as there are moments when human love hurts us when we take it.

That holy love constrains us. Its pressure pains the heart and grips the conscience. It hurts while it holds with a grasp we would not, if we could, escape. Yet it makes our hearts sore, not only with the sense of our unworthiness but with the sense of the summons to live as he lived. The cross, as Denney once said, only redeems those it inspires.

MEMORIAL DAY [1]

This day shall be unto you for a memorial. Exodus 12:14.

The text is more appropriate to the subject than may appear at the outset. The Jewish Passover, to which it refers, was a memorial by redemption of blood. Decoration Day, at which time we lay our fairest flowers on the graves of soldiers who died that we might live, is likewise a memorial by redemption of blood. Without the shedding of blood there is no remission, and without the shedding of blood there is no civilization.

I. MEMORIAL DAY IS A DAY OF RECOLLECTION

ON Memorial Day we ought to look back over the way we have come as a nation. Ours is a long history and a long tale. It takes us back into the German forests where a few Christian captives told the story of Christ. We trace the history of these converts into the British nation. We see them establish the Magna Charta, the greatest single institution in civic history. We follow them through the English Church to the days of the Reformation. Puritanism becomes established in America. There is the Continental Congress, the Bill of Rights, the Declaration of Independence. There is the War of Revolution, the Civil War, the World War, each bringing its own memories. Memorial Day is a day when we think of all these things.

II. MEMORIAL DAY IS A DAY OF DECORATION

The custom of decorating graves with flowers is wide in its practice. The Jews put the grave near the family home that it might be remembered. The Romans laid violets and roses on the graves of their dead. The Japanese observe death days when photographs of those who have passed on are very much

[1] By Herbert Booth Smith in the *Homiletic Review*, May, 1930.

in evidence. Shintoism has a sort of a decoration day. The souls of those who are dead are supposed to meet at a shrine, and an offering of fruit, rice, vegetables, and other foods is offered them. The Chinese erect buildings as memorials to their famous dead. The Christian custom of keeping the grass on the graves green and planting flowers, symbolizing the resurrection, is one of our most beautiful customs.

> "Salute the sacred dead,
> Who went and return not? Say not so!
> We rather seem the dead, that stayed behind.
> Blow, trumpets, all your exultations blow!
> For never shall their aureoled presence lack. . . .
>   They come transfigured back,
> Secure from change in their high-hearted ways,
> Beautiful evermore, and with the rays
> Of morn on their white shields of expectation."

III. MEMORIAL DAY IS A DAY OF RESOLUTION

There is always a to-morrow following hard on the heels of to-day. . . . Memorial Day ought to see us shake our clenched fists in the face of Mars.

Here is what some recent wars cost: Anglo-French War, 1793-1815, six and one-half billion dollars, two million lives; the Crimean War, 1854-1856, one and one-half billion dollars, one-half million lives; the Boer War, 1900-01, one billion dollars, 90,000 lives; the Russo-Japanese War, 1904-05, two and one-quarter billion dollars, one-half million lives; the United States Civil War, 1861-65, four billion dollars, 6,500,000 lives; United States Spanish War, 1898, $165,000,000, three thousand lives.

And it is estimated that the World War cost ten million lives and the nations will struggle for generations to pay the cost.

THE FIRE AND THE CALF [1]

So they gave it me: then I cast it into the fire, and there came out this calf. Exodus 32: 24.

Aaron was frightened at what he had done. He was afraid of the act himself, and he was afraid of what Moses would say about it. Like all timid men, he trembled before the storm which he had raised. And so he tried to persuade Moses, and perhaps in some degree even to persuade himself, that it was not he that had done this thing.

I. THE FURNACE DID IT

AARON's speech represents a common human disposition. We are all too prone to lay our own sins and shortcomings upon the flames. A man may be cruel and gross, licentious and sinful. But he will take refuge behind this old excuse, saying in our modern language, "I am a victim of circumstances."

And so with the woman of society. "The fire made me do this," she says of her frivolity and pride. And so of the politician and his selfishness and partisanship. "I put my principles into the furnace and this came out." And so of the bigot and his bigotry, the one-sided conservative with his stubborn resistance to all progress, the one-sided radical with his ruthless radicalism.

II. WE EXTEND THIS SAME PHILOSOPHY TO THOSE OVER WHOM WE HAVE RESPONSIBILITY

The father who has never done one thing to make his son an honorable citizen will say after the son has become a profligate that he cannot understand it. He says: "I put him in the world and this came out." The father whose son is a skeptic will say the same thing, though he has never done a thing to

[1] By Phillips Brooks in "Sermons Preached in English Churches." E. P. Dutton & Company.

direct him in the way of the faith. Perhaps he tries to place the responsibility upon the minister.

III. STREAM CURRENTS IN WHICH WE FLOAT LARGELY DETERMINE OUR ACTIONS

There are very few isolated instances of life.

There are currents flowing always in all bad directions. There is a perpetual river flowing toward sensuality and vice. There is a river flowing perpetually toward hypocrisy and religious pretense. . . . And when you have once given yourself up to any of these rivers, then there is quite enough in the continual pressure, in that great movement like a Fate beneath your keel, to make you lose the sense and remembrance that it is by your own will that you are there, and only think of the resistless flow of the river which is always in your eyes and ears.

The man who commits fraud to-day did not do it in a hurry. There is some precedent. There was a beginning. It is a self-deception. Yet it is not always complete. Men who read these words may be planning fraud, but the words check them. They have not so far yielded to the current but that they know the reality of the sin which confronts them.

IV. THE REAL SOURCE OF THIS SPIRIT IS FOUND IN A VAGUE AND DEFECTIVE SENSE OF PERSONALITY

Anything which makes it less clear to a man that he is a responsible individual, standing on his own few inches of earth, tends to demoralize the essential personality.

So the only hope for any of us is in a perfectly honest manliness to claim our sins. "I did it, I did it," let me say of my own wickedness. Let me refuse to listen for one minute to any voice which would make my sins less mine. It is the only honest and only hopeful way, the only way to know and be ourselves.

HOLDING GOD'S HANDS [1]

O, this people have sinned a great sin, and have made them gods of gold. Yet now, if thou wilt forgive their sin—; and if not, blot me, I pray thee, out of thy book which thou hast written. Exodus 32: 31, 32.

JEHOVAH is busy. He cries, "Let me alone;" but Moses persists. He is pleading, not for himself, but for the Israel he loves. Another prayer you will find in Exodus 32: 11, 12, which gives this same appeal.

I. THERE IS A LACK OF SELFISHNESS IN THESE PRAYERS

Moses asks nothing for himself. The fact that God would make a great nation of him does not seem to interest him in the least. He is not going to let himself take the position already given to Abraham. He is interested in Israel, his people. Jehovah has made him their defender, and he intends to act as defender and advocate. Jehovah would be dishonored among the nations if Israel failed. He must give them another opportunity. For this he pleads. He feels that in making the prayer he is putting himself in line with God's plan for his people.

II. THERE IS IN THIS PRAYER A DEEP LOVE FOR ISRAEL

He knows that Israel has sinned, and he does not belittle the offense. His good soul is aghast at their perfidy as shown in the making of the golden calf. They have indeed "sinned a great sin." But he pleads for forgiveness. Moses did not want to live if Israel was to be discredited. If they could not have a fresh start, then "blot me, I pray thee, out of thy book which thou hast written." With Moses God was first, Israel second, and Moses forgotten.

[1] By Enos Kincheloe Cox in "Where Is the Lord God of Elijah?" Bible Institute Colportage Association.

When a man prays who is willing to put God first in everything, and is willing to be blotted out rather than that his cause should suffer loss, and can be moved by no motives of self-interest, then by all the laws of his holy, compassionate nature God must listen to that man.

III. THESE PRAYERS GLOW WITH AN ABIDING AND CONSUMING EAGERNESS

Many of us think of Moses as a man of meek and quiet spirit. He has been pictured as one who was never swept by mighty passions. But this concept is wrong. His meekness was that of a God-taught self-control. Moses was a volcano within. He was an Etna or a Vesuvius, a great flaming furnace of a man whose nature ran deep and strong.

God is forced by his very nature to heed prayers like those of Moses. The wonderful thing about this is that Moses seemed unconscious of the wonderful thing that he was doing. Great prayers are usually self-conscious. People like Moses are willing to be called fanatics, but they have no time to worry about what people think of them.

Moses in prayer was a greater man than Moses as a leader. His prayers were great; he could pray anywhere. God and Moses were working at the same things. They frequently went into conference.

But the man who prayed like that could not die. In that cry is the very essence of all that makes for life eternal. The man who could so lose his life found it more abundantly and belongs to the ages.

THE TALEBEARER [1]

Thou shalt not go up and down as a talebearer among thy people. Leviticus 19: 16.

"Boys flying kites haul in their white-winged birds;
But you can't do that way when you're flying words.
'Careful with fire' is good advice we know;
'Careful with words' is ten times doubly so."

(Carleton.)

Dr. J. G. W. Ward, in his very interesting book, "Cameos from Calvary," relates a story concerning a talebearer that is much to the point. A certain woman became a menace in her neighborhood on account of her gossiping tongue. No one's reputation was safe, and no one could restrain her. Finally, in desperation, they brought her to her parish priest. He was an understanding man. He listened to the story and imposed upon her a strange penance. "Take," he said, "a hundred small feathers, and drop them one by one from this milepost to the next." That did not seem hard to do. "And then," he continued, "come back by the same way, and gather them up and bring them to me again." Some time later she stood before her confessor with only a few feathers in her hand, for as she had dropped them the wind had scattered them far and wide. "You see, my daughter, what this means," he said. "Your words lightly spoken are as feathers dropped by the way. But they are quickly carried far beyond the hope of recovery, and fall where we cannot trace them."

I. THE WORDS OF A TALEBEARER ARE SCATTERED LIKE FEATHERS IN THE WIND

HERE our figure breaks down, for they are not as innocent as feathers, nor do they fall so lightly. The psalmist likens them to flying arrows. And how deeply they wound! The recollection of them remains, like irritating bits of shot and shell

---

[1] By Costen J. Harrell in "Friends of God." Cokesbury Press.

which soldiers sometimes carry in their bodies after their wounds are outwardly healed. A backbiting tongue strikes at what we hold dearest, our good name and reputation, and it is easier for us to forgive and forget an act of injustice than to pardon a slurring remark or a libelous report. There are no wounds more irritating or more difficult to heal than the wounds which evil words inflict.

II. GOSSIPING IS THE MOST INJURIOUS PASTIME

Only God can measure the harm done in every community by men and women who find an unwholesome delight in dissecting their neighbors' reputation and spreading every evil tale. They "whet their tongue like a sword, and bend their bows to shoot their arrows, even bitter words" (Psalm 64: 3). A gossip-loving tongue is no respecter of persons. Often it smites the good name of the innocent. A multitude of men and women with a past would be able to live down the painful mistakes of other days and become an asset to their neighborhood were it not for little tête-a-tête gatherings where talebearers meet. We would do infinitely better if we would blot their transgressions out of our book of remembrance, as God does, and lend them a helping hand.

III. AMONG THE GRACES OF CHRISTIAN LOVE NONE IS MORE CHARM- ING THAN THIS: "REJOICETH NOT IN INIQUITY." (1 COR. 1: 13.)

It has no pleasure in discovering a sordid story or repeating it. A love-filled heart manifests itself in a love-controlled tongue. And this is the mark of a love-controlled tongue: It will not parade a brother's shame; it will not speak of it except to remedy a condition or to save another from evil, and then with greatest care. There is sound philosophy and religion in lines that appeared among the "memory gems" in old readers:

> "If wisdom's ways you wisely seek,
> Five things observe with care:
> Of whom you speak, to whom you speak,
> And how, and when, and where."

CONQUERING THE LAND OF PROMISE [1]

Let us go up at once and possess the land, for we are well able to overcome it. Numbers 13 : 30.

There are seven candlesticks in the perfect church, seven lamps in the perfect home, seven seals to the law, and seven colors to the rainbow; the children of Israel marched around Jericho seven times before it fell. So there are seven conquering words for taking the land of promise.

I. RECONNAISSANCE

MOSES was very wise to send spies to find out what sort of country it was that he was expected to take. And we need to make this study in regard to present-day conditions. Just what is America to-day? It is not the America of a generation ago; not the America of our own childhood. Perhaps it is sad that this change has come. But the first step toward righting it is to find out what the conditions are.

II. REVELATION

We must have a revelation of what God wants. Some years ago while hunting in Canada our dog with a long pedigree pointed at nothing but field mice and grasshoppers. Some people are like that. They see no mighty visions for the Church. They just see small things.

III. INSPIRATION

Pep is supplanting inspiration in our Church programs. But pep is nothing but physical energy. We need God inspiration.

"When an audience falls before a preacher like the autumn leaves before the north wind we may know that he is in tune with the infinite."

[1] By P. R. Knickerbocker in "The Southern Methodist Pulpit." Cokesbury Press.

In the day of Pentecost inspired men and women seemed as drunken. Our Churches need that same inspiration.

IV. REGENERATION

I believe in social regeneration, I believe in the great social movements; but back of them all and inspiring them all must be regenerated men and women. . . . The home with Christ in the midst must come back to its own.

V. REJUVENATION

The saddest day for any man is the day when the little boy in him dies. Moses was a little boy at eighty. He had the little boy's perpetual faith. David was a boy all his life. His wife was shocked at him at one time when he acted as a boy. But God loves the boy-man.

VI. AGITATION

We must sell Christ to the world. Joseph Parker said that when the Church goes stark crazy for God it will turn the world upside down. We need men crazy for Christ—as crazy as St. Paul. Wherever he went there was either a riot or a revival. If I am sane, two men can hold me. If I am crazy, it takes a roomful.

VII. DESPERATION

We must do or die. We must set our faces steadfastly toward Jerusalem. Sin must be driven out, though it means persecution, contempt, spittle.

It is five o'clock in the morning, and every day seems four hundred and forty-eight hours long. Woe be to the prophets who say that the Church is that strumpet that shall be spewed out of the mouth of God, and that this age of the Holy Spirit shall end in blood and failure.

OVERCOMING [1]

Now therefore give me this mountain. Joshua 14: 12.

"Caleb" means "capable." Unfortunately, every man does not live up to his prophetic name as Caleb did. He was a rare composite of *faith, courage, patience,* and *holiness.* The incarnation of these qualities in the souls of men has always characterized and qualified leadership, irrespective of race or space. Men thus endowed are masters and deal with mountains more easily than weaklings do with marbles.

I. CALEB REQUESTED THE MOUNTAIN OF GIANTS BECAUSE HE WAS A MOUNTAIN-TYPE MAN AND THEREFORE CAPABLE OF CONQUEST

His faith was a mighty pyramid towering toward the sky. The Lord had promised him this mountain forty-five years before, and he had never doubted that he would receive it. He had courage, faith, and patience; and, more than these, he followed the Lord. He was a man who believed in the promises God gave him.

No, Caleb, thy choice was not foolish. To-day, looking down through the valley of the years, our holden eyes are opened and we see clearly. Indeed, thy choice was wise. Thou hadst the faith of the pioneer which lifted thee into the glorious realm of vision.

> "God's promises are sure;
> He gains the prize who can the most endure,
> Who faces issues and never shirks,
> Who waits and watches and always works."

II. APPLICATION

1. Hard work is the open door to all greatness.

[1] By S. R. Bratcher in "Advertising Jesus." Cokesbury Press.

Some one has wisely said that there is always room at the top. But the elevator is not working, and the only way to get there is to climb. All of life is a climb and a struggle.

Learn a parable from the bluebell of Scotland. It lives in the ice and snow of the early spring. The power of existence is within.

"Mr. Riley," said an old friend to the bard, "what is the key to your success?" "The rubber end of the pencil," was his laconic reply. Measured by every standard, Gray's "Elegy in a Country Churchyard" is nearer perfection than any long poem ever written; but we should never forget that the author poured seven years of his busy life into its molding. Aristotle, illustrious teacher of Alexander, sat at the feet of Plato for twenty consecutive years. Here he learned "to labor and to wait," and here he learned also that patience—stretched-out courage, power of endurance—is the annealing furnace of all true greatness.

"The rougher the sea, the stronger the sailor must be," is an old sea adage.

2. Your character will surely be tested.

Character is like asbestos. The more it is used, the more valuable it becomes. All along the highway of life there is a testing. In Nashville I saw on the sidewalk a piece of linoleum which a merchant had put out for people to walk on to test it. Character is tested like that.

"He that endureth to the end shall be saved."

"For the high soul climbs the High way,
  And the low soul gropes the Low,
And in between, on the misty flats,
  The rest drift to and fro."

FIGHTING THE STARS [1]

The stars in their courses fought against Sisera. Judges 5: 20.

THE verse gives the Hebrew interpretation to a great battle in which the Hebrew forces were victorious. Just as the battle opened a heavy storm converted the black loam of the fertile field into a morass. The heavy chariots of the Canaanites sunk to the axles. The foot soldiers of the Hebrews could move more quickly. Chariots of iron proved a handicap. It was a storm of nature. But the Hebrews preferred to attribute the victory to God. The story does symbolize the great forces of the universe who fight for the man with righteous ideals.

I. WE CAN CO-OPERATE WITH GREAT NATURAL FORCES TO ACHIEVE THE ENDS SOUGHT

All about us are familiar forces which we do not originate, which we do not control—the light and heat of the sun, the power of gravitation, the movements of the winds, and the pulsating tides. We cannot control them, but we can adjust ourselves to them. There are other mighty forces which, from the beginning of time, have been moving the race onward and upward. Certain forms of evil have been driven out of society. Others are on the way.

> "There is a power not ourselves which makes for righteousness." (Matthew Arnold.)
> "There is an infinite and eternal energy from which all things spring." (Herbert Spencer.)

II. THE ANTAGONISM OF THESE FORCES SPELLS DEFEAT TO THOSE WHO DO WRONG

The stars never tarry long in bringing in their verdict upon the coarser sins of the flesh: murder, adultery, stealing, and

[1] Charles Reynolds Brown in "The Cap and Gown." Pilgrim Press.

lying. But they reach, as well, all the way down to the subtler sins of pride and envy, meanness and selfishness. No man ever outwitted the stars, and no man ever will. The sun rises when it is due, no matter how the individual man may set his clock. No man can outwit the moral order of the universe.

Go through any modern city with your eyes open, and you will see this statement about Sisera written out in a plain hand. You will find people, some of them well dressed, some in rags, with their hearts draped in wretchedness and despair. Poor, deluded mortals; they have been butting out their brains against the moral corner stones of the universe in the vain hope that possibly the way of the transgressor might not be hard for them.

III. THE ULTIMATE WELL-BEING OF LIFE IS SECURED THROUGH CO-OPERATION WITH THE STARS

The ship is in distress when the skies are clouded. But when the stars appear the mariner knows his way. Life is also guided by certain stars. We have to see them and understand them to coöperate with their purpose. There are many universal forces for us to use if we will. The forces of love, grace, forgiveness, and redemption are ours. When we use them they bring us peace and joy.

You can always trust these forces. They belong to that universe of God's which does not fail us.

(Samaria Baptist church, March 7, 1943)

AN OLD-TIME MOTHER [1]

For this child I prayed; . . . Therefore have I lent him to the Lord; as long as he liveth he shall be lent to the Lord. 1 Samuel 1:27, 28.

I. SHE LOOKED UPON MOTHERHOOD AS A PRIVILEGE

OF course she lived a long time ago when woman had but one vocation. That was home and motherhood. To-day loyalties are divided. Women are satisfied without children. But Hannah was not satisfied. And the modern woman who turns her heart from the cry to motherhood deliberately turns from her sublimest throne. The women to whom the world of to-day is most indebted are the women who bore children and rocked cradles.

We hear little of Mrs. Luther as a religious leader; but we know this, that she rocked a reformation in her cradle.

II. SHE WAS A PRAYING MOTHER

"For this child I prayed."

Can you say that? God pity the child that comes into a home where nobody prays. It seems to me that if nothing else in the world would lead us to pray, we might be led to do so by the heavy responsibilities of fatherhood and motherhood. We cannot hope to succeed in any other way. We need to be praying constantly the prayer of the friend at midnight. We need to remind God of the child that has come, and that we have nothing of spiritual bread to give except it be given from above.

III. SHE RECOGNIZED HER CHILD AS GOD'S CHILD

She believed that God loved him and had a place for him. She "lent" him to the Lord. Not long ago a Christian woman

[1] By Clovis G. Chappell in "The Village Tragedy and Other Sermons." Cokesbury Press.

41

remarked that she would hate to have one of her boys go into the ministry. Hannah thought nothing was higher or nobler for her own boy. The Christian Church and its missionary efforts would be hopeless without mothers and fathers who consecrate their children to God. Other parents hesitate to have their little children attend the Church services. They think that they should wait until older before starting the practice. I have learned that the time to break a colt is when he is young. The time to start the child on the right road is in the first years of his life.

IV. SHE SUCCEEDED

Hannah made good in the highest of vocations. The Bible tells us that all Israel knew that a prophet had risen. She had rocked him. You will miss the whole point of this story if you look upon Samuel as an abnormal boy. He was not born a saint. He was made one by home training.

It makes a difference what you teach your children regarding God. For a good Bible illustration take Lot and Abraham. Lot did not put God first. As a result he lost his influence over his children and saw them go to the bad. But Abraham's children for generations have risen up to call him blessed.

THE CALL OF DAVID [1]

So David prevailed over the Philistines with a sling and a stone.
1 Samuel 17: 50.

I. DAVID APPARENTLY HAD NOTHING TO RECOMMEND HIM TO GOD

DAVID was the youngest of the brethren and was despised by the others. Even his father did not bring him before Samuel.

In this country many are chosen, many are not; and why some are chosen and others are not we cannot tell.

We wonder sometimes why God chooses the people he does for baptism and the protection of the Church. Surely there are many worthy people outside of the Church.

II. GOD CHOSE ONE OF HUMBLE OCCUPATION

He passed by the rich and the famous to take a shepherd lad. He does choose the rich—the rich in faith and in the promises of the kingdom. But he passes by many so-called rich of the world.

III. GOD CHOSE DAVID THROUGH A MAN

He might have selected his king quietly, but evidently he preferred a voice. And when God chooses us he usually does so through this method. He sends his minister to speak the word. God is looking now for men and women to serve in his kingdom. He is sending voices to call them. Samuel was told to do only what Christ's ministers of to-day are told to do. The only difference is that he was sent to call one. The minister can call many.

[1] By John Henry Newman in "Parochial and Plain Sermons" (Volume VIII). Longmans.

IV. THERE WAS A VISIBLE ANOINTING

"Samuel took the horn of oil."

The minister likewise uses the visible sign in the ordinance of baptism. Samuel used oil. The minister uses water. There is nothing divine in either. Any power it possesses is given it by God. Water in the minister's hands, blessed by God, becomes something more than water.

V. NOTHING IMMEDIATELY CAME FROM THIS ANOINTING

David went back to caring for his sheep. Then Saul sent for him. He played for Saul and then went back again to his sheep. The Spirit of the Lord which came upon him did not make him, at once, a great prophet. So it is with Christian baptism. Nothing may show for a time, but the Spirit of God is dwelling in the heart of the child. But David later had his Goliath. So will the children we baptize.

VI. WHAT IS OUR GOLIATH?

The answer is plain. It is the devil. We have to fight Satan. We are brought forth to fight the devil immediately after baptism. But by degrees our work creeps up on us, and responsibilities are laid on our shoulders. As we grow, the Spirit of God placed there by baptism also grows.

VII. WHAT, THEN, OUGHT YOU TO DO, WHEN THUS ASSAILED?

Quit you like men, be strong. Be like David, very courageous to do God's will. Think what would have happened had David played the coward, and refused to obey God's inward voice stirring him up to fight Goliath.

PLAYING THE FOOL [1]

Behold, I have played the fool, and have erred exceedingly. **1** Samuel 26: 21.

THERE are a great many fools mentioned in the Bible. We can't mention each of them. But the ones which we will discuss have special prominence in the eyes of God.

I. THE ATHEISTIC FOOL

"The fool hath said in his heart, There is no God."

A fool is one who speaks and acts contrary to reason. The man who declares that there is no God is such a man. One might as well declare that there is no air. One does not debate the presence of air, he merely uses it. The Bible does not try to prove the presence of God. It uses it.

The best science can do is to lead us back to protoplasm and then say, "Evolution." But what is back of the protoplasm? The Bible gives the answer: "In the beginning, God."

II. THE CONCEITED FOOL

This is the man who believes in God and yet thinks that he can make a success without him. He substitutes self for God. This was the sin of which Saul was guilty. His head had been turned by victory. He took full credit for everything himself. Then the disastrous end came. He had played the fool.

A man without God is dead in sins and trespasses. He cannot perform his mission in life without the power of God animating him, controlling him, and making him equal to the task he has to do. Turn on the electricity, and the car moves along the track to perform its mission. Unite your soul through Jesus Christ to God, and his Spirit will come into your life and give you mastery over sin.

[1] By Russell M. Brougher in "What We Preach." Judson.

III. THE SELFISH FOOL

Jesus describes this fool in the twelfth chapter of Luke. He was the man who was successful. He was going to tear down his barns to build greater. He was to take his ease—eat, drink, and be merry. But God said unto him: "This night thy soul will be required of thee. Then whose will these things be?"

> "Death steals no man;
>   No plea, no prayer delivers him;
> From the midst of life's unfinished plan,
>   With sudden grasp it severs him;
> And ready, or not ready, no delay,
>   Forth to his judge's bar he must away."

IV. THE CARELESS FOOL

In the twenty-fifth chapter of Matthew you will find the story of the wise and foolish virgins. You will remember that the foolish failed to prepare for the future. When the bridegroom came they were not prepared. They could not go to meet him.

The world is filled with fools like this. They do not prepare for life. While great battles are to be fought they are "fooling around." Every day the crisis of life comes to some one. Are you ready for it to come to you? Have you built the reserves of Christian character so essential for this time?

RUNNING WITHOUT TIDINGS [1]

Wherefore wilt thou run, my son, seeing that thou hast no tidings ready? 2 Samuel 18: 22.

Ahimaaz was fully justified in his desire to run, and he had more tidings than the mere official announcement; he was eager to bring with him the joy of a great day on the one hand, and on the other the sympathy of a friend in an hour of great sorrow.

The old commander (Joab) was right, however, in one most important point. He had the vigorous common sense to see that a messenger must have a message—that if a man run, he must have tidings.

A YOUNG man being ordained to the ministry similarly must have more than a mere enthusiasm for a great cause. He must have tidings. The world will tell him that religion has run its course. He must know definitely where he stands.

I. HE HAS NO TIDINGS WHO HAS NOT A FIRM GRASP OF CHRISTIAN FAITH AS A SYSTEM OF HISTORICAL FACT AND REVEALED TEACHING

Christianity rests upon fact. It is true that other religions have a place in history, but their doctrines are not founded upon historical facts. For instance, the central promise in the Old Testament is a covenant between God and Abraham. Now, if Abraham did not exist as a historical person, what becomes of the promise? St. Paul touched the vital point when he said in speaking of the resurrection, "Then is our preaching vain, and your faith also is vain."

The historical facts are the basis, but they are not, alone, enough; interpretation is needed. That comes through the inspiration of Scripture.

[1] Albertus Pieters in *Moody Bible Institute Monthly.*

"The longer I live, the more it seems to me that this is the fundamental problem of theology: Has God spoken?" (James F. Zwemer.)

II. HE HAS NO TIDINGS WHO HAS NOT EXPERIENCED SAVING GRACE

Christianity is the power of God as well as the wisdom of God. There are many things about Christianity which can be learned from study. But Christianity, itself, can only be learned from experience. One of the evils afflicting the Christian Church is the presence in the pulpit of so many ministers who have not been born again. It is not enough to say, parrot-like, that Christ is your Saviour; he must have saved you from something.

III. HE HAS NO TIDINGS READY WHO HAS NOT BEEN ADEQUATELY PREPARED TO EXPOUND THE DOCTRINE

It pleased God to reveal himself through the medium of Hebrew and Greek. This means that a fair proportion of the clergy should be able to understand the original writings in those languages. There are many different literary forms in our English Bible, and the literary qualities must be duly appreciated. A general knowledge of history is necessary to appreciate the setting for the Scripture story. And only by a thorough knowledge of Church history can one know of the work of the Holy Spirit.

We must seek the grace of God that we may continue to have, in ever-increasing measure, men who are fitted to run with the message of the gospel because, in addition to knowing a living message, they are also well trained to carry it.

THE SIN OF BEING TOO BUSY [1]

As thy servant was busy here and there, he was gone. 1 Kings
20:40.

EVERY one thinks at times that he is the busiest person in
town. Entering the office, store, or mill, one hears the statement, "This is my busy day." Approach the ordinary individual
concerning some project aside from the regular routine, and
he will likely say, "I haven't time."

> Because folks are busy with big business is no reason
> why they should neglect the claims of the biggest Man in
> the world. Jesus Christ was both big and busy—none
> were bigger nor busier. Yet he always found time to be
> about his Father's business.

Our text springs from the story of battles. The Israelites
had beaten the Syrians. The captured leader was marked for
punishment and intrusted to Ahab. Upon a flimsy pretext he
let the captive escape. His excuse was that he had been too
busy for his chief duty.

I. THIS IS THE NOTABLE SIN OF MANY

We are always busy—too busy to accept Christ or lead others
to him. Jesus warned against the high crime of preoccupation. In the parable of the soils, he lamented the highest life
being choked out by the pursuit of other things.

Clutching at the throat of spiritual life are three death-
dealing hands. One of them is worldly cares. This means, of
course, unnecessary anxiety. It is unrelaxing attention to material things to the exclusion of preparation for the eternal.
Subtle in their lure and, promising joy, they become gay de-
ceivers.

[1] By Roy Irwin Farmer in *Church Management.*

There is deceitfulness of riches. Christ was speaking of the fruitage of worldly toil. The glitter of gold may be as deceptive to one receiving fifteen hundred dollars annually as it is to him who receives fifteen thousand dollars. Christ warned the prosperous farmer that he could not feed his soul on corn. Unless he controls both production and use of every income, it chokes out eternal life.

Then Jesus rebuked the excessive pursuit of things. This may be nothing criminal—just things displacing him. It may be only tasks, social engagements, business committees—one after another until preoccupation leaves no room for him. Only the dregs of time, talents, or money are left for the world's Saviour.

II. THE SIN OF BEING TOO BUSY OFTEN LEADS TO DODGING DUTY

Humanity crowds the court room when God holds court with sinners. Though not rebellious against God, we may simply kick duty under the bed while we imagine God is not looking our way. Setting profit or pleasure above the welfare of our fellows is sinful. We love God and serve him only as we love and serve our neighbors. "He that loveth not his brother whom he hath seen, how can he love God whom he hath not seen?"

III. CHRIST NEEDS BUSY PEOPLE

Christ needs big men—busy men of big business. His is the biggest business in the world. It is winning men to Christ instead of letting them go to hell because we are too busy. When Lord Kitchener was once approached by a subordinate officer with a recital of reasons for not obeying an order, he replied, "Your reasons for not doing it are the best I ever heard; now go and do it." Our Christ speaks likewise to us.

May we preserve our moral equilibrium, speed up our spiritual development, and live happier lives because we find time for Christ. With Shakespeare, may we realize that "In persons grafted in a serious trust, negligence is a crime."

WHERE IS THE LORD GOD OF ELIJAH? [1]

Where is the Lord God of Elijah? 2 Kings 2: 14.

At the present hour many of God's people are cast down and discouraged. The Elijahs are gone. The fires upon the altars of their Carmels have gone out, and the ashes of their sacrifice are cold. They see no fire coming down from heaven, but they hear the exultant shouts of the enemy, and see temples of numberless false gods. The cowardice of Ahab and the audacity of Jezebel are yet abroad in the land.

I. WE ARE CONFRONTED WITH SEEMINGLY OVERWHELMING OPPOSITION

There are gigantic industrial conflicts on every side. The fires of the World War hatreds still smother. The East has grown tired of the exploitations of the West and is arousing from its slumbers. The yellow peoples are developing a new race consciousness. There are social evils which attack our race from the inside. Wealth is allied with ruthless greed.

Our cities must fight the rottenness of the stage and the movies. Present-day literature has sunk to a very low depth as it advertises unchastity and sex. The modern dance is lower than that of the old ballroom. And crime is rampant. Racketeering and shooting occur in every great city. Then the basic philosophy which is supplanting the older way of thinking is basically unchristian. Little wonder that we should ask, "Where is the Lord God of Elijah?"

II. THIS IS A TIME OF KNOWN AND CONFESSED WEAKNESS

The forms of religion remain much the same, but the flame of holy zeal and burning ardor is lacking. Many who are cry-

[1] By Enos Kincheloe Cox in "Where Is the Lord God of Elijah?" Bible Institute Colportage Association.

ing for the growing kingdom are looking for better living conditions and are not interested in a righteousness growing out of regenerated lives. Churches are distinguished by broad tolerance rather than deep convictions.

Our missionary enterprises have become philanthropic movements with a laudable desire that the heathen should have the comforts of our Western civilization. There is a persistent clamor that Christianity should shape itself to meet the needs of the day. Yet the early apostles did not fit the gospel to Greek demands of their time.

Somehow or other the note of authority is being lost from Church and preaching. We have eloquent preachers, but the zeal of soul-winning is lost. Perhaps the pulpit has more of beauty than virility. "Repentance" and "conversion" have become weak words in numerous theological vocabularies. Penitent sinners are an unusual sight in these days.

Our God has given us in hours of need such men as Knapp, Finney, Earle, Moody, Spurgeon, Chapman, Torrey, and a host of others. Has his power departed from them? "Where is the Lord God of Elijah?" Yes, the God of Whitefield, of Carey, of Judson, of Moffatt, of Livingstone? Was he mighty only while they lived? Has the God of Elijah abdicated or forgotten his promises? Only by laying hold of the power of the living God, as furnished by the dynamic of the ageless gospel and the enduement of the Holy Spirit, can our victory be won.

THE SOUL'S VISION [1]

And the Lord opened the eyes of the young man; and he saw. 2
Kings 6: 17.

Physical blindness is never so hard or dire in its results
as spiritual blindness. The souls of men are greater than
their bodies. Men have overcome physical blindness. . . .
But spiritual blindness has no remedy.

I. IF WE HAVE THIS SPIRITUAL VISION, WE MAY SEE THE UNSEEN

SPIRITUAL sight allows us to see the unseen, know the un-
knowable, and use the impossible to attain the impossible for
God. It gives us the far view of opportunity. There is much
in society to discourage one to-day. If he sees only the close-up
view, he may rest in lethargy, imagining that things can never
be any better. But when he sees with the far vision he becomes a fighter for righteousness.

Most things worth while have been seen with the far view.
It took generations to build the world's great cathedrals. What
system of education is worth the paper it is written on unless
it is founded on the far view?

II. THE VISION OF THE SOUL FACES THE IMMEDIATE CONDITION AND PRESENT LIGHT OF GOD

> "Careless seems the great avenger;
>   History's pages but record
> One death grapple in the darkness
>   'Twixt old systems and the Word;
> Truth forever on the scaffold,
>   Wrong forever on the throne;
> But that scaffold holds the future,
>   And behind the dim unknown,
> Standeth God within the shadow,
>   Keeping watch above his own."
>   (James Russell Lowell.)

[1] By John Timothy Stone in "Places of Quiet Strength." Doran.

III. SPIRITUAL VISION MEANS MATERIAL LEADERSHIP

In every human crisis when leadership has been needed in the affairs of men a man of vision has met the need. Read your lists of the world's leaders. See how many had the spiritual vision to see beyond the present.

IV. SPIRITUAL VISION HAS INITIATIVE

It is this initiative which suggests the remedy for the situation. Who ever dreamed that Elisha could escape? What chance did he have when surrounded by a great army of a mighty commander? But spiritual vision saw the way when every other means failed. It possessed the initiative for making the effort.

V. THE VISION OF THE SOUL GIVES TO MEN POWER IN PRAYER

Men who have no use for law ridicule the law. Men who practice law believe in it. Men who do not pray laugh at prayer. Men who pray, know.

In preparing this sermon, I looked over some letters received from the front [this sermon preached in war time], from boys of this Church, boys of different types and kinds. Many had the requests, "Pray for us," or, "We are glad the Churches are remembering us in prayer."

IV. THE SOUL'S VISION GIVES US RELIEF AND VICTORY

Who among that Syrian host ever dreamed that they would be led by the surrounded prophet into the land of Samaria? But the power of answered prayer led that great host because the man of prayer was a man of initiative.

"O Lord, open our eyes, that we may see."

THE DRIVING OF JEHU [1]

*And the driving is like the driving of Jehu the son of Nimshi;
for he driveth furiously.* 2 Kings 9: 20.

JEHU was evidently a careless driver. But his driving was
characteristic of his entire life. He drove his chariot furiously.
When he took vengeance upon his enemies, he took that furiously also. He had the ability to sweep aside obstacles which lay
between him and his ambition. He represents, in a broad way,
the strength and weakness of his type of character.

I. THE JEHU TYPE OF LIVING

This is very evident in our civilization of to-day. We are
living in a day of speed.

> "In the year 1800 there was no system of highways
> which equaled the Roman roads, no posting service as quick
> as Cæsar's, no method of signaling which could compare
> with the semaphore 'teleography' of the Persians, and
> probably no ship which could not have been overhauled by
> a Phœnician galley in a moderate sea." (Lothrop Stod-
> dard.)

But look at the world now. Radio. Airplanes. Rapid
transit. Fast mail. Ocean liners. Subways. These react
upon personal habits. The modern man must learn to eat
breakfast in a few minutes. We take our vacations furiously.
We are too hurried to be polite. Preaching gives way to
snappy sermons or sermonettes.

II. THE JEHU TYPE OF MIND

There must be a Jehu type of mind to go with the Jehu type
of living. They are inseparable. Fortunately, the Jehu type of

[1] By Umphrey Lee in "Jesus the Pioneer." Cokesbury Press.

mind was not characteristic of the Hebrews. They live to-day because of the meditations of Amos, because of the philosophic debates of Job, because of the psalmists. Jehu did not produce Psalms.

But in our day Jehu comes to his own. We rejoice in furiousness. We like the wit who comes back quickly and slays his opponent. There is little opportunity given the average man for reflection. John Wesley had his coach fitted up with bookshelves and read as he rode around England. One can't read as he rides in an automobile, which demands all of his time and attention to handle.

The Jehu mind crowds out those deeper fellowships of the soul which arise only with courtesy and culture.

III. JEHUISM IN SOCIAL RELATIONSHIPS

Here lies the greatest danger from Jehuism. We cannot turn back the centuries, but we can adjust ourselves so as to protect our social heritage. Business men are finding that they must have time for recreation and exercise. Women are finding that periods of leisure are necessary to preserve their mental sanity.

Never has there been a more opportune time for the emphasis upon the quietness of worship. We need the inner adjustment which only worship can give.

> "Drop thy still dews of quietness,
>   Till all our strivings cease;
> Take from our souls the strain and stress,
> And let our ordered lives confess
>   The beauty of thy peace."

THE PEOPLE HAD A MIND TO WORK [1]

The people had a mind to work. Nehemiah 4: 6.

I do not know of any story which applies so well to the tragic situation in which our country finds itself to-day—and our city, too—than this story of Nehemiah and his reconstruction task. Nor do I know any text which more accurately suggests at once the spirit of the people and the tragedy of unemployment than the words, "The people had a mind to work." The people of America, the people of our city, have a mind to work; but there is no work for them to do. The economic walls of many people have broken down, and hordes of poverty, despair, immorality, starvation, and death are pouring through as the Babylonian soldiers poured through the break in the walls of Jerusalem some twenty-five hundred years ago.

I. THE PROBLEM OF UNEMPLOYMENT IS A RELIGIOUS PROBLEM

RELIGION has to do with life everywhere. If religion is less than this, it is a specialty. To think of religion in the terms of specialization is a sacrilege. Every social problem is a religious problem. Unemployment defeats the high purpose of whole families, smashing into fragments the dreams of parents, opening doors to the wolf of starvation. It is distinctly a religious problem.

There is a distinct relationship between the spiritual and the physical life, between a man's stomach and his soul. Social workers everywhere will say that unemployment increases immorality.

Many who do not enter the ranks of the criminals become a part of the great army of the useless. The tragic fact is that the unemployed tend to become the unemployable.

[1] By Norman D. Fletcher in the *Christian Register*.

II. UNEMPLOYMENT IS DUE TO SOCIAL CAUSES AND NOT INDIVIDUAL ILL-DOING

There are people who seem to think that men and women who are seeking jobs are the ne'er-do-wells, hopelessly inefficient and lazy. But this attitude is unjust and is based upon ignorance. Personal defects are factors in the situation, but they are very minute factors. There is not a social worker in the country who would agree that the causes of unemployment are personal. Many of the unemployed are skilled workers who own their homes. They have a mind to work. They are the victims of a maladjustment in the social order. Religious people need to take an attitude toward the situation which is consistent with their religious ideals.

III. PERMANENT RELIEF IS ESSENTIAL

Religious people everywhere should try to relieve the unemployment as they have opportunity. To help in the emergency is a religious obligation. But more than this is needed. We must try and build into our economic system those qualities which will make impossible a repetition of this situation.

In this matter of unemployment America is not unlike the little village of renown that had in its precincts a highway which ran over a dangerous cliff. Instead of putting a fence along the highway to prevent accidents, the community put an ambulance at the foot of the cliff! We need the ambulance of relief, but we must have also the fence of prevention.

THE PENALTY OF HATE [1]

Yet all this availeth me nothing, so long as I see Mordecai the Jew sitting at the king's gate. Esther 5: 13.

There are spots in the sun; and if you think you see the spots, you will come to see nothing but the spots when you look. There is some drawback in the fairest prospect, and when the eye once catches it there is no getting rid of it—we come back to it again and again to be irritated afresh.

I. THE BLACK SPOT IN HAMAN'S SUNSHINE

HAMAN had many things to make him happy. He was the favorite of the king. In addition, the favorite wife of the king had been impressed by him and had invited him to dine with his royal master. This would seem enough to make the most envious man happy. But there was one thing—a little thing at that—which spoiled the entire thrill. It had to do with a Jew, one Mordecai, who would not bow to him. Everybody else bowed, but Mordecai refused to bow.

All the splendor of the court favor, the sunshine of the king's smile which does so much for courtiers, could not take away the sting of the tacit insult that Mordecai had not bowed to the great man and done him reverence. It took all the sap out of his pleasure, a gnat's bite that took away all his comfort.

II. THE PERSONAL APPLICATION OF THE STORY

The lesson of this story comes close home to each of us. We know from experience about this spot in the sunshine. Some one offends us, wittingly or unwittingly, for good cause or no cause; but it stings. Some one does not show us sufficient honor or reverence. Or he says something unkind and

---

[1] By Hugh Black in "Listening to God." Revell.

critical. Or there is envy of some one else's position or good fortune. No matter what it is, it eats like a cancer until it colors our whole being.

1. Malice makes a man lose perspective. It magnifies the one petty thing and blinds the eyes to everything else. It is like the closed room in the story of Bluebeard. Though every other room is open, that is the one we must see. It is like a disease. It works its way through the body until the entire body is diseased tissue. Haman could not enjoy his great success because of this one grievance. "All this availeth me nothing, so long as I see Mordecai the Jew sitting at the king's gate."

2. Malice leads to self-deception. Haman was a man who was supposed to know the "ropes" of politics and intrigue. He entirely missed the purpose of the queen in having him at her table. Self-deceived, the gallows he prepared for his victim was destined for his own carcass.

"Anger is like rain; it breaks itself on what it falls." (Seneca.)

III. SALVATION FROM THIS MALICE

It could only come by understanding; never by indifference or pride. He could not pass him by and pretend that he did not see him. But if he had made an effort to really learn about this man Mordecai and get his point of view—see his heart—it would have made all of the difference in the world. Love is the only antidote to hate.

THE NEED OF AN INTERPRETER [1]

An interpreter among a thousand. Job 33: 23.

But it is not of the interpretation of sorrow and pain in particular that I want to speak just now—but of the broad truth that, for full understanding of most things, an interpreter is necessary; and I want especially to show how this was true of God and how it still holds true of Jesus. God needed an "interpreter" to explain himself to men, and Christ still needs "interpreters" if he is to be understood and received as Lord of mankind.

I. THINGS MUST BE INTERPRETED TO US BEFORE THEY ARE RIGHTLY UNDERSTOOD

TAKE the radio. We sit in our homes and listen to pleasant programs from many cities. But an expert comes in and tells us about wave lengths and ether vibrations. Until then, as much as we have enjoyed the programs, we have not understood the secret of their possibility. The same thing is true when we consider the birds and insects; it holds when we study the stars or the seasons. It is true of the seasons of the year. And the truth likewise applies to mankind. How could we understand one another unless there was speech to tell what we are and what we are thinking?

Without the aid of words we should live in an intolerable isolation and loneliness, and should spend our lives complete and utter strangers to one another. Speech is the interpreter which enables us to understand and appreciate one another.

II. INTERPRETATION IS NEEDED IN THE HIGHEST REALM

(1) Nature is a partial interpreter of God. Men have never been able to contemplate the world seriously without thinking

[1] By J. D. Jones in "The Inevitable Christ." Richard R. Smith.

of him.   (2) Then man's own soul is a partial interpreter.
Any man who listens to his conscience knows something of
God.   (3) Saintly and gifted men are also interpreters.
Through the Old Testament and in the history of the Church
there have been such interpreters.

But the only complete interpreter is Jesus Christ.   He is the
"Logos"—God's Word.

> There are lots of things in life I cannot explain; there
> are lots of things in nature that baffle and perplex me, but
> I turn from life and nature to Jesus, and, in spite of all
> the bewildering and baffling things, I know that God is
> love.   Jesus is an "interpreter" among a thousand.

III. JESUS HIMSELF NEEDS TO BE INTERPRETED

This is the urgent need of our day.   Men of the world do
not know the real Jesus.   They have seen a caricature of him
and think they know him.   If an interpreter should arise who
can show him as he really is, men would rise up and follow him.

> "The dear Lord's best interpreters
>   Are humble human souls,
> The Gospel of a life like hers
>   Is more than books or scrolls.
>
> For scheme and creed the light goes out,
>   The saintly fact survives;
> The blessed Master none can doubt,
>   Revealed in holy lives."

OPPORTUNITY [1]

The Lord is the portion of mine inheritance and of my cup: thou maintainest my lot. The lines are fallen unto me in pleasant places; yea, I have a goodly heritage. Psalm 16: 5, 6.

Genuine contentment is a rarely beautiful characteristic. Of course I do not mean the stagnant contentment that succumbs to environment, but the progressive, lively spirit that is busy availing itself of to-day's opportunities, beating unruly conditions into shape, and at the same time anticipating better things for to-morrow.

> "I would have gone; God bade me stay:
>   I would have worked; God bade me rest.
> He broke my will from day to day,
>   He read my yearnings unexpressed
>   And said them nay.
>
> Now I would stay; God bids me go:
>   Now I would rest; God bids me work.
> He breaks my heart tossed to and fro,
>   My soul is wrung with doubts that lurk
>   And vex me so.
>
> I go, Lord, where thou sendest me;
>   Day after day I plot and moil:
> But, Christ my God, when will it be
>   That I may let alone my toil
>   And rest with thee?"

CONTENTMENT is only found in the assurance that God controls our lot and that for us the best opportunity that we could have to-day is that which we have. The world is filled with opportunities that become visible only when we think of leaving them to go some place else.

I. THE SOUL OF OPPORTUNITY IS CONTENTMENT

Contentment is concentrated enough and sufficiently keen-eyed to survey the immediate landscape. It becomes

[1] By Charles H. Brent in "Prisoners of Hope." Longmans.

familiar with all it sees and learns to use to the best advantage all that it touches. It finds treasures in waste that the careless discard as useless or of small value. After all, opportunity can be found only by those who possess character. There is no opportunity anywhere for the querulous and vicious—they spoil all they touch. They turn a garden into a desert and make a fruitful tree barren.

II. OPPORTUNITY LIES HERE, NOT YONDER

A little boy dreamed that he saw a beautiful castle across the fields from his home. One day he went in search of it. Instead he found a farmhouse very similar to the one which he left. But he found a playmate, and the day was happily spent. He told his new friend about the castle he had seen. "I will show you where it is at sunset," said the new friend. As the sun sank in the west he pointed across the field at the home the boy had left. Opportunities in life are like that. We must leave and look back to truly appreciate them.

III. AN OPPORTUNITY IS GREAT IF ATTACHED TO A GREAT CAUSE

Duties are simple. But they become mighty when they are tied to a great cause.

We are Americans. We would die to preserve the nation. But we fail to appreciate that simple loyalty to the social duties of life is one of the things which make the nation. The growing disrespect of social customs is dangerous. As the family life is weakened, so the nation is weakened.

Contentment and its handmaid, Opportunity, lie at our feet, in homes, in offices, and activities. Let us disperse each one of us to our own house and, I think—I hope— that it will be a house with windows of gold and diamonds.

PROVIDENCE [1]

He leadeth me. Psalm 23: 3.

"THE world could better spare many a large book than this sunny Psalm," says Dr. Alexander Maclaren concerning the twenty-third Psalm. "It has dried many tears and supplied the mold into which many hearts have poured their peaceful faith." It is a song of perfect trust. The singer is sure of the Lord. "The Lord is my shepherd; I shall not want." He is so sure of God that he is haunted by no anxieties.

The Psalm is divided into two distinct parts. The first four verses speak of the Lord under the figure of a shepherd who with watchful solicitude tends his sheep. In the last two verses the figure is changed from shepherd to host. The host is one who provides a home for man and lavishes his gracious kindness upon him. "Thou preparest a table before me. . . . I will dwell in the house of the Lord forever." The first four verses portray in clearest fashion the ways into which God leads us. David sings to us across many centuries, and his shepherd song is so simple and so personal that it has come to be the most universal of all the Psalms.

I. GOD LEADS US INTO JOY

"He maketh me to lie down in green pastures: he leadeth me beside the still waters." A broad pasture land, carpeted with tender green and skirting quiet waters, is a joyful retreat. It is typical of the pleasant pastures into which God is ever leading us. His kindness is infinitely more evident in this world than his severity. Because our sorrows weigh heavily upon us, we are likely to exaggerate them. The sorrow which one suffers in the loss of any treasure is not so great as the joy he has

[1] By Costen J. Harrell in "Friends of God." Cokesbury Press.

previously experienced in the possession of it. Elizabeth Barrett reminds all persons who are disposed to exaggerate their misfortunes that the blue of heaven is far bigger than the clouds. The joys of God's children outweigh their sorrows. Home and friends, the beauty of the world, the presence of God, and the settled peace which nothing can destroy—into all of this the Good Shepherd leads us.

II. GOD LEADS US INTO RIGHTEOUSNESS

"He leadeth me in the paths of righteousness." Through his providence runs a holy purpose. His purpose is to make us righteous as he is. Therefore, the Good Shepherd leads us into the strait and narrow way. The paths of right are not always attractive. Often they are hard and steep. But one who follows the leadership of God must walk in the ways of righteousness. It is a difficult way, but we do not tread it alone. Our Leader and Deliverer is with us. When we are faint, his grace will sustain us. When the way is too steep for human strength, he will help us up the grade and set our feet on higher ground.

III. GOD LEADS US THROUGH SORROWS

"Yea, though I walk through the valley of the shadow of death: . . . thou art with me." These words are possibly more accurate rendered "through the valley of deep darkness" or "through the valley of shadows." Through every dark valley into which the path of life may dip, God is with us. No trial is too hard if he is there to comfort us with the rod of his grace.

The providence of God covers the whole range of human experience. The sunny pasture lands, the shadowed valleys, the rugged climb toward righteousness—these make up the whole of a good man's life. We may set the message of the shepherd's song to words more modern, and sing,

> "Whate'er I do, where'er I be,
> Still 'tis God's hand that leadeth me."

THE LIFE OF TRUST [1]

Commit thy way unto the Lord; trust also in him; and he shall bring it to pass. Psalm 37: 5.

I may be permitted to remark on a text that has entered more than any other into my personal history. By it I have been literally saved from death, hell, defeat, and despair. By it I also have assisted others out of gloom, discouragement, desolation, suicide, and damnation.

II. IS YOUR WAY AN ANXIOUS WAY?

WHO hasn't been anxious? Do you remember the time you left home for college and choked back the tears? Do you remember when you started in business? A thousand anxieties haunted you.

Then most of us are worried about the future. We do not know what it holds in sadness or gladness. But this is in God's hands.

> "I know not where his islands lift
> Their fronded palms in air;
> I only know I cannot drift
> Beyond his love and care."

II. IS YOUR WAY A DIFFICULT WAY?

Then take faith in God as your first essential. By it men have removed mountains. If God is your Partner, no task is too difficult. "I can do all things through Christ which strengtheneth me."

III. IS YOUR WAY AN UNEQUAL WAY?

Have you done, as most good men have—looked around and seen the prosperity of the wicked? Have you asked why condition does not conform with conduct?

[1] By J. M. Dawson in "The Light That Grows." Sunday School Board of the Southern Baptist Convention.

Despite all temporary conditions Infinite Love rules, righteousness is gain, all sin is tragic loss. The coming years will reveal the justice of time.

IV. IS YOUR WAY A MISUNDERSTOOD WAY?

Have you seen a vision which is not seen by others? Have your motives been misunderstood? Have you been misrepresented and maligned? If so, you have the consolation that nearly everybody else that has ever seriously tried to serve the world and live worthily has suffered the same misfortune. But cling to the text. God will vindicate you and establish your character in the noonday. The mists and clouds may obscure the sun, but they cannot permanently hide it.

V. IS YOUR WAY A TROUBLED WAY?

In answer to Queen Victoria as to the search of his matchless exploration and evangelization in Africa, David Livingstone said that it was the inspiration of Christ's promise, "Lo, I am with you alway, even unto the end of the world." "That," said Livingstone, "is the word of a gentleman of the strictest honor, so that is the end of the matter."

VI. IS YOUR WAY A SINFUL WAY?

We are living in a day when many remedies for sin are proposed. There is salvation by sanitation and salvation by legislation. But, after all, there is only one real salvation. That is the salvation through Jesus Christ. Eugenics, social service, pleasant thoughts, and talking spirits do not save. Jesus saves from sin.

> "In vain I've tried a thousand ways
> My fears to quell, my hopes to raise,
> But what I need *through all my days*
> Is Jesus."

TRANSFORMED BY GRACE [1]

I waited patiently for the Lord; and he inclined unto me, and heard my cry. He brought me up also out of an horrible pit, out of the miry clay, and set my feet upon a rock, and established my goings. And he hath put a new song in my mouth, even praise unto our God; many shall see it, and fear, and shall trust in the Lord.
Psalm 40: 1-3.

Within the compass of these three brief verses such great subjects as sin, salvation, security, song, and service are treated.

I. SIN

SIN heads the list. Under the figure of a horrible pit filled with miry clay, into which the unwary traveler sinks to his doom, the subtle workings of sin and Satan are seen. Sin is a treacherous bog. Its dangers are not apparent to the light-hearted men and women who argue that they can do certain things that they know to be wrong without being harmed by them. There are hundreds of people who are not holden in the bonds of sin who would have been repelled by the picture of themselves a dozen years before. I can think of nothing worse than a place of eternal sin. Hell is such a place.

II. SALVATION

Salvation is sin's antidote. Or to carry on the figure, it is deliverance from a horrible pit.

"This poor Chinaman was in a deep well. I cried for Confucius to help me. He came and looked at me and said, 'Poor Chinaman, it is too bad that you are down so far. If you could only get out, I could help you, and I could keep you from getting in again.' But I could not get out. He could not reach me, and so he had no help for me. Then I cried for Buddha. He came and wept

---

[1] By P. W. Philpott in "Is God Still Speaking to Men?" Revell.

over me and said, 'I am sure that I could help you if you could only get out.' He, too, was unable to reach me. Finally I heard some missionaries talking about one Jesus who comes right down where men are and lifts them out of the horrible pit. I cried to him, and he came to the place where I was and lifted me." (A Chinaman's interpretation of Salvation.)

III. SECURITY

"He set my feet upon a rock, and established my goings."

Men and women hesitate to yield to Christ because they fear that they will make a shipwreck of their faith. They dread a falling away and a return to sin. They fail to realize that the keeping power of Christ is as great as his saving power.

"He is able to keep that which I have committed unto him against that day." (St. Paul.)
"Kept by the power of God." (St. Peter.)

IV. SONG

"He hath put a new song in my mouth."

"Birds with gladder songs o'erflow,
    Flowers with deeper beauty shine,
Since I know, as now I know,
    I am his and he is mine."

V. SERVICE

"Many shall see it, and fear, and trust."

When a poor, hopeless, worthless sinner is established on the Rock of Ages, he ceases to be a liability and becomes an asset to society. He is saved to serve. I once met a remarkable group of such transformed men. They were superintendents of city missions, gathered in conference. Some of them had been notorious leaders in crime. Their pictures had decorated rogues' galleries. But they had been saved by the grace of God. . . . They might have been mistaken for bank presidents.

HOW TO FACE LIFE WITH STEADY EYES [1]

God is a shelter and stronghold for us, we shall find him very near; therefore we never fear. Psalm 46: 1, 2 (Moffatt).

THINK of Jerusalem being surrounded by a mighty army. Everywhere there is consternation. Panting refugees arrive telling of the horrors which await the besieged. Those who were acquainted with the French villages during the War know the terror under which the people lived who feared the coming of the German forces. But in all this there was one man who moved—calm, cool, and unafraid. Why? Religion.

I. THE RELIGIOUS MIND KEEPS ONE COOL AND BRAVE WHEN OTHERS FALTER

It is not easy to face life. The ancients had an appalling notion that there are about us evil spirits which plague and distress us. And too often we find that life itself substantiates such an idea. Disease, madness, hatred, calamity, and death spring at us from the dark. But the religious-minded know that the greater unseen force is God. It is he who says: "Peace I leave with you; my peace I give you." And with Jesus we call him "Father."

II. THE RELIGIOUS ATTITUDE IS THE REASONABLE ONE

Once, speaking to a mass of men, scores of them unemployed and sick at heart, I happened to say that a great preacher had begun a famous sermon by remarking that one thing absolutely certain in the future was temptation, and ventured to add that that, while a fine stoic saying, just left out the whole of Christianity, everything that Christ came to tell us. For, says he, there are some things ahead of us more certain than temptation, most sure al-

[1] Arthur J. Gossip in "The Hero in Thy Soul." Charles Scribner's Sons.

though that is—the love of God to hearten us, and his
presence to strengthen us, and his hand always there
reached out to help us up all the steep places of the way.
We can be certain about that. And at that the Church
burst into applause. And one looked proudly at the men
facing their difficult lives so bravely. Yes, and happily
across at Jesus Christ, as one turns eagerly toward somebody one loves, hearing him praised and honored. It was
not for nothing that you died. Here are men to whom what
you did and said and were makes all the difference.

III. PROMISES OF GOD ARE SURE

No matter what the future may bring in temptation or failure, remember that it also brings the promises of God. They
are sure. "To-day," said Rainy, "I have a committee, to-
morrow I preach, one day I shall have to die. Well, we must
try to do each duty as it comes as well as we can." "From the
bottom of my heart," wrote Luther to Melanchthon, "I am
against these worrying cares which are taking the heart out of
you. Why make God a liar in not believing his wonderful promises?"

THE INVESTMENT OF THE YEARS [1]

We spend our years as a tale. Psalm 90: 9.

OUR earthly lives were intended to be measured. In heaven there will be no limitation and no death. Here it is a matter of cycles and of years. We speak of youth, maturity, and old age. We speak of dawn, noon, and evening, and also of spring, summer, and winter. We speak of years. We spend our years as a tale that is told.

I. HOW THE YEARS MAY BE SPENT

They may be spent as a miser spends. That means that no investment in life is made. Like the man in the parable, the miser buries his talent in the ground. Life is hoarded, not spent. The man who lives just for himself and the woman who lives only for herself or her family hoard life.

Then there are those who spend life like a spendthrift. The spendthrift in life is characterized by lack of economy in the present. There is a virtue in economy. There is a lesson in the parable of the loaves. "Gather up the fragments which remain, that nothing be lost." The man who spends his time in idle, useless recreation, when there is work to be done and life to be constructed, is a spendthrift of time.

Then there is the Christian way of spending the years. It is as stewards of the manifold gifts of God. The Christian is a citizen of two worlds. When any question arises as to the best method of investing his talents, it is easy to see that they are to be invested in those things which will pay dividends in both worlds.

[1] By John M. Vander Meulen in "The Southern Presbyterian Pulpit." Revell.

II. THE TALE TO BE TOLD

We found that there are three ways of spending life. There are three tales which life may tell.

To some life must be a love story. Love is the sweetest story ever told—especially when it is lived in the two worlds. But the love story which has no connection with heaven has little to offer to a permanent life on earth. Bertrand Russell writes: "I shall not teach my own children that faithfulness to one partner is in any way desirable, or that a permanent marriage should be regarded as excluding temporary episodes." That is not the sweetest story.

Others will want to write an adventure story with their lives. The spirit of adventure is strong in life. Joseph wrote such a story, as did David. But as with the first story, the adventure story must be one which can be written in the two worlds. There is an adventure of helpfulness which is pleasing to God.

But there is still another story, and it is greater than these. It is the story of the gospel. Jesus spent his years in that sort of a tale. I am wondering if you are writing yours in the same way. I am wondering if your life, as you live it day by day, is telling the greatest story ever told. Are men led through you to Jesus Christ?

GOD'S PROMISES [1]

Because he hath set his love upon me, therefore will I deliver him: I will set him on high, because he hath known my name. He shall call upon me, and I will answer him: I will be with him in trouble; I will deliver him, and honor him. With long life will I satisfy him, and show him my salvation. Psalm 91: 14-16.

Once I was in a town in Iowa, and right around that town there had been no less than seven cyclones, and every time there came up a little cloud people were alarmed. They seemed to be in constant dread of some terrible calamity. I have an idea that this Psalm was written on some occasion of that kind.

THERE are seven things in these verses that He says he will do.

I. "I WILL DELIVER HIM"

I have no sympathy with the thought that God comes down here and saves us and leaves us in bondage to any besetting sin. He will not leave us in bondage to a bad, irritable disposition, to bad temper, to lust, to our passions, to our appetites. He can break the strongest chain the devil can forge and set every captive free.

II. "I WILL ANSWER HIS CALL"

Has there ever been a time when a man, no matter how black his sin, has called on God for mercy and has not received it? "Whosoever" is a sweeping word. It includes the drunkard of the streets and the thief on the cross. When people really pray, God hears them.

III. "I WILL BE WITH HIM IN TIME OF TROUBLE"

I was greatly cast down on the vessel. My wife and children were on this side. I had been away from my

[1] By Dwight L. Moody in "Thou Fool." Published by the *Christian Herald*.

country a long time and was coming home. I just longed
to get to my family. I was awake one morning, Saturday
morning, at daybreak, and the old boat shook. . . . Sunday
afternoon came, and we got the people together, and I
read the ninety-first Psalm. And when I got to the verse,
"I will be with him in the time of trouble," the burden
rolled away and light burst in upon me, and from that
hour I was as calm as if I were a babe in his mother's
arms.

IV. "I WILL DELIVER HIM"

The next day, before daybreak, my son—one of my sons
was with me—came and woke me up and said, "Father,
there's a light." I sprang up, and there was a little star. I
said, "That's the Star of Bethlehem." Just a little light
bearing on me. He was with me at that time. I would be
meaner than any infidel that ever walked the earth if I
doubted it. He made that pillow as calm and peaceful as
any pillow I ever had in my life.

V. "I WILL SATISFY HIM WITH LONG LIFE"

That doesn't mean threescore years and ten. The great
trouble here is that everything soon comes to an end. The seal
of the past is upon us. But God has everlasting life.

VI. "I WILL SET HIM ON HIGH"

When God sets us on high, we shall be among the stars.
Perhaps you have seen or read of the coronation of kings. I
have seen three Tzars crowned in my day. They were raised
up on high for a short time. The glory of the world doesn't
amount to much, does it? But when God sets on high we shall
be above angels.

VII. "I SHALL SHOW HIM MY SALVATION"

O man, cheer up. Begin your life anew. What will it
be, to be the Son of God, and to be set on high? It is
only a little while, and then we'll be called to the everlasting glory.

THE RETURN TO THE ALTAR [1]

O worship the Lord in the beauty of holiness. Psalm 96: 9.
For the Father seeketh such to worship him. John 4: 23.

Whatever else man may be—vile, lustful, cruel, vain—
the story of his religion is enough to prove that he is not
wholly base. Rites horrible, rites unspeakable may have
been a part of his earliest ritual; but if the history of past
ages had left us nothing but the memory of a race at prayer,
it would have left us rich.

I. FROM EARLIEST TIME MAN HAD TWO BASIC INDUSTRIES: TOOL-MAKING AND RITUAL-MAKING

RITUAL-MAKING preceded theology. These rites were not
so much attempts to placate the gods as expressions of com-
munal life. They were celebrations of its great events, such as
marriage, birth, and death; an effort to secure its social sanctities by social safeguards. It was an attempt, through ritual, to
reach the Divine. So interpreted, the ritual is organized mys-
ticism. It dramatizes faith, hope, and the spiritual dreams of
men. It gave a reality to the unseen forces which otherwise
might be unreal.

II. THE THREE ELEMENTS WHICH ENTER INTO WORSHIP ARE ADORA-TION, INQUIRY, AND ALLEGIANCE

At a high level of adoration we see life in truer perspective
and proportion. The problems of faith and duty are plainer.
When the gentle, troubled singer of the seventy-third Psalm
felt his faith wavering, he went into the sanctuary. The Bible
calls the inquiry which takes place in the sanctuary the confession of sin. "Search me, O God, and know my heart."
And there at the altar we take a new oath of allegiance.

[1] By Joseph Fort Newton in "Things I Know in Religion." Harper

III. THERE IS AN APPALLING NEED FOR A RETURN TO THE ALTAR IN THIS HURRYING, UNWORSHIPFUL AGE

Never has there been an age when mankind has found itself so harnessed to mechanical tasks as this. Because we live so much in the exterior of things the unseen forces seem unreal. Man does not know how to be alone. He has not found the force which unifies life. The newer tendency in our Churches to provide the proper setting for music comes for just this time. It is the only thing which can save the individual and our Christian culture.

IV. WORSHIP IS AN ACT, SOLEMN, SPECIFIC, SACRIFICIAL

Worship is more than an attitude; it is an atmosphere in which the heart is made pure and the mind clear. Air is one thing and charged everywhere the same, but an atmosphere is charged with a quality of its own, benign or blighting. There are thoughts which we do not think in the holy atmosphere of the altar, imaginations which take flight at the mention of the magic name of Jesus. Finally, worship is more than an atmosphere. It is an act, solemn, specific, sacrificial, not merely a conception but a perception of God, not simply a yearning but a yielding of the whole being in deliberate self-surrender to one higher, wiser, and holier than ourselves.

To sum up, worship is to life what distance is to art, what the measureless is to music. Here under the hospitable roof of God life reveals its true proportions and dignity. . . . Here our hearts melt in song, and those ineffable truths which on other days seem dreary and dim renew their reality, and we dare to read the meaning of life by what is highest.

SIX WARNINGS [1]

The generation of the upright shall be blessed. Wealth and riches shall be in his house. Psalm 112: 2, 3.

He that getteth riches, and not by right, shall leave them in the midst of his days, and at his end shall be a fool. Jeremiah 17: 11.

When justly obtained and rationally used, riches are called a gift of God, an evidence of his favor, and a great reward. When gathered unjustly and corruptly used, wealth is pronounced a canker, a rust, a fire, a curse.

I. I WARN YOU AGAINST THINKING THAT RICHES NECESSARILY CON-FER HAPPINESS, AND POVERTY UNHAPPINESS

PURSE rich does not always mean heart rich. Wealth will do little for lust but hasten its corruption. There is no more happiness in a foul heart than there is happiness in a pestilent morass. On the other hand, poverty is not a waste and howling wilderness. There is a contented poverty in which industry and peace rule.

II. DO NOT ATTEMPT TO BECOME RICH TOO QUICKLY

He that hasteth to be rich hath an evil eye. It leads to incorrect vision. He seeks to prosper by crafty tricks rather than by careful industry. The prosperity which grows like a mushroom is as poisonous as the mushroom. When God sends wealth to bless men, he sends gradually, like a gentle rain.

III. COVETOUSNESS

"Thou shalt not covet" is a law by which God sought to bless a favorite people. The Bible meets it with significant woes, God's hatred, solemn warnings, denunciations, and exclusion from heaven. Covetousness breeds carelessness. It works the mind to a fever so that the judgments are not cool or calm.

[1] By Henry Ward Beecher in "Twelve Lectures to Young Men." American Tract Society.

It breeds misery. He who covets shall be buried with the burial of an ass (Jer. 22: 19).

IV. SELFISHNESS

This is one of the curses of business. Men consider life as a battle. They are to beat the other man and get from him what they need. "Every crevice of the heart is calked with costive maxims, so that no precious drop of wealth may leak out through inadvertent generosities."

> The heart of an avaricious old age stands like a bare rock in a bleak wilderness, and there is no rod of authority, nor incantation of pleasure, which can draw from it a crystal drop to quench the raging thirst for satisfaction.

V. COVERT DISHONESTY

It is neither necessary nor profitable. Industry, honesty, kindness, taste, genius, and skill are the only materials for rightful competition. But even if we assume that victory is not possible without guile, who can justify victory at the cost of virtue?

VI. VIOLENT EXTORTION OR FLAGRANT VILLAINY

The Bible overflows with warnings to those who gain wealth by those methods. What can justify the man who slips from under the poor their possessions? Or he who steals the patrimony from the simple? Or those who feed upon the sensual, the low, and the debased in humankind? Riches got by these methods cost the man who secures them plenty. Unjust riches curse the owner. They curse his children. He fills his coffers, but he empties his soul.

THE MINISTRY OF SONG[1]

Thy statutes have been my songs in the house of my pilgrimage.
Psalm 119: 54.

"GIVE me the man that whistles while he works," said
Carlyle. This same thing is true in a much larger sense. We
need to-day a new Pentecost, where, despite our variety of language, we learn the song of angels, good will among men.

I. RELIGION HAS ALWAYS BEEN ASSOCIATED WITH MUSIC

"It has a mystic power: it carries us to the verge of infinity
and allows us for moments to look into it." (Carlyle, speaking
of music.) What a vehicle of the Spirit song has been.
Take the Psalms: every human passion is expressed in them.
The children sleep believing that the good shepherd of the
twenty-third Psalm is keeping watch over them. The penitent
prays in the language of the fifty-first Psalm: "Have mercy
upon me, O Lord." The exile sings: "My heart is athirst for
God." Every prayer or human hope can find a Psalm which
portrays the mood.

II. THE INSPIRATION OF SONG DID NOT CLOSE WITH THE HOLY WRIT

The early Church used many of the old songs, to be sure,
but new ones were born in the new burst of happy experience.

There is no greater composition than the *Te Deum*. Age
after age has augmented the music of the Psalms. Cromwell's
Ironsides charged down to battle with songs upon their lips.
They come as songs in the night.

I have witnessed the power of our national songs and
great hymns of the Church in the training camps, at home
and on the battle fields abroad. The battle done, the tempo
changes, and the demand is—

[1] By Cornelius Woelfkin in "Religion." Richard R. Smith, Inc.

81

"Not for the grand old masters,
Not for the bards sublime,
Whose distant footsteps echo
Through the corridors of time.
For, like strains of martial music,
Their mighty thoughts suggest
Life's endless toil and endeavor;
And to-night I long for rest."

III. THE CHURCH STILL SHOULD LEAD IN THE ARMISTICE OF SONG

Jehoshaphat set the choirs to the front and retired the spearmen. This is a good procedure for the Church. In a world of divisive thought songs unify and inspire. When we sing in our churches, using hymns of many denominations, do we ask the theology of the authors of our hymns? Catholic and Protestant are side by side. Liberal and conservative walk together.

"Song has come to us from the angels. Christianity invented the organ and gave sighs to brass. Wherever she has erected her altars, there have arisen a people who sing as naturally as the birds of the air. Song is the daughter of prayer. The Iriquois, who could not take the doctrines of the Church, were overcome by her songs. Love and harmony are the things it has taught to men. Music noted down her hymns: sculpture wrought out her meditations. Architecture reared her temples as sublime and melancholy as her thought." (Chateaubriand.)

THE VIRGIN BIRTH OF JESUS [1]

The voice of him that crieth in the wilderness, Prepare ye the way of the Lord, make straight in the desert a highway for our God. Isaiah 40: 3.

Behold, I will send my messenger, and he shall prepare the way before me: and the Lord, whom ye seek, shall suddenly come to his temple, even the messenger of the covenant, whom ye delight in: behold, he shall come, saith the Lord of hosts. Malachi 3: 1.

Behold, a virgin shall conceive, and bear a son, and shall call his name Immanuel. Isaiah 7: 14.

The most important subject that could possibly be discussed is the Virgin Birth of Jesus Christ. It is the battle ground of belief, and within the confines of its discussion are to be found two contending forces—the enemies of God and the children of God.

I. THE VIRGIN BIRTH IS PROPHETICALLY STATED IN THE OLD TESTAMENT

WHAT is the string of prophecy? (1) The seed of the woman shall bruise the serpent's head. (2) It is to be the seed of Abraham. (3) It must come through the seed of Judah. (4) The heir is to be born in Bethlehem. (5) He must have a forerunner. (6) He must be called Immanuel. (7) He is to be born of a virgin.

These prophetic utterances are there, and no Jew on earth can deny them, and no one who can read history can deny them—they are there. Well, they must be there for a definite reason. They must have been placed there by Almighty God. They were supernaturally written, they reveal a supernatural fact and a supernatural line, for the purpose of bringing a supernatural person into existence.

II. THIS DOCTRINE IS HISTORICALLY STATED

There is a great conflict around this point. The Bible states

[1] By Mark A. Matthews in the *Presbyterian* (December 18, 1930).

very clearly that all of these prophecies were fulfilled. But men question. They say that the statement that Jesus was born without a father is unscientific. The Bible does not say that Jesus was born without a father. It specifically states that God was his Father.

There is not a line in Scripture that ever intimated that Joseph is his father. But every line speaks of Mary as his mother. What else? Every line in Scripture in which the statement is made speaks of God as being the Father of Jesus Christ. Not only did God say that he was the Father, but he never said or intimated anything else.

Again, Jesus never, at any time, intimated that he was the son of Joseph. He says that he is the Son of God. To be true he speaks of himself as being the Son of Man. That was possible because of his human motherhood. He was both human and divine.

Now, it is a fact that the credibility of Scripture rests upon the virgin birth of Jesus. On the fact of the virgin birth rests the sinlessness of Jesus. If you bring Jesus into existence with a human father and mother, he is going to come with a sinful body.

The supernatural Son of God, supernaturally incarnated, supernaturally sacrificed, supernaturally raised, is supernaturally coming, will supernaturally gather you unto himself, because he is the Son of God.

THE PRACTICAL VALUE OF RELIGION [1]

They that wait upon the Lord shall renew their strength; they shall mount up with wings as eagles; they shall run, and not be weary; and they shall walk, and not faint. Isaiah 40: 31.

Grant the utmost that can truthfully be said of the inadequacy of our worship and preaching, and still it is true that the practice of religion, just as it is, with all its defects, has values no one can afford to miss.

WHAT are they? This text tells. Life makes terrific demands upon us. Strength must be renewed. It shall come by waiting upon the Lord.

I. THEY SHALL MOUNT UP WITH WINGS AS EAGLES

The man who wrote that looked in the heavens and saw the eagles. Perhaps his spirit had been weary. "So I would rise," he said, "and soar in the higher atmosphere. To-day we see men who have this faculty of rising. What is the secret? Power. The famous flight of the Question Mark was possible only because some one found a way of renewing its reserves of power.

What a parable of the living. We are not balloons. We are "heavier-than-air machines." It takes strength, continually renewed, to keep us in the higher atmosphere.

Ask yourselves if it is easy to keep in the high moral atmosphere. Life is a busy place. How can one keep above the details?

II. THEY SHALL RUN, AND NOT BE WEARY

There comes a time when we face an emergency. We must be a contestant in a race. We must have stamina and strength.

[1] By William Pierson Merrill in "Great Themes of the Christian Faith." Richard R. Smith.

How are we going to secure it? What would it be worth to anybody to have the spiritual reserves to meet the great crises of life? The answer again is, by waiting upon the Lord.

I recall the day when William R. Harper came in where a little group of us were meeting and told us that he had an incurable disease and must soon leave us. I know what sustained that man and gave him his victory. For years it has been to me one of the proofs of the glory and power of our religion. He asked one or two Christian men whose faith seemed most real and clear to come and talk with him; and with them he faced the whole problem of life and death; he made his plans for the future life as calmly and sensibly as he would have planned a trip to Europe; he sought God and found him, and died as he had lived, in the strength of friendship with the unseen Father.

III. THEY SHALL WALK, AND NOT FAINT

It is not alone in the great crises of life that the practice of worship helps. There are seven days in the week. Each of these days is filled with duties. One walks better because of the practice of religion and worship. A man who sought Church membership said: "I have found, by actual test, that when I go to Church and pray I can do things I couldn't do otherwise."

It may be that two young men, or two young women, came down the avenue this morning. At the door of the church they halted. One came in to worship, the other went to take a walk, to call on a friend, to do any number of things. Now you may ask me, "If you should inspect each of these two to-morrow, could you tell which of them had been to Church to-day?" No, probably not. But let them keep on doing that, week after week, year after year, one keeping up the practice of religion and the other neglecting it, and anyone could tell the difference.

VERDICTS OF HISTORY REVERSED [1]

He was despised and rejected of men. Isaiah 53: 3.
The name which is above every name. Philippians 2: 9.

The favorites of one generation are often unknown **in** the next. In 1792 Paris unveiled a marble tablet, having in gold letters certain names that France would hold in everlasting remembrance. Unfortunately, the next generation pulled down the tablet; to-day the names of these immortals are unknown. In sculpture, men do not know their own leaders. In Paris the Salon refused Rodin's first model of the "Thinker," and urged the sculptor to stick to his brick and mortar; but Rodin was not a hod carrier. Now he ranks with Phidias and Michelangelo. On a winter's day Rembrandt took a painting to the burgomaster. The rich ruler scoffed at the canvas, but offered the painter a gulder for a loaf of bread. The time came when Holland paid 100,000 gulders for the rejected canvas.

I. HISTORY HAS REVERSED ITS VERDICT ON THE CHARACTER AND CAREER OF JESUS

THE chief rulers took him for a young carpenter and nothing more. He carved yokes, laid floors, and hung doors. His formative years were filled with toil, and he had no opportunity for books or travel for which his heart dreamed. He was of the common people. He knew them and loved them, and his entire life was tied up with them. Perhaps the common people heard him gladly, but the rulers decreed that he was to die. But generations afterwards the case was reopened. His friends urged a reversal of judgment. They urged that he brought men three gifts—God, freedom, and immortality. Now the ablest men of letters vied to pay him tribute. But the first judgment was scorning and crucifixion.

[1] By Newell Dwight Hillis in "Anglo-American Preaching." Harper.

II. HISTORY HAS REVERSED ITS JUDGMENT AS TO JESUS' METHOD OF HUMAN CONTROL

There have been many plans for ruling states. Kings have ruled by regiments and dungeons. Soldiers have ruled by swords and fagots. Plato named one kind of ruler an "autocrat"; another group of rulers he called "aristocrats"; the third group he called "the democrats"; but every one of these states enforced their laws by swords or clubs or bombshells.

But Jesus proposed to rule society by the omnipotence of great ideas.

First idea was: Man is the Son of God and therefore he must be free.

Second idea: The equality of the classes.

Third idea: The equality of the races.

Fourth idea: The equality of the sexes.

Every one of these ideas cut like a sword into the conventional thinking of the times. Here was one who bases a new republic upon the quality of mankind. Where did he find precedent for this alliance with the poor? But history has decreed that Jesus was right. Ideas have come from the poor. Inventors from Watt to Edison have come from the poor. Every great painter and sculptor began his life in poverty. The same is true of authors, historians, philosophers, and poets.

"Call the roll of the kings. No one of them ever invented a steam engine, or a telegraph, or a printing press, or a ship."

THE MIGHT OF PUBLIC OPINION [1]

No weapon that is formed against thee shall prosper. Isaiah 54: 17.

PUBLIC opinion is the mind of any society, tribe, or nation in full and imperative expression. We have in the career of Jesus two supreme instances of the power of public opinion— his death and the preservation of his teaching. Pilate appealed to public opinion, and the answer was, "Crucify him." On the other hand, the teaching of Jesus has been preserved through generations because public opinion has recognized the worth of the teachings.

I. PUBLIC OPINION MAY BE IMPROVED

This is true in every phase of life. Take the change in the attitude of America, north and south, toward slavery in a few generations. Without this hope the world would surely be a dark place. The deepest faith in the first prophets of Christianity was this: "The public mind is all and desperately wrong, but it can be renewed"—and here is our basis for hope and motive for work.

II. INDIVIDUALS MAY CHANGE AND IMPROVE THE PUBLIC MIND

Henry Ward Beecher was but one man, a tired man at that. But as a lecturer for humanity he influenced public opinion against slavery in England and America. Alexander Hamilton was but one man. But when the national mind was in darkest despair, he brought light and restored confidence in our national resources. Abraham Lincoln was but one man. But he united the divided North at the time of the Civil War.

III. THE BETTER INSTINCTS OF THE RACE UNDERMINE THE WRONG PUBLIC MIND

One of the wonderful things in human history is the way

[1] By George A. Gordon in "Anglo-American Preaching." Harper.

that right has of eventually supplanting wrong. Christianity, which at one time was hated and distrusted, has become the flower of civilization. Man's nobler instincts will not allow him permanently to side with falsehood against truth, evil against goodness, the criminal against the citizen who orders his life in industry and progress.

IV. LAPSE OF TIME WILL DEMOLISH WRONG PUBLIC OPINION

When I was a home missionary in Maine about fifty years ago, there was in full swing a great economic heresy. Get a mill running well and print greenbacks by the hundred million; then all the people will have all the money they want all the time. All the forces of economic enlightenment then available went forth against this absurd state of mind, but at the polls the economic heresy won. The state of Maine was disgraced. Her educated men and her intelligent citizens were ashamed. Many of them fell into despair; to my knowledge some of them died of grief over this insane public mind. What could reason do? As well reason with the Penobscot and Kennebec Rivers. . . . "Give men rope enough, and they will hang themsleves"; so runs a wise old proverb. . . . Few living to-day remember the Maine craze. It went its way as time became wiser and brought a saner heart. . . . Time is great, because God is in it; as the Time Spirit in Faust sings:

> "At the whirring loom of Time unawed
> I weave the living mantle of God."

FOR THE LAST DAY OF THE YEAR [1]

The harvest is past, the summer is ended, and we are not saved.
Jeremiah 8: 20.

The books have been closed; the account has been balanced; the time for payment has expired; we are declared defaulters for the year.

I. THE LESSON OF THE YEAR

THE text refers to a regretful survey on the part of a nation which had neglected opportunities until they had passed forever. Jeremiah speaks but the bitter truth. Life presents just two conditions out of which we must mold our faith. We will note just what they are.

II. THE MEANING OF THE HARVEST

Some years ago Dr. William Osler made the statement that after forty years of age a man's opportunities, as far as originating anything, are practically at an end. Dr. Osler was severely and unfairly criticized. He did not mean, as some supposed, that at forty years of age a man is useless, or that he should be put out of the way. He meant that in life there is a period corresponding with the summer in nature when a man is at his best. His years after this period are full and plentiful if he has lived courageously and worth while in the spring and summer of his life. Harvest in life, as in nature, is merely a revelation of what a man has been.

III. HARVEST A PERIOD OF OPPORTUNITY

In the world there are many kinds of grain for the harvest. Some of the labels are Wealth, Pleasure, Ambition, Power. But there is one of more importance than all these. It is the harvest of the future. Shall I live for the Hereafter?

[1] By Frederick D. Kershner in "Sermons for Special Days of the Year." Doran.

When the end of life draws near, men count failure not in terms of dollars, but in terms of character and life. A girl who committed suicide wrote her friends: "Do not tell my mother what a failure I have made of my life." In the last day there was but one thing which counted. That was character. As he was dying, John Randolph, the great American statesman, insisted on his doctor writing one word. The word was: "Remorse."

IV. HARVEST AND TIME

Life not only means the use of strength and its opportunities. It means also time for them. The wise man has altogether too little time to do the things he wishes to do. The hours of life are precious, and he who fills them full of good things will have the good harvest. Many times we do not appreciate the value of time until it has flown.

"If I could be spared for only a few years, I would give all the wealth I have amassed in a lifetime," said a millionaire as he neared his end.

V. THE CONCLUSION

We are not saved. These sad words are for those who realize their failures in character too late.

TRUST [1]

Leave thy fatherless children, I will preserve them alive; and let thy widows trust in me. Jeremiah 49: 11.

You will find the word "trust" is used in the Old Testament as a general thing where the word "believe" is used in the New Testament. In the Old Testament you read about "turning to the Lord"; in the New Testament it is "Repent." In the Old Testament "distrust," in the New "disbelief."

I. WHOM NOT TO TRUST

IF we trust ourselves, our strength may fail. If we trust friends, they may turn against us or may die. Many a man has been disappointed who has put his trust in money. If you trust in fame and reputation, some slandering tongue may blast them. Trust must be in something beyond this life.

II. WHOM TO TRUST

I would rather have trust in Jesus Christ than any bank. We are to trust him at all times.

We are to trust God. Christ urged it. He said: "Have faith in God. Some think that it is unreasonable, but I think that it is the most reasonable thing in the world to trust the God of the Book.

I think I can doubt my existence about as easy as I can doubt God. It is not a hard thing to put your trust in him.

III. WHEN TO TRUST

We are to trust Him at all times.

There is a common saying, "I wouldn't trust that man out of my sight." That is the way a lot of people treat Almighty God.

[1] By Dwight L. Moody in "Thou Fool." Published by the *Christian Herald.*

You have heard of the woman whose horse ran away with her. She was asked, "What did you do?" She trusted in the harness until it broke. Then she trusted in the wagon till it smashed. At last she called on God and was saved.

IV. HOW TO TRUST

There is just one way. That is to trust him with your whole heart. No one is ever barred out of heaven who trusts with his whole heart.

"I want to tell you of a great mistake made in my life. If I had my life to live over again, I wouldn't make it. I haven't served God with all my heart." (Statement of a prominent physician of Glasgow in Mr. Moody's meetings.)

V. WHO WILL TRUST

Those who know Him will trust. The reason an infidel cannot trust God is because he does not know him. If you find a man or woman who believes the Bible and reads it constantly, he can trust. Unless people come to God and get acquainted, they are hardly in a position to trust him.

VI. THE FRUIT OF TRUST

It is luscious fruit.

Probe the human heart, and you will find down in its depths a want, a cry for rest. Where can rest be found? Here it is, right here. Put your trust in the living God with all your heart, mind, soul, and strength, and you will have peace. Don't think to keep it; it keeps you. . . . There is a place within reach where you may have perfect peace. The world cannot take it away. That is what He wants to give you.

WHAT YOUR FACE REVEALS [1]

They had the face of a man, the face of a lion, the face of an ox, and the face of an eagle. Ezekiel 1: 10.

During his captivity in Babylon the prophet Ezekiel had a wonderful vision of four creatures, each with four faces.

I. FACE OF A MAN

> "You don't have to tell how you live every day,
> You need not reveal if you work or you play:
> A trusty barometer is always in place—
> However you live, it will show in your face."
>
> (C. F. Cross.)

"No sunrise, mountain top, or June blossom is so beautiful and so inspiring by its beauty as human faces at their best." (William C. Gannett.)

"I want every Englishman to know that when he is looking into my eyes, he is seeing into my soul." (General Botha.)

THE most wonderful face is the face of Jesus Christ. And John tells us that the blessedness of heaven is linked with that face. (Rev. 21: 2; 22: 3, 4.)

II. FACE OF A LION

The lion has always been the symbol of courage. Courage is not the absence of fear, but the overcoming of fear. Mr. Spurgeon at one time remarked that the reason the lions could not eat Daniel was because he was mostly backbone and grit. But the lion is also cautious. His character is a combination of these two qualities.

Robert E. Lee, according to Frederick B. Maurice, had a faculty for "calculated daring." Even Napoleon is credited with saying that, "in order to win, one must sometimes be very

[1] By W. J. Thompson in *Church Management.*

prudent." Success demands both boldness and prudence. One must dare, but not recklessly. One must be prudent, but not faint-hearted.

III. FACE OF AN OX

The ox symbolizes patient, plodding perseverance. There are circumstances which must be met with the policy of the lion. But more often we win with the methods of the ox.

"My imagination would never have served me as it has but for the habit of daily, humble, commonplace, patient, drudging attention." (Charles Dickens.)

Lyman Beecher was once asked how long it took him to prepare a certain sermon. He replied, "Forty years."

Judson toiled seven years in Burma for the first convert. Morrison waited seventeen years for the first convert in China. They used to speak of David Livingstone as "the man who would go on."

"Then remember this, my brother,
Don't give up—whate'er you do:
Trust in God and keep on going—
See things through.

Be persistent! And your Saviour
Will your faith and hope renew.
Jesus Christ will never fail you—
See things through."

IV. FACE OF AN EAGLE

The eagle is the emblem of keen vision and lofty flight. We need these powers in order to see beyond our limitations to the wonderful freedom of life; to look beyond the temporal to the Eternal; beyond the power of sin to the glorious salvation offered us by Christ our Redeemer.

THE SOUL'S OPEN WINDOWS [1]

Now when Daniel knew that the writing was signed, he went into his house; and his windows being open in his chamber toward Jerusalem, he kneeled upon his knees three times a day, and prayed, and gave thanks before his God, as he did aforetime. Daniel 6: 10.

I. IN DANIEL'S CAREER APPEAR THREE STAGES OF TESTING

(a) THE trial of flesh. Daniel dines with the rich in the city where the tables groan under the weight of good things. There are wines and rich foods. Even though he might not care for these things, there is the temptation to yield for the sake of convention. But Daniel did not yield. He refused their wine and their rich foods.

(b) The trial of intellect. This has to do with his ability to interpret the dream of Nebuchadnezzar. It was a serious thing for Daniel. The king used those harshly who failed him in the time of need. Daniel probably did not fear for himself, but he did fear for his fellows. But he stood the test.

(c) The trial of spirit. This is the story of the text for the sermon. The enemies of Daniel tried to find that wherewith they could entrap him. Feeling that his religion might offer the opportunity, they succeeded in having the king decree that anyone who worshiped any god but himself for thirty days should be thrown into a den of lions.

II. WHAT THE OPEN WINDOWS REVEAL

(a) Daniel's belief in God. When a busy statesman can find time to kneel and pray three times a day, he is a believer. In this instance it was a revelation of his belief in the God of his childhood and his homeland.

(b) The windows symbolize his religious faith. The faith

[1] By Samuel Judson Porter in "Lamps of Gold." Sunday School Board of the Southern Baptist Convention.

must have open expression. Faith does not grow when concealed under a bushel.

(c) The windows reveal Daniel's estimate of spiritual reality. He was in a land which had every appearance of wealth and power. The king had bestowed great honors upon him. On the other hand, Jerusalem was desolate. Yet Daniel believed that Jerusalem had a spiritual reality which Babylon did not possess.

(d) The open windows reveal a belief in spiritual fellowship. Daniel prized his religion and kept it up to date. He had daily communication with headquarters.

(e) The open windows suggest a better life beyond the present.

We feel that Daniel's open windows are but the Old Testament way of saying we look for a city which hath foundations, whose builder and maker is God. . . . In all probability he was never permitted to return to the city of his childhood; but when the hour of his releasement came, we may be sure that his tried, purified spirit found its radiant way to that better Jerusalem home toward whose shining portals he had been facing during all his exiled years.

> "Do you fear the foe will in the conflict win?
> Is it dark without you—darker still within?
> Clear the darkened windows, open wide the door,
> Let the blessed sunshine in."

THE SOUL WINNER [1]

And many of them that sleep in the dust of the earth shall awake, some to everlasting life, and some to shame and everlasting contempt. And they that be wise shall shine as the brightness of the firmament, and they that turn many to righteousness as the stars forever and ever. Daniel 12: 2, 3.

Now, mark you, these are not the words of some hot-headed evangelist, the words of some young man in the flush of youth; but they are the words of an old statesman, who stood as high in his day as Bismarck ever stood in Germany, or Gladstone in England, or any statesman that we ever had in this country.

I. EVERY ONE LIKES TO SHINE

ALL business men are trying to get to the head. Go to the university, and you will find each professor seeking to become a leader in his profession. Every newspaper man wants to be the greatest newspaper writer in the world. Every soldier wants to be a general. Every statesman would like to get into the White House.

And the mother, she has a boy at school, and if he gets to the head of the class, she manages to let everybody know it. If he is valedictorian, she will let it be known. You all want to be known. You all want to shine.

But we are not told that business men are going to shine forever and ever.

II. IT IS THE SOUL WINNER WHO IS WISE AND WILL SHINE FOREVER

"He that winneth souls is wise."

I experienced a Minnesota blizzard some years ago. They told me a story of a man who was lost in one. Just as he was

[1] By Dwight L. Moody in "Thou Fool." Published by the *Christian Herald.*

about to give up all hope he saw a light and made his way to a cabin. Some one there had left a light burning, thinking it might help some poor soul who was out in the storm. After the man got out of the storm he became wealthy, and he built a great house. He put a lighthouse on top of it, so that any one who might be lost would have a light to lead him on his way. His light shone in righteousness.

I used to have a rule that was a wonderful help to me; it was never to let a day pass without speaking to some one about his eternal welfare; and if I didn't do any good to anybody else, it kept me warm. It was great exercise for me, and it kept my interest in others, my sympathies alive.

III. MANY SMALL LIGHTS MAKE A GREAT LIGHT

When I first went West and got into those log school-houses, I was a drummer. I used to speak, if I got a chance, for Christ. On one occasion a man asked me: "Will you speak again this evening?" Then he added: "My young brother from Chicago is passing through our town, and he has promised to speak here to-night at early candlelight." That's the way he gave it out, you know. We always used to go around a little ahead of time, and a man would turn up with an old, dingy lantern he had to feed his cattle with, and he would stick it up upon a bench to light the schoolhouse. I hadn't a light, but they brought their light. Then a woman would come with a lamp filled with sperm oil, and she would bring it out from under her shawl, and she would put it on a school bench, and then another a tallow dip, a candle, and how it would sputter. And by the time we got the old schoolhouse filled, we had plenty of light. If everybody had a little light, it would light it. If you can't be a lighthouse, you can light up your tallow dip. They burned up Portland with a firecracker. Do what you can!

SPIRITUAL POVERTY [1]

Can two walk together, except they be agreed? Amos 3: 3.
I have called you friends. John 15: 15.

I. WHERE THERE IS BEAUTY, ORDER, AND TRUTH, THERE IS HARMONY

WHEREVER unity is, there God is. Wherever there is discord, there God cannot exist. For he laid the keynote of all harmonies; he planned all the perfect combinations.

> "And wheresoever in his rich creation,
>   Sweet music breathes—in wave, or bird, or soul,
> 'Tis but the faint and far reverberation
>   Of that great tune to which the planets roll."

II. THE KINGDOM OF GOD WHICH OUR LORD CONSISTENTLY PREACHED WAS AN IDEAL OF ORDERED AND HARMONIOUS LIFE

The Church is to be the outward expression of this Kingdom. It is the family of faith. Here the children are to find their highest expression of unity in a definitely social act—the sacrament of the body and blood. They are charged to show to the world a oneness of heart and purpose. "By this shall all men know that ye are my disciples, if ye love one another."

III. THE WORDS OF JESUS, "I HAVE CALLED YOU FRIENDS," IS THE LAW OF CHRISTIAN LIFE

It is of more than passing interest to note that he did not ask to have all his disciples alike. Personality was not to be submerged. But, differing in temperament and personality, they were to be friends. They were people of strong and varied opinions. Arguments were a foregone conclusion. There would be occasional friction. But the word "friends" created the unity.

[1] By Charles L. Warr in "British Preachers, Third Series," edited by Sir James Marchant. Revell.

IV. THIS IS THE GOSPEL WHICH OUR TURBULENT AGE HAS FORGOTTEN

Uniformity is a dreary business. There is little uniformity in nature. There is little in personal experiences. It is probably not to be desired. We shall continue to have our differences in nations and Church divisions. It is not the divisions which are to be regretted.

It is the suspicion, the greed, the selfishness that blaspheme that friendship to which Christ called his followers. These have created the barriers between man and man, class and class.

V. WE CANNOT FULFILL OUR CHIEF END UNLESS OUR SPIRITS BE IN HARMONY WITH THE SPIRIT OF CHRIST

The unity of friendship is not of opinions, but of the heart. If we take life with any degree of gravity, and if we are sincere, we will find to whatsoever religious or political party we belong our common idealism is centered in a great historic fact —namely, the sacrifice of Jesus Christ and all that implies for humankind.

VI. THERE ARE SIGNS THAT THIS GENERATION IS LOOKING AND LISTENING FOR THIS "FRIENDS" PHILOSOPHY

Let us hope that this is true. The Church must learn that the better ambition is to grow, not with authority, but with humility. Nations must learn that their greatness will be found in the moral greatness of their people. Commerce must learn that humanity is first, profits second.

But when these are learned, and they are being learned, we can find the whole world united in the adoration of the Father, everlasting.

A MESSAGE FOR GRAY DAYS [1]

If the vision tarry, wait for it, for it will come: and it will not be late. Habakkuk 2:3 (Moffatt).

Age after age, apparently earnest souls feel hotly that the world is out of joint, that something must be done to mend things; yes, and they see what that is, and start up eagerly to set about it, sure that they can put it through. And, age after age, in a little they are standing puzzled, and daunted, and confused, with their resolution oozing from them, tired and dispirited.

I. THE MESSAGE OF "WAIT" IS ONE OF GOD'S MOST COMMON THROUGH THE AGES

And yet this is the hardest thing in the world. When the doctor says, "There is nothing we can do; we must wait," it brings nerves to the tensest point. That brings agony. Yet God asks just this thing continually. It is not that we are to dawdle about and do nothing. In this time we are to prepare ourselves so that when God calls for our coöperation we can act. We are to build into our characters that poise and assurance which will sustain our faith. Nor is it that God does not want the thing done. But he knows that it will take longer than we think.

This is true in our own lives. "We all thought," said Baxter, in speaking of the civil war, "that one battle would end it; but we were all very mistaken." Ananda, Buddha's favorite disciple, saw comrade after comrade reach Nirvana, yet the years slipped by, and it seemed far away for him. Such is life for most of us.

> "Love, love that once for me did agonize,
>   Will conquer all things to itself. If late
> Or soon it be, I ask not nor advise.
>   But, since my God is waiting, I can wait."

[1] By Arthur John Gossip in "The Hero in Thy Soul." Scribner's.

103

II. GOD ALSO SAYS: "IT WILL COME"

"All that hoped or dreamed of good," says our brave poet, "shall exist not its semblance but itself. The hard that proved too hard, the heroic for earth too high," will all come truly—will surely all come true. I promise it, says God. If you will play your part, you can depend on me. It is upon the road, though you see nothing; the seed is living, is springing up, and will flower.

It is well to be reminded of this, for there is much in the world of affairs to make us cynical. Here are experts who assure us that since the time of Henry VI there have been twenty-six attempts to eliminate war by international agreement. Twenty-five times before the present effort the vision has been seen. But on the other hand, the Reformation broke out at least that number of times before Luther nailed his theses. No effort in the cause of truth is ever useless. Every new attempt revives the idea in men's minds and brings the ideal near to fruition.

But history also makes heartening reading. There were once horrible diseases rampant, leprosy for one of them. Many a country church still shows the old leper's window through which outcasts partook of the communion. Yet this disease is gone—gone like a hideous nightmare from which one awakes. Yes, humanity progresses. "It will come," says the prophet. "In God's name I promise it."

Up! up! and back into the quick of things with steady hearts and quiet eyes. And even "if it tarry, wait for it, for it will come: and it will not be late."

PLAY [1]

The streets of the city shall be full of boys and girls playing in the streets thereof. Zechariah 8: 5.

Children play. They all do it. That is one of the very first things they do. Their parents know they are going to do it, and so they lay in a stock of toys in advance. How disappointed a child would be if, on opening his eyes, there were not a toy anywhere within sight. He would say: "What kind of a world is this, in which there is nothing for me to play with? I am sorry I came!"

I. PLAY IS A PART OF LIFE

SOMEBODY has said that the world is a workshop. Well, it is also a playground. People are not alone here to work. They are also here to play. Many parents would be better if they understood this. A play room is as necessary as a parlor. If you do not provide a place for your children to play, they will find a place outside of the home. If you do not provide them with companions, they will find their own. If you do not give them time for play, they will steal it from time allotted for other things.

But, of course, one cannot play all the time. To try that becomes tedious and sickening. There is a time to eat, a time to sleep, a time to work. And there is a right time for play.

II. GOD LIKES TO SEE YOU PLAY

Your earthly father likes to see you play. If you did not play, he would be worried. Well, your heavenly Father also likes to see you play. Jesus always said that you should think of God as you think of your own father.

God gives us the play instinct, so he must like it. Indeed,

[1] By Charles E. Jefferson in "Under Seventeen." Revell.

God plays. He plays after the fashion of deities. For instance, he plays with colors. A sunset is not work for God; it is play. The next time you see a sunset remember that it is God playing. Adults ought to play as well as children. Their play will not be like the play of children. A sixty-year-old woman does not want a doll to play with, nor will a man of seventy want to match marbles. But there is a play for these years, and those who are wise will take advantage of it.

III. THE LAWS OF PLAY ARE THE LAWS OF LIFE

As one learns to play he learns to work and to live. It is a law of God that one should work with all his might. We learn that as we play. It is a law of God that one should not cheat in his work. We learn that in our play. One who cheats at his play is soon in disgrace. It is a law of life that one should not become sour and grumpy in failure. We learn that in play. One learns that bragging and strutting do not pay, nor does peevishness when he can't have his own way. Play is a great school for learning the ethics of coöperation.

There is a vivid and unforgettable picture in the old book of Zechariah which I presume hardly any of you have ever read, the picture of a beautiful city which does not exist yet, but which some day is going to be. The prophet painted a picture for the encouragement of the men of his day. The city in which he lived had been having a hard time. It had gone through the horrors of war. It had suffered the ravages of pestilence and famine. Hardly anybody in that city lived to be old. The aged had wellnigh disappeared, and so also had the young. The city was made up of men and women in middle life; tribulation had killed off all the rest. But the prophet gazed into the future and saw that a better time was coming. . . . The streets will be full of boys and girls playing in the streets thereof.

ROBBING GOD [1]

Will a man rob God? Malachi 3: 8.

This is one of several unanswered questions in the Bible. Jesus says, "What shall it profit a man if he gain the whole world and lose his own soul?" St. Paul asks, "How shall we escape if we neglect so great salvation?" Peter cries out, "If the righteous scarcely be saved, where shall the ungodly and the sinner appear?" The prophet Malachi exclaims, "But who shall abide the day of his coming, and who shall stand when he appeareth?"

I. THERE ARE TWO PARTIES TO THIS QUESTION

MAN and God. Man is marvelously created and adapted.

"Man is the conservation of all **perfection** as an instrument." (Sir Charles Bell.)

God is the Creator. He gives all of his forces without stint. He might have produced the world so that living is pain, but instead he made it joy. He has adapted it for our comfort and ease.

We start a rock on the mountain side, but gravitation puts its shoulder under it and multiplies its speed a thousand times. We launch our ships upon the seas, and he sends the winds to push them on their way. He unlocks the prisoned sunshine of past millenniums fastened for ages in the black coal, and steam is generated from it, which moves the giant screws and moves the steamer onward through the billows.

Can man rob such a God?

II. WHAT GAIN CAN COME TO MAN FROM HIS OPPOSITION TO GOD?

He can't rob God by force. God is strong. The forces of

[1] By Charles L. Goodell in "Life Reveries." Revell.

all nature are his, and man cannot array his own strength
against such forces. Nor can he rob God by stealth. Men
may sleep, but God never sleeps. Darkness and light are the
same to him. Then who would think of stealing from a judge
who is to try his case? No, God is not robbed in this way. It
must be some other way. History is full of stories of strange
perfidy, and among the most amazing of these are the ways in
which man has found to rob God.

"When Jesus came to Golgotha they hanged him to a tree,
  They drove great nails through hands and feet, and made a Calvary;
  They crowned him with a crown of thorns, red were his wounds and deep,
  For they were crude and cruel days, and human flesh was cheap."
                                                      (Studdert-Kennedy.)

III. WE ROB GOD BY DENYING HIM THE LOVE HE CRAVES

God says: "My son, give me thy heart." We answer, "Soul,
take thine ease; eat, drink, and be merry." God says, "It is
time to seek the Lord." We say: "Go thy way for this time.
When I have a convenient season I will call for thee." God
says, "Thou shalt love the Lord thy God, and him only shalt
thou serve." Man says, "I love pleasure and self, and these
will I serve." God wants what you want—*love*.

What does a husband or a wife or a brother or a sister
want most? What avails it if we have every comfort in
life if we do not have love? A loveless heart is a pauper,
no matter what else it has. What we need in our homes
is not so much better furniture, or larger rooms, or finer
food. What we want is love.

Love is what we must have, and it is what God wants!
It is love that makes sacrifice easy. It is love which
makes life anew.

THE HUSHED PROPHETS [1]

And he shall turn the heart of the fathers to the children, and the heart of the children to their fathers, lest I come and smite the earth with a curse. Malachi 4: 6.

THIS is the last verse in the Old Testament. It will be four hundred years before a note will be sounded which is important enough to put in the canon of the Scripture. In four hundred years Christ will be born and the prophetic voice will again be heard. But for these four centuries the prophet voices are hushed. Why?

I. MAYBE THEY ARE HUSHED BECAUSE THEY ARE TALKED OUT

Perhaps they have told their story. If they talked on, it would be merely to gabble or babble. They would say nothing new. The revelation they had received they have given. Not one jot or one tittle can be added to it.

II. MAYBE THEY ARE SILENT BECAUSE THEY HAVE FULLY MAPPED THE FUTURE

The prophets were an intelligent group, and they knew that they were shaping the morals of the future. They were walking in the centuries. Socrates' ethics are gone. Plato's ethics are a jest. The ethics of Solon are all vanished. But the book of God, containing the codes spoken by these prophets, have been indelibly written in human history. No one single item has vanished from the Decalogue. Now that they have told all that they know the prophets are silent. The future will complete the story.

III. PERHAPS THE NEARNESS OF JESUS HAS SMOTE THEM DUMB

He is four hundred years away. But they hear his footsteps

[1] By William A. Quayle in "The Healing Shadow." Copyright, 1923. Used by permission of the Abingdon Press.

and are on their faces. Have you not noticed that the birds are mute before the coming of a storm?

In four hundred years there will come a singing woman. The angels will then stop their singing to listen to one who carries a babe on her heart. Before this scene—though it is four hundred years away—the prophets are dumb.

IV. MAYBE THEY ARE HUSHED BECAUSE THEY SAW THE SUNRISE

There is the Sun of Righteousness who is to arise with healing in his wings, the night is dark, but the morning cometh.

That is enough, Malachi. Come, sit silent forever, Malachi. No more words from you. You have told it all. It was a dark night; now it is daylight. "Shall the Sun of Righteousness arise with healing in his wings?"

V. MAYBE THE PROPHETS ARE SILENT BECAUSE THEIR MUSIC WAS COMMONPLACE

Suppose that the organist's organ were beside the sea. And as he played the organ of the sea began to play. Would he not stop as God pulled out the stops of the great organ, and the tremolo began to play and the lyric voice started to sing? The prophets were in the position of the organist. Their music seemed commonplace compared with that which God started through Jesus Christ.

And the organist Christ is playing yet, "Come unto me, all ye that labor and are heavy laden, and I will give you rest."

And the prophets all are hushed, but Christ's voice and music are not hushed yet, nor will be to-morrow, nor will be forever, and forever, and forever. Amen!

AS I SEE IT [1]

Follow me, and I will make you fishers of men. Matthew 4: 19.

The one thing Christ seemed to be asking me, when I came to that moment in my life, was: "Have you the courage to follow me?" No doubt many men are unconscious that they have ever come to a crisis of this kind, and yet somehow have imbibed the spirit of the Master, which makes them follow him and so entitle them to be called Christians, whether they label it or not. Thus, for example, we always have working for us men and women of all kinds of affiliation, or of no affiliation, serving in almost every capacity just for the love of it. . . . Afterwards most of these have found out that it was the leadership of Christ, visualized unconsciously somehow, that had brought them to what superficially might be regarded as making a sacrifice for others.

I. IT IS SERVICE, NOT INTELLECTUAL ATTITUDE, WHICH COMMENDS ONE TO GOD

ONE reason I am sure of this is because my own intellectual attitude changes from year to year. I have made it a practice to mark my Bible as I read. The first one with every page marked was presented, upon request, to a Boston museum. Since then I have marked and laid aside several. But if I would compare one of the newer ones with that first marked Bible, I would find that the comments differ in many ways. The intellectual attitude has changed. The law of service does not.

The older I grow the more convinced I am that my teachers were wrong when they taught me that we had nothing to do because it was all done for us. I believe now that what we do is of utmost importance to Christ and his kingdom.

[1] By Wilfred T. Grenfell in "British Preachers, Third Series," edited by Sir James Marchant. Revell.

111

II. THROUGH HUMBLE AVENUES OF SERVICE COMES THE VISION OF GOD

On another occasion a poor fisherman had taken me across a bay to see a dying man. He apologized when I got to his house wet and cold because the hot tea he offered me had neither sugar nor milk. There were several children in the room partly grown up and miserably clad. In the attic I found an old fisherman dying of cancer of the throat, and his wife, blind with cataract, crooning from her broken heart over the partner of her life. After doing what I could I came down the ladder that served for the stairs and asked my friend whether this was his father. "Only a neighbor," he replied. "How long has he been in your house?" I asked. He replied that the man had been there about a year. I said: "Do they pay anything for food?" "They have nothing to pay." I then asked him: "Why do you do it, seeing you and your children are so much in need?" The man looked into my face and said: "What would you do, doctor?"

There was a lesson such as one would not get in church or cathedral. The vision of God arose from the fisherman's hut. This was not an isolated instance. [2] Such are more common than unusual.

Life is a field of honor. What Christ's teaching leads me to do in life is the gauge by which I should be judged. It is unquestionably the gauge by which men appraise any claim to the title Christian.

What Christ seems to be asking me for every time is not comprehension but apprehension, not belief but courage. His religion is not the emotion which seeks to save itself, but that ennobling one which in willingly laying down life for others finds its own salvation.

[2] At this point Dr. Grenfell gave several similar instances.

BLESSED MOURNERS [1]

Blessed are they that mourn; for they shall be comforted. Matthew 5: 4.

Of course Jesus does not mean that every mourner is necessarily blessed. Tears are not good in and of themselves. There are tears, thank God, that seem to wash bright the eyes and spread beauty of the cheeks as they flow. They seem to water the gardens of the heart and set the fields of the soul to flowering. But there are other tears which leave the eyes smarting and blinded. They fret channels upon the cheeks and scorch and wither the verdure of the heart. There are, then, mourners whose mourning brings them no comfort. There are others whose mourning is the open road to heavenly consolation.

I. THE MOURNERS WHOSE MOURNING LEAVES THEM WITHOUT COMFORT

1. The deliberate pessimist. There are those who are veritable gluttons for wretchedness. They are never so happy as when they feel that they have a perfect right to be miserable. They are never so miserable as when they feel duty bound to be happy.

2. Those who mourn over some thwarted ambition. It would be hard to find a more tragic mourner than Napoleon.

3. Not always are those blessed who have suffered the loss of a loved one. Instead of being made tender by the loss, they are made bitter.

4. Those whose mourning is born of remorse. They do not hate evil, they hate its effects.

II. THOSE ARE BLESSED WHOSE MOURNING LEADS THEM TO JESUS CHRIST

THESE are the ones who mourn for their own sins and the sins of others. Many are they who can testify that the darkest

[1] By Clovis G. Chappell in "The Sermon on the Mount." Cokesbury Press.

days of their lives have brought them new visions. The very thing you thought would make your ruin made you instead. "Blessed is the man who is conscious that he is not what he should be." And especially blessed is the individual who can enter into the sufferings of others and share them. Jesus was that kind of a mourner.

III. THE NATURAL OUTCOME OF SUCH MOURNING IS COMFORT

1. This is true of those who mourn for their own sin. The outcome of that mourning is reconciliation with God. It ends in pardon and a peace that passeth all understanding.

Remember this suffering is for the sin and not for the consequences. Saul mourned for the consequences and was not blessed. David mourned for sin itself and was blessed. Peter mourned for his sin, and Jesus brought him words of comfort when he broke the bands of death. Judas mourned for the consequences and got little comfort.

2. Those who suffer for the sins of others share the blessing of Jesus. Paul was a mourner after this fashion. In his solicitude for others he had great "heaviness and continual sorrow." But it was the kind of mourning which was blessed, and he was the most happy of men. "For as the sufferings of Christ abound in us, so our consolation also aboundeth by Christ." Those who enter into the fellowship of Christ's suffering do find comfort.

SALT [1]

Ye are the salt of the earth. Matthew 5: 13.

This figure of speech is plain and pungent. Salt is savory, purifying, preservative. It is one of those superfluities which the great French wit defined as "things that are very necessary." From the very beginning of history men have set a high value upon it and sought for it by caves and by the seashore. The nation that had a good supply of it was counted rich. A bag of salt, among barbarous tribes, was worth more than a man. The Jews prized it especially because they lived in a warm climate where food was difficult to keep and because their religion laid particular emphasis on cleanliness and because salt was largely used in their sacrifices.

I. THINK, FIRST, OF THE INFLUENCE FOR GOOD WHICH MEN OF INTELLIGENCE MAY EXERCISE IN THE WORLD IF THEY WILL ONLY PUT THEIR CULTURE TO THE RIGHT USE

HALF the troubles of mankind come from ignorance. There are certain diseases which would go out of existence in ten years if people would only remember what they have learned. There are political and social plagues which are propagated only in the atmosphere of shallow self-confidence and vulgar thoughtlessness. Men of intelligence and training ought to have an antidote for these dangerous things. Having been instructed in the lessons of history and science, they are bound to contribute their knowledge to the service of society. College men should be the most conservative men in their communities; that is to say, the men who do most to conserve it.

Passion is equally dangerous with ignorance. Take, for illustration, the time of war. Educated men should be the steadiest opponents of war when it is avoidable. But when it

[1] By Henry Van Dyke in "The Open Door." Westminster Press.

becomes inevitable, they should be the most vigorous advocates for carrying it to a swift, triumphant, and noble end.

The culture which leaves a man without a flag is only one degree less miserable than that which leaves him without a God.

II. THINK OF THE DUTY WHICH MEN OF MORAL PRINCIPLE OWE TO SOCIETY IN REGARD TO EVILS WHICH CORRUPT AND DEGRADE IT

Men who love an orderly life are in great danger of doing nothing else. We have our cesspools in society. Thousands of our fellow men are living in darkness, confusion, and bitterness. Even in what we call respectable society, forces of corruption are at work. The question for men of salt is, "What are we going to do to stop these forces and remedy these conditions?" It is not enough to decide that the thing is unclean and we should leave it alone. On the contrary, when salt touches decay it checks it.

What the world needs to-day is not a new system of ethics. It is simply a larger number of people who will make a steady effort to live up to the system we have already.

III. THINK OF THE PART THAT RELIGION OUGHT TO PLAY IN THE PURIFYING, PRESERVING, AND SWEETENING OF SOCIETY

The loftiest reach of reason and the strongest inspiration of morality is religious faith. In society religion should be a balancing, compensating, regulating power. It should keep the relations between man and man, between class and class, normal and healthy and mutually beneficent.

Some people think that we are near a social revolution. I do not know. But I know that there is one thing that can make revolution needless, one thing that is infinitely better than any revolution; that is a real revival of religion.

BREAD, WORK, AND LOVE [1]

Give us this day our daily bread. Matthew 6: 11.
But my Father giveth you the true bread. John 6: 32.

THE struggle for bread is a naked fact, and we must face it and face it naked, stripped of the garments of make-believe that we too often weave in our minds to hide it.

I. BREAD

The materialistic conception of history would reduce every human endeavor to a struggle for bread—a struggle for existence. And there seems to be much to justify this point of view. The story of mankind is not a pleasant one. Brother fights against brother, family against family, clan again clan, race against race. Each one is seeking material prosperity for itself. The competition for bread enters into modern business life. When a person gets a job it means that some one else who sought the same position does not get it. One gets bread; one fails in his quest. Indeed, it seems difficult to reconcile human history with the ideal of love as expressed by Jesus Christ.

II. WORK

But there is something degrading about getting bread dishonestly. Stealing is morally and spiritually wrong. And it is hard to justify begging. Giving away money or bread is a dangerous thing if it creates paupers. Human society has reached a stage to-day where it recognizes but one way for the acquiring of bread. That is the way of work.

Men work together. Work is a social thing. Men may hunt

[1] By G. A. Studdert-Kennedy in "If I Had But One Sermon to Preach" (English Series). Harper.

or kill alone, but work is a coöperative enterprise. There was no harvest on earth until men worked. Men have learned to love each other by working together. The progress in this work shows how small the world is to-day. Not alone the single family works together. The whole world coöperates in the raising and distribution of food. The working unit widens, and with it grows the sweep of neighbor love.

III. LOVE

The materialistic conception of a struggle for bread disappears under the plan of bread-producing in the world to-day. It no longer satisfies. Men look back at the past and see the bitter struggle. But they prefer to look on ahead and see neighborliness.

The materialistic conception of history, which seeks to explain life in terms of hunger and the struggle for bread, is a particular and pernicious instance of this fallacy. Men are taught to explain the present in the terms of the past. Look back and you see a struggle between tribes, nations, and classes, a constant struggle for bread. The economic factor has always been final and decisive; therefore the struggle must continue and the economic facts always be final and decisive. . . . Against this ruinous disease of the mind and spirit Christian thought protests. It seeks to explain bread in terms of man and not man in terms of bread. It thinks of human evolution always as an ascension.

HOW TO GET RICH [1]

Lay up for yourselves treasures in heaven. Matthew 6: 20.

THESE words of Jesus point the way toward true economy in life. They not alone tell a man how to die happy; they inform him how he may live happily.

I. THERE IS AN INWARD TREASURE

Personal character and moral capacity are necessary to appreciate the things of the kingdom of God. Heaven or the Christian life would be of no use to the person who does not possess these things. I had a Greek professor who could not appreciate music. He did not distinguish one note from another. He missed the exquisite pleasure which music lovers enjoy because of his own limitations. The principle of taste and adaptation holds in spiritual things as well.

"The problem of existence is not how much I can get out of my threescore years and ten, but how can I fit and educate myself for eternity." (Bishop Remington.)

II. THERE IS A GODWARD TREASURE

It is the treasure of divine approval. What is more natural than for one to look for approval from God as the child looks for approval from the father?

How many Christians are like Mary?

Mary is a charming girl, and everybody knows it.
Mary has talent, and she knows it.
Mary is a member of the Church, but you do not know it.
Mary says she loves the Church, but does not show it.
Mary has time for social duties, but none for religious duties.

[1] By Oliver C. Horsman in "What We Preach." Judson.

119

Mary spends a lot of money on clothes, but she spends very little for Christ.

Mary used to attend worship regularly, but now she goes to the club or the lodge, or the theater.

Mary's example was once distinctly Christian, but you wouldn't guess that she was a Christian now.

III. THERE IS A MANWARD TREASURE

There are few pleasures in life to be compared to that which comes with the commendation from a friend.

In one respect my life has succeeded beyond dreams of my youth. I have never cared for money—nor for reputation—nor power. But I have desired friends; and it sometimes seems to me that no man ever had more friends than I have. I am often stopped on the street by a stranger who thanks me for some word of counsel or inspiration; and scarcely a week goes by that I do not receive a letter of grateful appreciation from some unknown friend whom I will never see here, and who, perhaps, has never seen me. (Lyman Abbott.)

IV. THE LORD'S COUNSEL IS MOST REASONABLE

My youngest son at the age of nine, on the morning after an operation for tonsils, having had nothing to eat for twenty-four hours, remarked feebly, "I feel like an empty peanut." . . . When you consider it, there is nothing much emptier than an empty peanut—unless it be a life in which these heavenly treasures of which we have been speaking are nowhere to be found.

The heavenly treasures, judged by time alone, are the most lasting. That is sheer fact. One man fills his coffers and dies. The other fills his life and finds peace, quietness, and happiness. The difference between the worldly man and the heavenly-minded man is largely a matter of horizon. The vision of one is bounded by the grave. The vision of the other extends into the infinite.

THE GIFT AND ITS RETURN [1]

For with what measure ye mete, it shall be measured to you again.
Matthew 7: 2.

"He that soweth sparingly shall reap also sparingly, and he that soweth bountifully shall reap also bountifully." (St. Paul.)

I. THERE IS A REBOUND OF NATURE TO THE GIFTS OF MAN

Three men stand in the same field and look around, and then they all cry out together. One of them exclaims, "How rich." Another cries, "How strange." Another cries, "How beautiful."

TIME passes, and the three men again meet. The earth has met the demands of each.

One cries, "Come here and see my barn"; another cries, "Come here and see my museum"; the other says, "Let me read you my poem."

Each got from the ground what he put into it.

> "One harvest from thy field
>   Homeward brought the oxen strong;
> A second crop thine acres yield,
>   Which I gather in a song."

II. THERE IS A SIMILAR REBOUND FROM HUMANITY

What does it mean that one man cannot go among any kind of men, however base and low, without getting happiness and good; while another man cannot go into the midst of the noblest and sweetest company without bringing out misery and despair and sin?

Both Jesus and Judas faced the same Pharisees. But from the environment the conviction of Jesus of his unique relation-

[1] By Phillips Brooks in "Sermons Preached in English Churches." E. P. Dutton & Company.

121

ship to the Father is strengthened. To Judas, however, there come only black dreams of treason and despair.

You hear men say to you: "Seek the society of noble men. Live with the true, the faithful, and the brave; so you will be true and brave and faithful. . . ." There are men enough in the world to-day being made worse by living with the purest and the best. Judas could never have come to be the wretch he was if he had lived out his quiet, stupid days among the men in Kerioth, and Jesus of Nazareth had never crossed his path.

III. THE SAME LAW APPLIES TO THE INTELLECTUAL AND SPIRITUAL ATTITUDES AND CREEDS

Creeds and occupations seem of vast importance. But of far greater importance is the character of the individual. A man is not made by his profession. The same calling reacts differently upon different characters.

Plenty of young men studying law and coming out full of prejudice and the very essential spirit of injustice; plenty of young men studying medicine and coming out coarse instead of fine, brutal instead of reverent; plenty of young men studying divinity and gathering unspirituality and uncharitableness out of the very marrow of the gospel; plenty of men, old and young, giving their days and nights to philanthropy and the public weal and growing more selfish and jealous out of the very substance of practical benevolence.

IV. THE SAME LAW HOLDS IN THE GIVING OF ONE'S SELF TO JESUS

Men come to Jesus with different motives. One seeks beauty; another an answer to curiosity; another safety; another all the Master has to give. To each Jesus gives just that which he is seeking. But before we receive we must give. It is the impact of personality upon personality.

THE CITY AND JESUS CHRIST [1]

And came into his own city. Matthew 9: 1.

THIS is the day of social workers. They have discovered, or think that they have discovered, many new things. The city to them is a problem. Believing that the city is a peculiar problem, they have little sympathy with the preacher of Christ. They give the impression that his message may be all right for the days gone by, but has nothing vital for the city generation of to-day. The social worker studies the city in the light of his theories. We Christians study the city in the light and name of Jesus Christ. The following observations are those of a minister of Christ who has lived in a great city for twenty-one years.

I. THERE IS NO CITY GENDER

Some folks seem to think that there is a country gender and a city gender. City folks, they feel, are different from country folks. Jesus did not think that way. He announced that there was just one gender, and that was the human gender. The only way the city differs from the country is that more people are piled up in a small space.

II. THE CITY HAS NO TRIBALITY OR NATIONALITY, BUT ONLY HUMANITY

Why should the foreigner in America expect to get his religion in a foreign tongue? To my mind the Christian Church would be better off in America if it had no foreign-speaking Churches. "One Lord, one faith, one baptism," and now in the American city we should add, "one language."

[1] By William A. Quayle in "The Healing Shadow." Copyright, 1923. Used by permission of the Abingdon Press.

III. WE MUST NOT BE SCARED OF THE CITY

I know its fury and fearfulness; I know its anarchy and murder; I know its squalor, filth, and perfidy; I know its lust and lechery, but I know too that for all these things the Christ is equal and for all these he only is the only cure. . . .

He is not afraid of the howling tempest of the Arctic sea; he is invited by it. He is not afraid of the city; he is invited by it. Christians consult Jesus Christ and not those fatalists who have no way out but a soup kitchen and an amusement hall.

IV. THE CITY IS NOT TO BE DEALT WITH ON THE LINE OF ITS SOCIAL OR INDUSTRIAL CLEAVAGE

Christian work in our cities has been mutilated and nearly slain by those who think that they must cater to class prejudice and hatred to get people into the Church. There are those who, in the name of Christ, think that they must become labor agitators and social agitators and strike promoters. Christianity is always with the man when there is a fight between the dollar and the man. Christianity is always against anarchism.

V. THE GOSPEL OF JESUS CHRIST IS OUR PREACHMENT

A company of country preachers freshly picked from the country bushes or pulled up from the country fields, and with their country freckles on their faces and on their hands, and no indoctrination in socialism and its accomplishments and embellishments, but just robust believers in the redemption of Christ, will do more to bring the city to its Lord than all the specialists ever trained in the world. The specially trained for the city are in deadly peril of knowing so much about what not to do that they never rise up and do the brawny things they ought to do.

FAITH REWARDED[1]

Then touched he their eyes, saying, According to your faith be it unto you. Matthew 9: 29.

THE profession of faith is not so much needed as possession of faith. But possession leads to profession. Faith is a possession. Faith is that which we seek and that which we attain. It is actual spiritual power. According to your faith be it unto you.

I. FAITH DOES NOT EXCLUDE THE USE OF MEANS, BUT DOES NOT STOP WITH THEM

Means were emphasized, and the disregard of means in the exercise of faith is dangerous. The Lord made "spittle and anointed the eyes" of another who was blind; the Lord "touched the eyes." God gave Moses a rod with which to exercise his command. The best medical skill should be accompanied by faith. It is unscriptural to disregard the means which God has provided, and, instead of lessening faith, they increase faith.

It is very necessary that Christians understand this in these days of so-called "faith healing." The applying of the oil was not simply a religious ceremony. It was the common means of cleansing. The disregard of means is unscriptural and unchristian.

"God does not give us ready money; he issues promissory notes, and then pays them when faith presents them at the throne. Each of us is given a check book." (Theodore Cuyler.)

II. THE ASSURANCE OF FAITH MUST BE OURS IF FAITH IS TO BE REWARDED

Let us take the following authorities.

Solomon in the first chapter of the book of Proverbs: "But

[1] By John Timothy Stone in "Places of Quiet Strength." Doran.

whoso hearkeneth unto me shall dwell safely, and shall be quiet from fear of evil."

St. Paul: "Your faith shall not stand in the wisdom of men, but in the power of God."

Author of Hebrews: "Who through faith subdued king-doms, wrought righteousness, obtained promises, stopped the mouths of lions," etc.

Job: "I know that my redeemer liveth."

Christ: "Be it unto you, even as thou wilt."

"There are three acts of faith: assent, acceptance, as-surance, and the assurance grows out of the other two." (John Flavel.)

III. FAITH MEANS LIVING THE SEEN LIFE IN THE UNSEEN GOD

We are living in a day when a great deal is said about re-ligion and practical affairs. Some feel that this is unscrip-tural, but they are mistaken. The words, "My citizenship is in heaven," do not mean that we are not to vote on this earth.

The religion of Jesus Christ does not go with poor sanitation, nor with a disregard of great moral law. The strongest human lives in their relationship to Christ are those which exercise the forces and power of the present in their confidence and belief and who in the unseen God have faith to make the seen world better.

"Preach faith until you have it, and then preach faith because you have it," said a Moravian missionary to John Wesley.

THE SUPREME LOYALTY [1]

He that loveth father or mother more than me is not worthy of me; and he that loveth son and daughter more than me is not worthy of me. Matthew 10: 37.

To the question, "What is your supreme loyalty?" there is, I venture to think, only one answer which those of us who are gathered here this morning would be willing to give. One after another, would we not promptly and unequivocally reply, "My supreme loyalty is to Jesus Christ"?

OF course Jesus, in the text, is speaking of himself not as an individual, but as a symbol of the kingdom of God.

I. SUPREME LOYALTY TO THE KINGDOM OF GOD GLORIFIES EVERY OTHER LOYALTY

For instance, when a man decides that his supreme loyalty is to Jesus Christ, the family does not suffer because of this loyalty. When a student decides that his supreme loyalty is to Jesus Christ, his university does not lose because of that loyalty. And when some patriot decides that his supreme loyalty is to Jesus Christ and not to the State, the State does not lose because of that stand.

"He who loves not his home and country which he has seen, how can he love humanity in general which he has not seen?" (Dean Inge.)

What has the country to fear from the man who puts Christ first? He will not be a profiteer. He will not put rotten shoes on soldiers' feet. He is not the man who will make a false entry in his income tax report. He is not the kind of man who would be involved in an oil scandal.

[1] By Ernest E. Tittle in "Best Sermons, 1924." Published by Harcourt, Brace.

II. THE HIGHER LOYALTY AND THE LESSER LOYALTY DO SOMETIMES SEEM TO CLASH

Suppose a man who has pledged loyalty to Jesus Christ should be asked by his superiors in business to do that which he feels is not honorable. How shall he meet that problem? Suppose that the commanding officer of the submarine which sank the Lusitania was a Christian. Suppose it was against his conscience to fire the torpedo. Should he obey the State or his conscience? Then there comes a time with some when the conscience says: "Love your enemies." The State says: "Hate your enemies."

Surely in a case like this it is not for the Church to bless that which promotes hatred. While the Church may not interfere with the individual decisions, it is time that she spoke out strongly against war.

III. FOR AN UNDERSTANDING OF LOYALTY FREE DISCUSSION IS NECESSARY

How very inconsistent the position of persons who demand a one hundred per cent loyalty to the Constitution of the United States and then try to limit the freedom of discussion.

Twenty years ago a theological student in Germany made a remark derogatory to the Kaiser. He was tipped off that the remark had been overheard and that he was to be arrested. So he hurried out of Germany into England. In London, in Hyde Park, he "cussed" the king to his heart's content. But is not the English method better than the German?

But there will come a time when loyalty to Christ will not clash with loyalty to Cæsar.

THE FINALITY OF CHRIST [1]

Art thou he that cometh, or look we for another? Matthew 11 : 1.

It is more than interesting that John the Baptist, who was the supposed forerunner of the Christ, should have some questions for himself regarding his genuineness. The situation is somewhat paralleled to - day by thinkers looking around in search of a new religion.

I. CAN WE CONTEMPLATE CHRISTIANITY AS TEMPORARY?

There are some conceptions of Christianity which accept this thought. To some Christianity is merely one of several great historical religions. Feeling that it is not meeting the spiritual needs of the times, they find that it rests on an infirm intellectual basis, or its views of morality do not fit in a freer and easier living world.

There are others who expect a reincarnation of the Christ. But they do not mean Christ in the sense that the title is used in historic Christianity.

There are others who expect to see Christianity produce its successor much as Judaism produced Christianity. It is not inconceivable that the New Testament should have a fulfillment in a new revelation just as the Old Testament did in the New.

But all these are based on the supposition that Christianity has failed. The answer that it has never been tried is not sufficient. Back of the supposed failure lies the idea that Christianity itself is an impossible religion. Some of these, however, take a more charitable view that it is the Church which

[1] By W. E. Orchard in "The Finality of Christ." George Allen and Unwin.

has died and not Christianity. Accepting all this and making it a starting place for the new religion means an admission that the noblest religion has gone wrong. It would mean that the greatest personage in history has confused his own cause.

II. WE MUST RECONSIDER THE CLAIM TO FINALITY

1. First, this cannot mean that the Christian revelation is exhausted. Christ is final. No one who has ever understood what is meant by the incarnation can conceive of its being repeated in an individual. But the meaning of Christ is inexhaustible. There is a new incarnation of Christ in the building up of his Church. The whole experimental side of Christianity has hardly been touched.

2. Christianity is final because there is nothing final about it.

> The great dogmas of the Church are not shackles, but axioms of freedom; they are not doors into a prison, but ways of escape into liberty; they are like buoys which mark the channel to the open sea.

3. The rediscoveries of our own time are promising.

It was left for the nineteenth century to rediscover the Christ and make him vivid for humanity. We are daily discovering the possibilities locked up in matter and the human mind. When these are geared to saintly pursuit the Christ and his religion will be revealed in their fullness.

COME UNTO ME [1]

Come unto me, all ye that labor and are heavy laden, and I will give you rest. Matthew 11: 28.

HERE is a message for the busy folks of to-day: The business man who comes home after a great business deal, yet knowing just how little the deal counts in the ultimate things of life; the society woman who gets inches of newspaper space with descriptions of her parties and gowns, and yet who has her moments of insight which show the worthlessness; young men and women, dizzy with the activities of a busy age, yet who have fears for the safety of the future in their moments of thoughtfulness—

It is to such as these, and to men and women of every class and type, that the message of my text comes; it can be universally applied and can be heard as a response to every aching longing from Park Lane to Whitechapel.

I. THE PREACHER'S MESSAGE STARTS WITH JESUS CHRIST

Christianity has one thing which no pagan religion can offer. That is Jesus Christ. And he is different from any other person in the world. This text is meaningful simply because he gave it. To deepen the Christ consciousness in the world is to deepen God consciousness. Back of all the theologies the thing that Christ has to offer is simply Jesus Christ. He it is who promises to bring rest to the weary.

II. TO ACCEPT THIS INVITATION MEANS A WILLINGNESS TO TAKE A DEFINITE STEP

We do not know just where that step may lead. It means accepting Jesus and following him wherever his mind and

[1] By H. R. L. Sheppard in "If I Had Only One Sermon to Preach." Harper.

thoughts may lead us. The "coming" is the first stage in the process of learning in which willingness to accept is called "taking the yoke." It seems like a tremendous demand. But upon second look it is similar to every other demand in life. The college student makes a yielding to the mind of his instructors when he enters as a freshman. If he did not agree to sit at the feet of his instructors, his learning would cease. So with those who follow the Christ.

III. CHRIST WILL BRING TO THOSE WHO ACCEPT THIS INVITATION PEACE OF HEART AND MIND

It does not mean that there will not be distress and sorrow, disturbance and misfortune. But he promises—and thousands have found that promise true—that in the distresses and anxieties of the world, even in pestilence and affliction, there will be peace of mind.

I know this. That there is no emergency in life which with him we cannot boldly meet; there is no problem to which he cannot supply the answer; there is no path so difficult, so intricate, so lonely, out of which he cannot smooth the roughness and over whose pitfalls he cannot safely lead us. If this is not rest, then I do not know what rest is.

CHRIST AS A SCHOOL OF CULTURE [1]

Learn of me; for I am meek and lowly in heart. Matthew 11 : 29.

GEORGE BERNARD SHAW says that he can find no meek and lowly Jesus in the Gospels. But here we have Jesus himself declaring that lowliness is one of his traits. Jesus has inspired more art than any other person who ever lived.

I. THERE IS NO BETTER SCHOOL OF CULTURE

1. Christ can show us what is meant by good taste. He once contrasted the flowers of the field with Solomon. What good taste he showed in the comparison. Solomon's robes were doubtless gorgeous, but Jesus preferred the simplicity in coloring and design of the lilies. Then take the instance when he defended Mary for spending her money for oil for his body. His defense was based on good taste. The artistic deed stands above the utilitarian practice he himself had commended. He was modest regarding himself. His confession that he himself was the Messiah had to be dragged out of him.

2. Christ can teach us good manners. When he went into the house of Simon he had to show him how he had not given him the usual courtesies offered a guest. He advised his own followers to wait until they were invited before taking the best seats. There is a story of a woman who was taken in adultery. Here again Jesus had to give a lesson in good taste.

II. THIS SCHOOL IS OPEN TO ALL

(a) It is the only one which is.
Learning itself cannot give culture.
It is an atmosphere which has to be breathed, a manner which has to be caught; it is a delicate refinement of un-

[1] By W. E. Orchard in "The Finality of Christ." George Allen and Unwin.

derstanding which only comes through the continual inter-
play of fine minds upon one another.

One cannot get culture by taking university courses. It is
not received from books. But there is one school of culture
which is open to every individual. It is the school of Christ.
If one has walked with Christ, he is at home in any company,
because one has no fears of anyone, and one has learned how
to behave.

(b) The Catholic Church is meant to be a school of the
best culture. It takes the poorest child, denizen of woods or
slums, and puts him in communion with the saints. It puts him
in touch with the culture of Greece and Rome. It offers him the
very best in architecture and art. It gives him prayers which
are the soul of propriety and good form.

That culture has been largely broken up by the terrible breach
of the Reformation. The Reformation cut off some of the
older Churches from the best in modern thinking; it cut off
some modern Churches from the best in ancient culture.

But this is merely to stress the outward observances
and the external considerations. Catholicism means nothing if it does not invite a man farther than that. It has
not only great art to show him, but it bids him seek for
the very inspiration of art, which Christ most certainly
has proved to be. It makes him not a connoisseur of art,
but an artist himself. . . . It introduces the soul to personal contact with all the company of heaven and to a
communion with Christ of the profoundest intimacy of
worship, friendship, and love.

WHY MARRIAGES FAIL [1]

What therefore God hath joined together, let not man put asunder.
Matthew 19: 6.

I. THE PETTY QUARREL

No couple is married very long before they find that there are many things on which they do not agree. Then comes the expressed difference in what we have come to call the petty quarrel. The great trouble with the petty quarrel is that it ceases to be petty and becomes serious. Petty quarrels become more serious and bitter as time goes on. Then the petty quarrel is very apt to develop into a quarreling habit. It is easy to let it grow until nagging and fighting become the order of the day. And third, when habit has been once established, a really successful marriage becomes impossible.

II. CHILDLESS MARRIAGE

I do not mean that the presence of children guarantees a happy marriage. But a childless marriage runs great danger of being unhappy. (1) Children serve as a safeguard of married life. When other influences seek to divide, children bind parents together. (2) Whenever you find a home that is deliberately childless, you know that it is the result of selfishness on the part of either husband or wife. Selfishness always makes for division. (3) This selfishness which is revealed in the childless marriage often leads to sin which divides.

III. NEGLECT

Neglect will kill any business or ruin any farm. It will also kill marriage. There is the neglect of attention on the part of husband and wife. Or there is the neglect of the wife

[1] By Clovis G. Chappell in "Home Folks." Cokesbury Press.

to make herself attractive to her husband. Or the husband becomes so busy that he is a boor and does not interest his wife. Dr. Banks tells the story of an eccentric man who made it a point to dress in his best every Tuesday evening and to ring the doorbell of his own home. His wife came to the door and invited him in. She entertained him as she did a sweetheart. Nothing was allowed to interfere with these Tuesday evenings. Whether or not you admire the method, you must appreciate the end attained.

IV. THE TRIANGLE

This is the case where the husband learns to love another woman or the woman another man. Sometimes the woman is guilty, but more often it is the man. If his wife should be guilty of the same indiscretions, he would shoot her dead. But what he does, he feels, is none of her business.

V. LACK OF FAITH IN GOD

Look over the broken marriages you know. In every one you will find that the break could have been avoided if the husband and wife could have met in mutual religious faith and talked and prayed things over. Marriage is a divine institution. As the divinity is lost from it, little hope can be held out for its permanency.

I therefore call husbands and wives to repentance.

REVERSAL OF JUDGMENT [1]

But many that are first shall be last; and the last shall be first.
Matthew 19: 30.

THE rich young ruler had gone away from Jesus sorrowing. The way of discipleship was hard. Jesus turned to the disciples and told of the handicap of riches. But lest self-complacency should envelop those who had left all to follow him he added this text as a warning. Though they were first in discipleship now, it did not mean that they would always be so. The last might be first.

I. EVEN HERE WE SEE THE TRUTH OF THIS STATEMENT

It is a commonplace of history and experience. The old fable of the hare and the tortoise is acknowledged by men to represent a fact of life. The clever boy at school is the one who is tempted to let things pass without sufficient application and thus go to the foot of the class. Small beginnings have ended in triumph while movements which began with the blare of trumpets have many times ended in smoke.

The stone rejected of the builders has become the chief corner stone. God put down the mighty from their seats and exalted them of low degree. Nations that seemed to stand strong and foursquare have tumbled like a house of cards; and the obscure and feeble people have grown into a world empire. A little one has become a thousand, and a small one a strong nation.

II. IT IS MUCH MORE TRUE IN THE SPIRITUAL WORLD

The judgment of God is unerring. Is it any wonder that the judgments of men may be reversed? The spiritual world is not a secret world. There an act is judged not by its size,

[1] By Hugh Black in "Listening to God." Revell.

137

not even by its good result, but by its motive alone. A man is judged not by the splash he makes in the world, but by his spirit.

A commanding character is not built at once. The great characters being produced in the world in which we live may lie in those quiet lives, unseen by many. In the judgment of men these lives are not considered. But they will be made known when God gives his judgments.

Even among the apostles, Peter was first in time. Paul was indeed born out of due time. He was the last. But we know which one God used most for the building of his kingdom.

III. VISIBLE REASONS FOR REVERSAL OF JUDGMENT

One reason is that men who feel themselves first easily succumb to self-complacency and sit at ease. Others grow. Sydney Smith, in speaking of the established Churches, remarked that endowed cats catch no mice.

Then it is difficult for us, even in the Church, to keep our minds on the things which place men first. We have men of great gifts, of eloquence, scholarly attainments, and other virtues whom we naturally put first. Take St. Paul's chapter in First Corinthians to tell the story. Love is the thing which counts. We have placed men first who have lacked it.

Christ's little ones, the nameless, fameless saints, the humble believers, who live their sweet, helpful, loving lives, may take courage that, however overlooked by the world, they are regarded in heaven; however misunderstood by men, they are understood by God. What he asks from all, the high and the low, the first and the last, is a sincere heart in which burns the pure flame of love.

WHO COULD IT BE? [1]

All the city was moved, saying, Who is this? Matthew 21 : 10.

I. A PAUPER

BORN of a poor woman in an outbuilding, He died not own-
ing six feet of earth in which to lay his body. At death his
whole estate was a seamless garment. Yet the amount of money
spent in his behalf makes Carnegie, Rockefeller, and Vander-
bilt appear paupers, ragged beggars in the street.

Who could this pauper be?

II. A FAME-KING

An infinitesimal few attain world renown, one or two in a
thousand million. After death their fame is soon forgotten.
One hundred years buries the most illustrious in obscurity.
Yet this poor carpenter, born without name, of inconspicuous
family, cut off as a malefactor in the pink of his manhood,
has triumphed over oblivion. Reversing Time's relentless laws,
his fame, renown, and praise have swollen as the ages rolled.
The largest library on earth will not hold the books written to
celebrate his honor.

Who could this fame-king be?

III. AN AUTHOR

An author seldom attains the half-million mark. One thousand editions is the climax of achievement. How different with
the words of this betrayed Galilean! Translated into five hundred tongues, published in more editions than man can number, in circulation for centuries, yet last year more than six-
teen million copies were sold! Scholars of his day called him
"Babbler, having never learned." To-day hut and palace warm
their hearts by his thought. Near by every hamlet in our land

[1] By S. B. Ghiselin in *Church Management*.

lies a field grown up with white granite on which are carved his sentences.

Who could this author be?

IV. A BUILDER

As a builder we know not that he ever built a house. Yet halls of wood and of stone, of brick and of marble, reared to his honor, are countless as the raindrops in an April shower. Though not a mason working with trowel and line in brick and stone, yet truly he is a builder. With faith and loyalty, love and devotion has he not built human temples—character masterpieces—memorials to the genius of a Hebrew Carpenter?

Who could this builder be?

V. A LEADER

"By my electric presence," says Napoleon, "I can inspire men to die for me." At his death his power ceased. Two thousand years after death, though offering neither power nor dominion, wealth nor fame, this Galilean peasant inspires countless men and women for his sake to die.

Who could this leader be?

"Liar! Devil! Man gone mad! Seeker for a crown," they called him. Taken to the edge of a cliff by old playmates to be killed! A price on his head! Suffering followed him as a shadow. Yet, in the climax of trouble with joy unquenched he comforts his close friends with this message: "Be of good cheer, I have conquered." With Gethsemane and Calvary just ahead, out into the night he walked singing a hymn.

Who could this sufferer be?

Pauper, Author, Builder, Leader, Sufferer,
Who could be it?
Pauper, you have made me rich;
Author, I have fed on thee.
Builder, you have builded me.
Leader, I do follow thee.
Who could you be but Jesus?

WORDS OR MARBLE [1]

Heaven and earth shall pass away, but my words shall not pass away. Matthew 24: 35.

When in Jerusalem in 1870 with a British Geographical Survey, we sought for the Temple. We could only find, here and there, little fragments of its pavements. Gone! Crumbled to dust, its marble pillars had disappeared, swept off into the dust of the air, away to the desert. But the words Jesus uttered remain with none the less force now than they had then.

I. WORDS IMMORTALIZED BY OCCASIONS

"England expects every man to do his duty." (Nelson.)
"Know thyself, O nation; know thyself, O man." (Demosthenes.)
"Liberty and union, one and inseparable, now and forever." (Webster.)
"Cæsar's wife should be above suspicion." (Cæsar.)
"The pen is mightier than the sword." (Lord Lytton.)
"Heaven and earth shall pass away, but my words shall not pass away." (Jesus.)

II. IF JESUS HAD NOT SPOKEN

What a different world this would be. How different your life and mine would be. Suppose Jesus had not told the story of the prodigal son. We would not have had a Wesley to preach over the English-speaking world. We would not have had a Spurgeon, a Newman, a Garfield, a Lincoln.

If Jesus had not said, "All things whatsoever ye would that men should do unto you, do ye even so to them," it would have made a great difference in the moral situation in most communities.

If Jesus had not said to the penitent thief, "This day shalt

[1] By Russell H. Conwell in "Borrowed Axes." Judson.

thou be with me in paradise," how hopeless this world would
be to men who sin.

Jesus saith, "He that cometh to me I will in no wise cast
out." There is scarcely a Christian who has not come to
Jesus because of that utterance. How different things would
be if he had not said it. And again he said: "Blessed are
ye when men shall revile you and speak all manner of evil
against you."

III. THE VINDICATION OF CHRIST'S WORD

How armies have marched, like Cromwell's, at the word of
Jesus! In obedience the Waldensians have met their foes or
hidden away in rocky mountains of the Alps, or have fled into
exile, and the missionary or pilgrim has gone into dark continents
and to distant lands. The heroes of the world have been made
by the words of Jesus Christ. Colleges have arisen; hospitals
have been built; the rich have reached down to help the fallen;
and the world has been wrought into a great beautiful brotherhood by the words of Jesus.

The Bible is better known, more read, more loved, more
closely followed in this world to-day than ever before. Its
influence over the earth is vastly greater, increasing with
every passing month.

THE DYING FLAME [1]

Our lamps are going out. Matthew 25: 8 (English R. V.)

THIS parable is peculiar to St. Matthew. But it may be taken as belonging to that class represented by the parable of the tares and the wedding garment, in which clear discernments are seen between good and evil.

I. THE FIVE FOOLISH VIRGINS WERE REBUKED BECAUSE THEY DID NOT BRING THAT TO FEED THE FLAME

They had their lamps, so did not err here. They slept, but the five wise virgins did also. They were not ignorant. For when they awakened and wanted oil, they knew where to go and get it. Their great failure was in going into a crisis in life without the oil necessary to keep their lamps burning.

They forgot that there is an awakening, and that every awakening is at an awkward hour. Every crisis is a midnight moment. It is the turn of the tide, to lose which involves either hard work at the oars, or waiting for the next tide, missing the grace of the present opportunity and the call of duty.

"They let God down."

II. THE DECISIVE THING IN LIFE IS THAT WHICH FEEDS THE FLAME

The decisive thing in a crisis is not the lamp, but that which feeds the flame—not the vessel, but what is in it—not the form, but the life—not the ritual, but the spirit—not the utterance of life, however sweet, but the fullness of the heart.

This parable has nothing to do with mere works. It goes much deeper. It deals with the preparation of life—the spir-

[1] Lauchlan MacLean Watt in "British Preachers, Third Series," edited by Sir James Marchant. Revell.

itual preparation. These foolish virgins were asleep when
they should have been awake. Not that we do not get tired
and need sleep.

Christ recognizes the necessity of rest and sleep. But he
does censure those who lie down and sleep when they are not
prepared for the emergencies which may arise.

III. WE CAN EXPECT THE AWAKENING CRISIS AT ANY TIME

Every day we are fighting a battle. There is no life which
will not have its crises. It is one's duty to be prepared for
them when they come. For these crises we need a vital living faith. The fact that we were born in a Christian family
is not enough. The theology of dusty books is not sufficient.
When the crisis comes the thing which counts is that we have
to feed our own lamps of life.

Each day takes us out on new duties.

> Before we go forth we must ask, "What of the sum-
> mons? What of the day or night before us?" We may
> need the lamp for threescore years and ten, or for twenty,
> or for one, or for a single day, or for a brief hour's watch.
> We do not know, as we go forward, where the slippery
> stone may be, or the string across the road in the night.
> Will the flame last through our necessity? Or, far from
> help, shall we see our lamp going out, leaving us blinded
> alone, with the unknown, which we cannot measure, clos-
> ing in upon us.

It surely takes a good measure of grace to get us by the
crises of life. The wise are prepared for these emergencies.

LOVE'S WASTEFULNESS [1]

To what purpose is this waste? Matthew 26: 8.

These disciples had forgotten one thing. They had forgotten that this woman's wastefulness was the native revelation of her love. There is a wasteful spending that is supremely selfish. There is a lavish giving that is disowned in heaven because the giver is always thinking of himself. But God suspends the pettier economies, and will not brook a single murmur, when he detects the wastefulness of love. It is the genius of love to give. It is love's way to forget self and lavish everything. And Mary's way was love's way when she brake the box and poured the ointment on the feet of Christ. And being love's way, it was God's way too.

I. NATURE IS PRODIGAL OF HER GIFTS

IN nature we find a similar instance of prodigality. The arithmetic of God is not ours. Things are not measured on fine scales. The spirit which breathes through nature is the spirit which brake the alabaster box. The heather at my feet is flinging off its seeds in such countless millions that this one patch could cloak the mountain side in purple. The birch which is shaking its head could seed the entire wood. The sun is shining upon the dead Sahara as well as on the living world which needs it. And the gentle rain which falls upon the green grass also falls upon the granite rock.

The world is very beautiful, but the beauty is not limited to places where it will meet the eye of man. There are vast regions in the tropics with beauty surpassing which the eye of man does not see. From a utilitarian way it is waste. But it is nature's way.

[1] By G. H. Morrison in "Flood-Tide." Hodder and Stoughton.

II. PROVIDENCE IS PRODIGAL IN ITS BLESSINGS

When aged Jacob sat in his tent in Canaan nursing the hope that Joseph was still living, he would have been content to have had his son again, though he came home in rags. And when the prodigal of the parable came hirpling home, ashamed of himself, and sorry for his sin, he wished no better chance than his father's kitchen. But God was lavish in his loving kindness and gave a prince and not a beggar back to Jacob. And the father of the prodigal was himself so prodigal of love that he must put a ring upon the truant hand and bind the shoes upon these wandering feet.

III. GOD IS PRODIGAL IN HIS GIFTS IN THE REALM OF GRACE

Now think: the death of Jesus is sufficient to pardon the sins of every man. There is no soul in the homeland so sunk that this pardon does not free him. There is no savage so degenerate that the grace of God is not sufficient. "God so loved the world, that he gave his only begotten Son, that whosoever believeth in him should not perish, but have everlasting life."

And why should Jesus suffer for those who will not accept his sacrifice? Because of love. Love never asks, How little can I do? but, How much? There is a mighty extravagance in love, whether it be that of Mary or God.

If therefore you believe that God is Love, if you take Love as the best name of the Invisible, then, looking outward to the world and backward to the cross, you can never ask again, To what purpose is this waste?

A LESSON IN PITY [1]

Straightway one of them ran, and took a sponge, and filled it with vinegar, and put it on a reed, and gave him to drink. Matthew 27: 48.

THERE is one voluntary act of pity in the passion of Christ. It rises as a single star on a night of darkness. An unknown man slips out from the crowd and places a sponge, filled with vinegar, on the lips of the crucified Lord. It symbolizes the quality of pity.

I. PITY IS BRIGHT-EYED

No Lazarus can lie at her gate in hunger and pain. She sees him while he is yet afar off and goes to meet him. For her, facts have loud voices which she cannot fail to heed. The spoken need is ever an unspoken request. To importune pity is to insult her.

There is both a depth and a height to pity. The depth is revealed in the miracle of the changing of water into wine. Jesus did this to spare the host humiliation. The height of pity is shown in the raising of Lazarus.

II. PITY IS QUICK-FOOTED

That unknown minister to Christ's need ran. But not as fast as Pity. But while Pity is quick she does not run so quickly as to trip. When Jesus heard that Lazarus was sick, he abode two days in the same place. Our pity for those who are the underdogs in the social struggle must not betray us to accept the first panacea which is offered for their release, even though it be the wrong one.

[1] By Charles H. Brent in "Prisoners of Hope." Longmans.

III. PITY IS QUICK-WITTED, FERTILE IN EXPERIMENTS

Christ thirsts. That which is near at hand must be used. There is a sponge and a jar of sour wine. There is a reed. The sponge is filled with the wine and by means of the reed raised to his lips. Pity must not lose her head, or she will not be able to think of these expedients.

The first trained Christian nurse was the man who gave Christ ⏤ sip of sour wine; the first hospital appliances were the sponge and the reed that afforded the means of ministering the needed refreshment.

IV. PITY IS INDIFFERENT TO OBSTACLES

She believes that there is a remedy for every evil under the sun. To her a discovered need is proof of an existing cure. She heeds not the cry of the crowd, "Let be, let us see whether Elias will come to save him."

There will be a cost to pay. Pity is not seldom weary. The gifts of healing exhaust. No true effort can be made without tiresome labor.

Two suggestions of a practical nature may help us more worthily to fulfill our function as ministers of pity: (1) We must look nearest to ourselves for our chiefest opportunities for bringing pity to bear on life. (2) We must never despise the privilege of giving something even less than a cup of cold water—perhaps that of moistening fevered lips with thin sour wine. . . . There is always a reed and a sponge somewhere.

THE ANGER OF JESUS [1]

And when he had looked round about on them with anger, being grieved for the hardness of their hearts, he saith unto the man, Stretch forth thine hand. Mark 3: 5.

I. ANGER, A NATURAL EMOTION

IT is a combative emotion. Compassion springs from love; anger is aroused by our antagonisms.

It gives physical courage, overcoming the paralyzing effects of fear, so that with blood boiling and swollen muscles a man in anger will hurl himself furiously upon an antagonist whom in cold blood he scarcely durst encounter. It reënforces moral courage, too. It gives outspokenness and telling force to rebukes which otherwise would remain unspoken, or would fall timidly and haltingly from the lips. It wings the orator to lofty heights in the denunciation of wrong and emboldens the satirist to tear the mask from hypocrisy, to lash the popular vices of society or the venerable follies of superstition.

But it also allies itself with the worst in human nature. It confuses judgment. Seldom do we see largely or clearly in anger.

II. THE GOSPEL INCIDENTS OF ANGER

Perhaps the hot anger of Jesus is shown best in the incident when he had to answer Peter, who suggested that it was not necessary for him to suffer. "Get thee behind me, Satan."

For an example of forked words driven by anger read the woes against the scribes and Pharisees in Matthew 23.

For driving anger take the cleansing of the temple in John 4. A most instructive instance is that recorded by Mark where

[1] By Robert Law in "The Emotions of Jesus." Charles Scribner's Sons.

he discusses **the Sabbath,** saying that the Sabbath was made for man.

III. ANGER AS A HOLY THING

The anger of Jesus was a holy thing. What we call anger in ourselves is usually but a display of bad temper. We are angry with people who are careless or inefficient. But Jesus did not display anger at such. He was never angry with his blundering, stupid disciples. His displeasure with them was sometimes hot, but he never took it as personal annoyance. He did not show anger when he was made the subject of gossip and bitter persecution. Even when they drove him to the cross he did not become angry, but he prayed for those who thus persecuted him.

IV. ANGER, THE REFLEX OF LOVE

Anger is the emotion produced by antagonism; and love by its very nature is antagonism to everything that works injury to life.

Look at the anger of Jesus. In every instance it is the anger of love. He loves men and he inflames with wrath against all inhumanity. He loves God, and therefore he dislikes all that desecrates God's house.

And those men in the synagogue, self-hardened against the truth:

Because he so yearned over them and so longed for the victory of truth and sincerity in their souls, therefore as he gazed upon them in their suicidal obduracy, his eye flashed with the instinctive wrath of love. He was angry as one might be angry at a sick man who in sheer adversity refuses the remedy in which lies his only hope.

THE MAN WHO TOOK THE BACK SEAT [1]

*And James the son of Zebedee, and John the brother of James;
and he surnamed them Boanerges, which is, The sons of thunder.*
Mark 3: 17.

And he killed James the brother of John with the sword. Acts
12: 2.

JAMES is famous in history as the patron saint of Spain.
But to readers of the Gospel he is famous because he belonged
to that inner circle of the disciples, Peter, James, and John,
which was permitted to share the closest intimacies with the
Master. Yet very little is known about James. There must be
some reason for it. History and tradition offer little account
of his life and work.

I. THE NAME JESUS GAVE JAMES

Boanerges might mean a great deal. It might mean only
that James and his brother were eloquent in the pulpit. But it
probably means that they were filled with a passionate zeal.
When they preached it was evident. And it was evident in
their lives. Like Cæsar, what he wished for, he wished strongly. Like John Knox, he preached with passion. There was a
resistless energy there which could not be denied.

It was a great gift. Would that we had more of it in
the Church to-day! Let us pray for a baptism of the Holy
Spirit, that we may have more of the holy fire for which
the prophet prays when he says, "Oh that thou wouldest rend
the heavens, that thou wouldest come down, that the
mountains might flow down at thy presence, as when the
melting fire burneth, . . . that the nations may tremble at
thy presence!"

[1] By W. Mackintosh Mackay in "The Men Jesus Made." Richard R.
Smith.

II. JAMES WAS INTOLERANT

James was not perfect, and intolerance was one of his imperfections. This was due, no doubt, to the very zeal of his character. There is a tolerance to-day which is due to the fact that its possessor has no strong convictions. James had convictions. Passionate convictions such as he had are apt to be accompanied with intolerance. Once he asked if he might not call down fire from heaven to burn offending villages. At another time he forbade those who were casting out demons because they belonged to another party.

III. JAMES WAS AMBITIOUS

It is but natural that when one gives all his life to a cause he expects a high place in it as a result. We can't be too severe with James and his brother. Perhaps the mother was more solicitous than the boys. But anyway it leaves a bad taste in the mouth—this appeal for supremacy in the Kingdom of God.

But the love for Christ transformed that ambition. Perhaps that is the reason we know so little about this man. Realizing the boldness of the earlier ambition, he learned to seek nothing but an opportunity for service. Love transformed a self-seeking bigot into a silent and self-sacrificing martyr.

"Love took up the harp of life and smote on all its chords with might,
 Smote the chord of self which, trembling, passed in music out of sight."

Surely this quiet man showed that he was able to drink of the cup of Christ and be baptized with his baptism.

GOD'S LAW OF GROWTH [1]

First the blade, then the ear, after that the full corn in the ear.
Mark 4: 28.

HERE we have the faith which prepares the soil, plants the seed, and waits for the harvest. We have the sacrifice in the seed for the planting. We have the industry in the labor of the sowing and the reaping. We have the obedience to law, which, while it cannot tell how or why, obeys and trusts. And we have the rewards in the full fruit and the harvest gathered.

I. GROWTH IS GOD'S LAW

Many never stop to get this fact. After man has dug the soil, placed the seed in the ground, and watered it, he still depends upon some force outside of himself. It must wait for that force. "It springs and grows up, he knoweth not how."

This law has more larger application than merely to a grain of corn. This growth is a law of all life. By God's law nations rise and develop. Evolution is merely another name for God's law. Jesus was speaking of God's law when he used this illustration.

II. EDUCATION IS MERELY ANOTHER PHASE OF THIS LAW OF GROWTH

The human life born into the world and advanced to young manhood or womanhood is one with the blade. The vocation chosen and thoroughly prepared for is not yet the full ear. Life has begun to take shape, but it has not yet acquired the full content.

But while this is true we must not minimize the fact that this formative period is a most important one in the maturing

[1] By Booth Colwell Davis in "Country Life Leadership." American Sabbath Tract Society.

of the grain. If education has been defective, if it has been misshaped by lawlessness or indolence or dishonesty, the full corn never will reach its full symmetry.

III. THE MATURE GRAIN

Men call it making good. Without the maturing process you have the blade without the ear, the blossom without the fruit. Five essential elements in the growth of the seed are:

Faith, which prepares the soil and plants the seed.

Industry, which labors to prepare the soil.

Sacrifice, which gives the seed to decay in the ground.

Obedience to law, which plants and waits.

The reward of the full grain in the harvest.

But the rewards I am thinking most of to-day are not in money or material wealth. They are in character. They are in soul assets. They may exist where but little surplus wealth has been acquired. They are the result of faith which reaches up beyond nature to God; of the sacrifice which forgets self that it may serve others; of the industry which toils for spiritual values; of the obedience to God and Jesus Christ, for our Lord says, "Son, daughter, give me thine heart."

You are now approaching the time of life for the maturing. May your reward be the full grain of character which will bring happiness to your homes and satisfaction to yourself.

WHEN CHRISTMAS COMES [1]

He took a little child, and set him in the midst of them. Mark
9:36.

EVEN in Fairyland no one ever heard a story as beautiful
as that of Christmas. It must be true, because no one could
build such a tale in the imagination. Think of the fantasy of
it. God incarnates himself in the being of a little babe.

I. THE INCARNATION INTO A LITTLE CHILD ACCOUNTS FOR THE HOMINESS OF RELIGION

If it were not for Christmas our conception of God might be
august and awful; it could never be homey and happy. A God
which only revealed himself in suns and planets could never
be intimately near. Christmas reveals a little God, a joyous
and gentle God, one who nestles in the heart. Christmas is the
appeal to the hidden child in us. The child is sleeping, but
never dead. Each Christmas season awakens the child and
we live in the childlike spirit again.

II. THE CHRISTMAS SPIRIT IS THE URGE TO A NEW CHILDHOOD

We must become as little children to enter into the Kingdom
of Heaven, Jesus told us. Perhaps we, like Nicodemus, have
grown wise with the years. It would have been interesting to
see the face of Nicodemus when Jesus told him that he must
be born again. What is it in the childhood that Jesus wishes us
to attain? Christmas makes the answer. It is the child attitude of wistfulness, of learning, of following.

III. CHILDLIKE, NOT CHILDISH, THINGS

There are childish things which we are to put aside. But
childlikeness is an entrance into the Kingdom. Tolstoi repre-

[1] By Joseph Fort Newton in "Things I Know in Religion." Harper.

sents the restlessness of our day, always going without arriving; always seeking without finding. Tolstoi came to Jesus, not in humility but in humiliation; and so missed a great secret. But Dostoievski won the child heart.

For some of us, something in the spirit of Christianity makes it plain that the cocksure sophistication of our day is pathetically superficial, its glittering cleverness profoundly stupid, and its towering pride tragically pitiful. As one listens again to the old immortal story, and sings carols that echo down the ages, the scene which many think is only a fairy dream which we have agreed to dream for a day, and then forget, seems nearer to the truth than all our dim philosophies.

IV. MEN OF SCIENCE ARE NEAR THE HEART OF JESUS IN CHILDLIKENESS

If a man would know scientific truth, said Huxley, he must sit down before fact as a child, eager, humble, teachable, rich in wonder, and pure in heart; and such a spirit is no less the secret of finding the truth of faith. Perhaps this is not so hard for the man of science, for in his laboratory he is always on the verge of discovery. New things reveal themselves. He is in the wonderland of Alice.

We should learn from this spirit. In the place of the childishness of fear and distrust we need the childlikeness of faith. Said Julian of Norwich: "To me was shown no higher stature than childhood."

THE CHURCH OF THE FUTURE [1]

My house shall be called of all nations the house of prayer. Mark 11:17.

As we read the gospel story we find many startling items. One of these is the account of Jesus's visit to the temple. Artists have called it "The Cleansing of the Temple," and have pictured Jesus angry of countenance, lashing right and left at the frightened money changers, the sellers of cattle and doves, and the rabble that gathered in the courtyard. It is a thrilling scene and one to be remembered, but the chief theme of this account does not concern Jesus's anger but his prophecy, "My house shall be called among the nations the house of prayer."

I. THE HOUSE OF GOD IS THE HOUSE OF PRAYER

THERE may be much difference of opinion regarding just what the house of God shall be. Some Churches feel that this text prohibits the use of the church building for social purposes. So they will not permit socials, bazaars, suppers, and other events. There is another group which seems willing to open the church building for anything of this nature, not even barring gambling games and prize fights. But in reality these are aside from the point. Jesus's anger was not because he found business activities in the church, but rather because he found there an organized gang of robbers. This group was organized to cheat the honest pilgrims who came to worship.

Here Jesus gave his definition of the church. It was to be a house of prayer. Now, what is prayer?

II. PRAYER IS ADJUSTMENT TO GOD

Here are some pictures of prayer.

Take "The Angelus." The evening bell is heard from the

[1] By Walter H. Stark in *Pilgrim Church Messenger*.

distant church tower, and the peasants cease their toil and lower their heads.

Take a great cathedral. Scintillating beams of light find their way through the rose windows. The air, filled with incense, vibrates with the music of the organ around wistful worshipers.

There is the soldier in the field of battle praying in agony.

On Calvary are three crosses. One blasphemes, another cries for mercy and pardon. The third prays for forgiveness.

In a home the parents ask God to spare the life of the little child who lies in the cradle.

All these instances are prayer. They show men and women trying to adjust themselves to God.

III. THE MISSION OF GOD'S HOUSE IS A MISSION OF ADJUSTMENT TO THE PURPOSES OF GOD

"A Church can do a lot of good if it does not care who gets the credit."

There are two ideas of service by the Churches. The first says that we will serve the people if they and their children will join our Church and subscribe to our creed. For every dollar expended the question is asked: "What will this mean to our Church and our school?"

The second idea says: "We will work, organize, promote, and sustain any piece of work in harmony with the principles of the Kingdom of God, for the sake of the work itself.

Prayer, after all, is not contained in the uttering of a few words, sincere as they may be; but prayer is the practice and development of an attitude in life which makes the most of every opportunity in a righteous way.

RECKON ON GOD'S FAITHFULNESS [1]

And Jesus answering saith unto them, Have faith in God. For verily I say unto you, That whosoever shall say unto this mountain, Be thou removed, and be thou cast into the sea; and shall not doubt in his heart, but shall believe that those things which he saith shall come to pass; he shall have whatsoever he saith. Therefore I say unto you, What things soever ye desire, when ye pray, believe that ye receive them, and ye shall have them. Mark 11: 22-24.

Years ago Hudson Taylor called my attention to these words of our Lord and told me of the immense blessing they had been to him in the early days of the China Inland Mission. He said that on his return from his first visit to China he was deeply impressed with the need to plant missionaries in Inland China. Up to that time they were principally located on the coast. It seemed to him the Saviour said to him: "Hudson Taylor, I am going to evangelize Inland China; if you will walk with me, I will do it through you." The challenge and promise were gladly accepted, and before that faithful servant of Christ passed home one thousand missionaries had commenced the work of inland evangelization.

I. RECKON ON GOD'S FAITHFULNESS

As did Samuel's mother when she prayed that a son might be given her. As did the nobleman who came from the bedside of his dying boy to ask the help of Jesus. As did Paul when he quieted his fellow passengers in the storm. As did Ruth when she followed Naomi.

II. RECKON ON GOD FOR FORGIVENESS

There are those who can never forget the sins of their lives. There was the man who asked God's forgiveness each night for the same sins. Was not that a slur on God's faithfulness? Surely, on confession of our sins, he blots them out forever.

[1] By F. B. Meyer in "Five Musts of the Christian Life." Bible Institute Colportage Association.

If a child should break a vase and come for forgiveness, it would be forgiven him. But if he came each day asking forgiveness when no further sin had been committed, it would cut one to the quick.

III. RECKON ON GOD FOR ANSWERS TO PRAYER

When once thoroughly, deliberately, and believingly one has handed a matter over to God, must he not believe that he is faithful to do his part? Prayer is coöperation of the human spirit with the divine. True prayer has two characteristics. First, we must allow the Holy Spirit to winnow away what is inconsistent with God's will to grant. Second, we must cease to worry. However long the interval may be between the prayer and the answer, we must keep faith with God.

IV. RECKON ON GOD'S GUIDANCE

There is an immense realm within us known as the subconscious self. It has been suggested that this is concealed from our knowledge as seven-eighths of an iceberg are concealed beneath the surface of the ocean. By our surrender to Christ we give him access to these hidden depths. Presently we become aware that our course is being charted for us. Tens of thousands have felt and obeyed the Spirit to their everlasting joy.

Don't worry! Don't anticipate! Don't fear! Don't, like Saul, offer the sacrifice precipitately before Samuel arrives. Sit still, my soul, sit still! Jesus, whom thou trusted, will not fail thee! He will not rest nor fail till he has finished that which thou hast committed to his care! Reckon on the faithfulness of the faithful Creator and Saviour! He cannot fail thee!

OBEDIENCE TO GOD THE WAY TO FAITH IN CHRIST [1]

When Jesus saw that he answered discreetly, he said unto him, Thou art not far from the kingdom of God. Mark 12: 34.

In these words, then, we are taught, first, that the Christian's faith and obedience are not the same religion as that of natural conscience, as being some way beyond it; secondly, that this way is "not far," not far in the case of those who try to act up to their conscience; in other words, that obedience to conscience leads to obedience to the gospel, which, instead of being something different altogether, is but the completing and perfection of that religion which natural conscience teaches.

I. THE BIBLE TEACHES US THAT OBEDIENCE TO GOD IS THE STANDARD OF HOLINESS

"Be not conformed to this world: but be ye transformed by the renewing of your mind, that ye may prove what is the good and acceptable and perfect will of God." (Rom. 12: 2.)

"Circumcision is nothing, and uncircumcision is nothing, but the keeping of the commandments of God." (1 Cor. 7: 19.)

"Whosoever shall keep the whole law, and yet offend in one point, he is guilty of all." (James 2: 10.)

Also see 2 Peter 1: 5-7; John 14: 21; Matthew 5: 19.

Christ also is to be sought by obedience to the law of God.

See John 6: 45; John 3: 21; John 7: 17; John 15: 23; John 8: 19; 1 John 2: 23; 2 John 9; 2 Corinthians 4: 4.

II. THE HISTORY OF THE CHURCH CONFIRMS THIS POINT OF VIEW

As far as we can trace the history of the Christian Church we find that it was made up of people who were in the habit of

[1] By John Henry Newman in "Parochial and Plain Sermons" (Volume VIII). Longmans.

obeying their consciences carefully. Zacharias and Elisabeth, to whom the approach of Christ's kingdom was first revealed, were described as "both righteous before God, walking in all the commandments and ordinances of the Lord." Joseph, Mary's husband, was a "just man." Simeon was "just and devout. Nathanael was "an Israelite in whom was no guile." Cornelius the Centurion feared God. Paul addressed his arguments to those who were just. Christ held out hope to sinners, of course. But to secure salvation they must first turn from their sins.

III. THE CONSEQUENCES OF FOLLOWING THIS GREAT GOSPEL TRUTH

(a) We see the hopelessness of waiting for any sudden change of heart. People deceive themselves by this expectation. Salvation comes from obedience. There are those, many of them, who have been waiting for this experience. Now is the time for them to awaken.

(b) It is wrong to live in sin while waiting for the coming of the spirit of penitence. Among those who are thus deceived are the young, those who have no time for the service of worship, those who desecrate the Sabbath, those who violate their own consciences, and many others.

Hence, in false religions some men have tortured themselves and been cruel to their flesh, thereby to become as gods, and to mount aloft; and in our own, with a not less melancholy, though less self-denying, error, men fancy that certain strange effects on their minds—storing emotion, restlessness, and an unmanly excitement and extravagance of thought and feeling—are tokens of the inscrutable Spirit.

THE FEAR OF FREEDOM [1]

Thou that destroyest the temple, and buildest it in three days, save thyself, and come down from the cross. Likewise also the chief priests mocking said among themselves with the scribes, He saved others; himself he cannot save. Let Christ, the King of Israel, descend now from the cross, that we may see and believe. Mark 15: 29-32.

We like very often to capture people's imagination or to violate their freedom, to win their judgment by some ways that we hardly realize are a little illegitimate, or not quite fair to the person we are trying to convince. Still we do realize as a principle that people should be free to judge, to judge for themselves, even to make their own mistakes. It was better for Judas to reject Christ than to accept him because he could exercise some magical power.

I. FEAR OF FREEDOM IN SOCIETY

THE mother fears to let a child run alone for fear he will fall. Yet it is the only way he can learn to walk. The father who lets the prodigal son leave home is doing the wise thing, though he does it fearfully. Social workers tell us that there comes a time with some girls when the only possible solution is to let them go—and hope they will come back. But they cannot restrain them any longer. There are slaves who fought against their own freedom. There are women who fought against their political franchisement. Everywhere there are people who are enslaved who prefer their enslavement to freedom. There are those who wish to be told how to make up their minds and how to think. They have not learned to use their own freedom.

[1] By Maude Royden in "The Friendship of God." G. P. Putnam's Sons.

163

II. SPIRITUALLY FREE

There has always been a human demand for some miraculous method of enforcing belief. "Let Christ the King of Israel descend from the cross that we may see and believe." Would they have believed if he had descended? Probably. But it would not have been through intellectual freedom.

Christ stayed on the cross. If he had descended, men might have said it was a trick. But he stayed, suffered, and died. The only message in this is the message of love. There is no attack on the mind. But love wins its way.

There are many social problems which folks think God should solve for them. "Why does a just God have wheat in America while people starve in Russia?" asks one. They expect God to work some moral trick to even up the inequalities of men.

There comes a time when people as much as say: "If God wants me to understand him, why doesn't he make me understand him?" That they have some obligation to help with the understanding doesn't seem to reach them.

Anything less than the eternal patience of God, and your moral judgment would cease to exist. Your personality would be stunned by the greatness of God. Does it ever strike you what infinite fineness there must be in the love of God that he does wait for you to "come to yourself"?

THE CRY OF DERELICTION [1]

Jesus cried with a loud voice, My God, my God, why hast thou forsaken me?" Mark 15: 34.

"THE most appalling sound that ever pierced the atmosphere of this earth." (James Stalker.)

"The saddest utterance man ever made." (Nathaniel Hawthorne.)

And yet the man who spake it deserved not the worst, but the best of life.

The words of this cry are the opening words of a Hebrew Psalm. People have said, therefore, that this is not a cry of dereliction. Jesus was harking back to a song of his nation learned in boyhood. He repeated its first words aloud and the rest of it silently for his comfort. But the gospelists do not so understand it.

I. WAS IT A CRY OF WEAKNESS?

It was a cry partially from weakness, but it was not a cry of weakness. Jesus was never weak in purpose. But now he was physically weakened. He had hung six hours on the cross. His wounds were burning, his limbs cramped. The slightest movement meant agony. Pain notoriously clouds the mind and distorts its images.

Yet the cry was not mainly from weakness. It came with a loud voice. He had refused the opiate which was offered him. The words of Browning found their best example in him.

> "I was ever a fighter, so—one fight more,
>   The best and the last!
> I would hate that death bandaged my eyes and forebore,
>   And bade me creep past."

[1] By George A. Buttrick in "Great Themes of the Christian Faith." Richard R. Smith.

165

This cry was alive, writhing, challenging—like a lightning flash in storm over a waste land at midnight.

II. THEN WAS HE FORSAKEN OF GOD?

No, he was not forsaken by God. God was never more near his Son than at Calvary. But it would seem that Jesus felt himself forsaken of God. Why?

He was born of woman and, like all others, was a child of doubt. Every man has questionings. For some the doubts are few and mild. For others they are sharp and bitter. The universal prayer is, "Lord, I believe; help thou mine unbelief."

Every one had forsaken him—his family, his townspeople, his Church, his nation, his disciples. Perhaps God, too, had forsaken him. Jesus put to God the only question he ever asked him. And there was no answer except darkness over all the earth.

In the play, "Green Pastures," it is the shadow of Hosea, the man of forgiveness and love, which keeps showing upon the scene. God tries many things to keep his people from sin. But there is only one common method which every one understands. That is the message of love and suffering.

The cry of dereliction? Better call it the "Cry of Victory." When God seemed farthest, God was nearest. When the flower was crushed, it yielded its fragrance to the world. When Jesus felt his spirit floundering in an angry sea, his feet suddenly touched solid ground. Even in his doubt there was something to cling to; for did he not even then say, "My God"?

THE CALL OF THE DEEP [1]

Put out into the deep, and let down your nets for a draught. Luke
5 : 4.

It is clear that the fisherman may greatly err, as these
apostolic fishermen seemed to have erred, by plying his trade
in shallow waters. The best fish are not found there. He
may catch a few minnows from the coves and a few cun-
ners from the rocks; but if he expects to win the haddock
or the cod or the bluefish, he must go out to sea beyond the
line of the breakers.

I. THE GREAT ACHIEVEMENTS ARE NOT FOR THOSE WHO CLING TO THE SHORE

THE men who made history pushed from the shore. They
were the Norsemen who dared to sail west in search of new
lands, the Phœnicians whose mastery of the Mediterranean
made it possible for them to push beyond the Pillars of Her-
cules. What sent Columbus forth on his great voyage? Faith
and science combined to urge him.

Man has two conflicting instincts. One urges him to keep
himself safe; the other sends him out to do great things. This
second instinct makes him raise his eyes toward the horizon
and wonder what lies beyond. It bids him go.

II. THIS IS TRUE IN INTELLECTUAL LIFE

There are a great many thinkers who insist on keeping close
to the shore in all their thinking. They are only waders or, at
best, coasters. They must stay where they can touch bottom. The man who pushes out soon finds himself thinking of
the things which lie beyond the horizon.

"Scorning the narrow measure of individual wants, human curiosity flies out, with wing more eager as the air

[1] By Washington Gladden in "The Interpreter." Pilgrim Press.

grows strange, unto fields remotest from the homesteads of personal and social life." (Martineau.)

III. BUT THE TEXT IS MOST PERTINENT IN THE MORAL REALM

The prime characteristic of much of our modern life is shallowness. There is little depth to convictions—nor to affections. The preacher in the Hebrew satire represents himself as one who has gathered all kinds of material good and sensuous pleasure and found it all emptiness. Yet there are some people who think modern life is broader and ampler than that of the past. These people are huddled together on the shore of the sea. They dare not launch out in the deep. Yet they think they have seen all that there is to life. They toil all night and they take nothing.

We live on the edge of mighty oceans, but we are unmoved by them. We are the children of eternity, but we are investing all of our resources in the things of time and sense. We are fishing for minnows or wading in the pools which the receding tide has left. And beyond lies life.

"Many a man is ineffective because he does not let down his nets as deep as they were meant to go." (Professor Peabody.)

> "To some thou givest at ease to lie
> Content in anchored happiness;
> Thy breath my full sail swelling, I
> Across thy broadening seas would press.
>
> For veils of hope before thee drawn,
> For mists that hint the immortal coast
> Hid in thy farthest, faintest dawn—
> My God, for these I thank thee most.
>
> Joy! joy! to see from every shore
> Whereon my step makes pressure fond,
> The sunrise reddening still before!
> More light, more love, more life beyond!"

THE UNEXPECTEDNESS OF JESUS [1]

And they were filled with fear, saying, We have seen strange things to-day. Luke 5: 26.

The Greek word which is translated "strange" is a word which is reproduced in our English word "paradoxical." The word literally means "contrary to opinion" or expectation and almost to belief. This is how Dr. Moffatt translates the sentence: "We have seen incredible things to-day."

BUT this is not the only time that people have seen incredible things in Jesus.

I. THE UNEXPECTEDNESS OF HIS BIRTH

The birth of the Messiah had been foretold, and for ages the Jewish people had awaited the event. The entire nation was on tiptoe. But they expected the event to be ushered in with pomp. Instead he was born of a peasant mother in a stable of Bethlehem. It surely was an unexpected way for the Messiah to come.

And yet it was the link with the masses of humanity. He was not isolated with greatness. Had Jesus been born in the home of a king it would have been more difficult for him to appreciate the struggles of human life.

II. THE UNEXPECTEDNESS OF HIS SPEECH

"Never man spake like this man."

The words startled, shocked, and amazed the people. This man from Nazareth challenged their conventions. He repudiated their popular ideals. In a day of war he called for meekness. It made it difficult for the rich to get into the Kingdom

---

[1] By J. D. Jones in "The Inevitable Christ." Richard R. Smith.

of Heaven. Take, for illustration, the story of the rich young
ruler.

III. THE UNEXPECTEDNESS OF HIS CHOICE OF FRIENDS

A corporation usually tries to get men of standing upon its
board of directors. Jesus selected twelve men of modest position. Only one had any standing, and he (Judas) proved to
be the one who was false.

"Hath any of the rulers believed on him, or of the Pharisees?"

And throughout his life he seemed to cultivate the friendship
of the social inferiors. He was the friend of publicans and
sinners. He was accused of being a glutton and a drunkard because of the company he has kept. But this helped to equip him
to understand the world's outcasts.

IV. THE UNEXPECTEDNESS OF HIS DEATH

He chose to save the world by dying for it. That was hardly
the method the Jews had expected. They had looked for him to
take possession by conquest.

There was power to convert and redeem men in that
atoning death. I don't know what would have happened
if Jesus had chosen the method expected of him. Thousands of swords would have leaped out of their scabbards,
and the Romans would have had a troublous time. But
of one thing I am certain—we should not have been thinking about him and thanking God for him to-day.

STRAITENED [1]

And it came to pass, when the time was come that he should be received up, he steadfastly set his face to go to Jerusalem. Luke 9: 51.
I have a baptism to be baptized with; and how am I straitened till it be accomplished! Luke 12: 50.

From the beginning the life of Jesus had been a going up to Jerusalem, like a stream which, with all its windings, is always making for the ocean. At first unconsciously, then more and more consciously as the Father's will unfolded itself to him, and at last, with deliberate intention, he takes the predestined way.

That face of Jesus, lips clenched, eyes fixed and gleaming, every feature tense with the emotion of the resolute, unyielding purpose, is one of the greatest pictures of the Gospels.

I. STRENGTH PERFECTED IN WEAKNESS

SOMETIMES it is given God's saints to sacrifice their lives in a moral issue which arises unexpectedly. More often they must show their bravery by going on, day after day, in a quiet, plodding way. But different from both of these is the way Jesus must take. He knows what lies ahead. He had seen men crucified. He had heard their cries. There is no mystery about the path ahead. But he decides that he must go.

Yet there are some to-day who talk of the weakness of Jesus. Could any task demand greater strength than this? It required an effort and consecration to make this decision. It was not reached in a minute.

Were there no such thing as fear, there could be no moral grandeur in courage; no natural shrinking from pain, then no such virtue as fortitude, which is not insensibility to pain but triumph over it; no natural tendency to succumb to

[1] By Robert Law in "The Emotions of Jesus." Charles Scribner's Sons.

difficulties, then no such virtue as perseverance. Strength always needs weakness as a background for the display of its loftiest perfection.

So when we see the steel-set face of Jesus we understand the story back of it. He is determined to move on his way to Jerusalem and to the cross.

II. THE SOURCE OF STRENGTH

The will is moved by our emotions, and our emotions are fed by our thoughts, our visions, and ideals. Strong and persistent effort of will is the only active outcome of prolonged and repeated concentration of the mind upon the end we have in view.

So it was with Jesus. Before him are the dust and smoke of battle. But far beyond that lie joy and triumph and peace. The way is before him, and he is straitened. He is a prisoner. It is not bars of iron, but moral bonds which hold him in. He is held in by a strong compelling motive. The Epistle of James speaks of the double-minded man. He is compared to the surge of the sea, driven by every wind which blows.

But there is something greater than this moral steadfastness. Jesus knows the love of God. Moral background is to God what the moon is to the sun. The sun is the ultimate source of power; the moon reflects it. We know the vast power of sin over men. But it never sent a man to crucifixion for the sake of his indulgence. It takes a greater power than that.

"Be strong in the Lord and in the power of his might."

THE MEASURE OF A MAN'S LIFE [1]

For a man's life consisteth not in the abundance of the things which he possesseth. Luke 12: 15.

The curse of things is upon us. Things are in the saddle. They chock and stifle, cramp and restrict life. Harold Bell Wright speaks with the insight of the prophet when he says: "Eyes blinded with the fog of things cannot see truth. Ears deafened by the din of things cannot hear truth. Brains bewildered by the whirl of things cannot hear truth. Hearts deadened by the weight of things cannot feel truth. Throats chocked by the dust of things cannot speak truth."

I. KNOWLEDGE AS A MEASURE

KNOWLEDGE is a better measure for life than possessions. A man's life does consist, in part anyway, in the abundance of things he knows. Between knowledge and life there can be no conflict. Half learning is not enough. We must know things thoroughly if knowledge is to aid in real living. A man may own a great violin, but if he knows nothing of music, he possesses but a bit of wood and string. But the same instrument in the hands of a man who does know may be worth its thousands. The same is true of a great painting or a book.

II. WHAT HE DOES AS A MEASURE

This is a very practical way of measuring a man's life. It can be overdone if we are not careful. We are not to do another's tasks for him. By doing that we rob him of life's value. We may do things for our children which rob them of their initiative. But there is a real joy in production.

The man who knows how to use his hands sees the product of

---

[1] By George Buckner in "The Measure of a Man's Life," in the *Homiletic Review*.

his labors. The farmer enjoys life because he sees the seed he planted grow. A beautiful house given to the newly wedded couple may mean less to them than a humble cottage would to a couple who had worked for years to secure it.

III. WHAT HE LOVES AS A MEASURE

The things he loves reveal the depth and breadth of his life. Our lives are tempered by our affections.

Love money, and your friends will perceive, if you do not, how your life grows cold and hard and metallic in its nature. Love noble books and live among them, and they soften and mellow your very soul.

Love not only measures life, but expands it. Like mercy, "it blesses him who gives and him who takes." It pushes back horizons and multiplies all values.

"I love God and flowers and little children." (Walt Whitman.)

IV. ASPIRATION AS A MEASURE

There is a measure which seems vague and indefinite. Yet it is real.

"All I could ever be,
All men ignored in me,
This, I was worth to God, whose wheel the pitcher shaped."

Measure men by their possessions, and Nero ranks high, while Paul remains a pauper. Measure them by the things to which they aspire, and Paul takes rank with the immortals, while Nero sinks to the level of beasts with whom he held in common the deepest longings of his nature.

With new experiences there come to our lives new aspirations—new ideals. The triumphant life is the one which adjusts itself to these ever-changing things. How large is man? As great as his aims, his hopes, his ideals, his aspirations? His life is measured by the abundance of the things to which he aspires.

THE CHURCH AS A PROMOTER [1]

Whereunto shall I liken the kingdom of God? It is like leaven, which a woman took and hid in three measures of meal, till the whole was leavened. Luke 13: 20, 21.

What the promoter is in the business world the Church is in the ethical world. It has been and should always be the pioneer, the innovator. By the Church aggressive, I mean, of course, that minority, that very small minority, which, led by religious zeal, undertakes tasks which seem to the world foolishness—for the first few hundred years. That any person should devote his life to the care of the sick and the permanently disabled; that buildings should be erected where the blind, the deaf, and the insane are well treated; that defenseless women and children should be given a protecting refuge; that the criminal should find sanctuary; all these seemed very strange and vain proceedings when they were novelties.

I. THE CHURCH AS A LEADER IN TEMPORAL THINGS

THE world laughed at it when the monks spent their time in reading and copying manuscripts instead of waging war. But there came a time when art, drama, music, and architecture burst from the monastic cell as a butterfly from its chrysalis. Schools and colleges are now supported by everybody. Once it was only the missionary who was interested in anthropology, but now we have our bureaus of ethnology and societies devoted to the study of folklore. Our form of representative society is a gift from canon law to common law. Internationalism had its birth in religious aspiration. Professor Van Tyne, of the University of Michigan, has found that the origin of the American Revolution lay chiefly in the nonconformist Churches.

[1] By Edwin E. Slosson in "Sermons of a Chemist." Harcourt, Brace.

175

II. SPIRITUAL AND INTELLECTUAL LEADERSHIP NEEDED TO-DAY

There seems to be some evidence that the ministry of to-day is not giving the intellectual leadership equivalent to that of days gone by. In a vote by the *Independent* to find out the general opinion of the greatest men in the world, a study of one thousand ballots showed the names of but three ministers. What generation of the past would have shown so low a percentage of ministers in a similar vote?

Yet we are in the greatest revolution of thought the world has ever seen. The Einstein theory of relativity, the Planck theory of quanta, the chromosome theory of heredity, the hormone theory of temperament, the new knowledge of the constitution of the universe—these ideas are going to influence the thinking of to-morrow. Edwards, Berkeley, Calvin, Aquinas, Augustine, or Paul would have been interested if they were the theories of their days.

If the Church is to be anything more than a Boosters Club of Zenith City, there has got to be some hard thinking done by those at the head of it during the next twenty years.

The living Church must have its school of prophets as well as its caste of priests; its innovators as well as its conservators. The prophet must rouse the people against unsuspected sins, sting them from their apathy, and prevent formalism from putting the Church to sleep.

Since the Church has been largely relieved of the educational and eleemosynary burdens, which it had formerly had to bear alone, it may again become the pioneer, pressing forward into unexplored territory and gaining higher ground. If the Church is crowded out from its previous occupations, there is always room at the top.

THE USE OF MONEY [1]

I say unto you, Make to yourselves friends of the mammon of unrighteousness; that, when ye fail, they may receive you into everlasting habitations. Luke 16: 9.

It is termed "the mammon of unrighteousness," because of the unrighteous manner wherein it is frequently procured, and wherein that which was even honestly procured is generally employed. "Make yourselves friends" of this, by doing all possible good, particularly to the children of God; "that when ye fail"—when ye return to dust, when ye have no more place under the sun—those of them that are gone before "may receive you," may welcome you, into "everlasting habitations."

I. GAIN ALL YOU CAN

GAIN all you can in your vocation, but do it honestly. We are not to hurt our own bodies and souls or the bodies and souls of our neighbors to acquire wealth. Those businesses which are injurious are to be avoided. We are to avoid those professions which lead one to atheism or deism. We must not enrich ourselves by devouring the lands or homes of our neighbors. Thus pawnbroking would be excluded, for all know the misery it creates.

Gain all you can by common sense, by using in your business all the understanding God has given you. It is amazing to observe how few do this; how men run in on the same dull track with their forefathers.

II. SAVE ALL YOU CAN

This is the second rule of diligence. Do not throw the results of your efforts into the sea. Do not throw it away on idle expenses. Expend no part of it merely to gratify the flesh. I do not mean only that you are to avoid gluttony and drunken-

---

[1] This is the famous sermon by John Wesley.

ness. An honest heathen would avoid these. Despise delicacy and variety, and be content with what plain nature requires.

Among the things for which we should not spend our gains are curious adornment of houses, superfluous and expensive furniture, expensive wearing apparel, painting, gilding, elegant rather than useful gardens.

Much of the expenditure for the things which are unnecessary does bring the applause of others. They admire your wealth. But that admiration is to be avoided. The gratification of these desires merely creates greater desires. Some pamper the pride of their children by buying them expensive clothes when they would not spend the money on themselves. This is wrong. If your children do not know the value of money, and if your money were left them on your death, it would only put temptation in their way. In that case leave to each one sufficient to keep him from want and use the rest in such a way as will be to the glory of God.

III. GIVE ALL YOU CAN

This is an important part of stewardship. First provide all things for yourself. Secondly, provide for your wife and children and your own household. Then, if you have anything left, do good to those who are of the household of faith. If there still be a surplus, do good to all men. Remember that you are a steward of God.

Render unto God not a tenth, not a third, not a half, but all that is God's, be it more or less; by employing all on yourself, your household, the household of faith, and all mankind, in such a manner that you may give a good account of your stewardship, when ye can be no longer stewards.

WHY WE BELIEVE [1]

Increase our faith. Luke 17: 5.

ONE result of underbelief in our day is the tragedy of trying to live a maximum life on a minimum faith; and it cannot be done. The ultimate truth can never be uttered. It can only be acted.

I. WHY DO WE BELIEVE IN GOD?

As far back as human records go men lived and died by faith in God. That belief was not put there by logic. No man was ever argued into faith in God, and probably no man was ever argued out of it. The sources of belief go back into human experience. When a man loses faith in God, it is not some logical process, but because of some inner disaster in his life—some betrayal or neglect.

II. WHY DO WE BELIEVE IN JESUS?

Take the experience of those who walked on the earth with him. In fellowship with him a change was wrought in their lives. They saw something more Godlike in him than they had seen before. Up to the cross they saw him go facing all that fate and his foes could do, trusting the power of love alone. They saw him die, and then defeat was turned into victory.

Those of us who have had fellowship with him believe in Jesus because we cannot help it. We cannot deny his purity, his pity, his holy kindness.

III. WHY DO WE BELIEVE IN THE BIBLE?

The writers of the Bible did not argue; they obeyed. They lived before they wrote. They were men of like passions as ourselves, of like faiths and fears and failings.

[1] By Joseph Fort Newton in "Things I Know in Religion." Harper.

They wrestled with reality. They were sorely tried, and their cries of anguish echo to this day—deathless trumpets from the oblivion of olden time. . . . What they needed they found in God, the Eternal, and in God alone, and they set down in simple words—gritty with reality, wet with tears—what they learned of his will, his love, his plans for them, and their duty to him. In short, they showed us in actual life how the victory is won, how truth is known by living, and how the face of God shines in the purest vision of man, as the clouds contain the sunlight.

IV. WHY DO WE BELIEVE IN PRAYER?

"Men pray because they cannot help praying." (William James.)

Prayer is primarily a personal experience. It is not getting something from God. It is asking him to do something in us and through us. We are not to ask for something for our own ends, but that he use us for his ends. We must not pray for anything just for ourselves. We must pray as well for our fellow men.

Prayer is another thing we cannot argue about. But those who practice it know its value.

V. WHY DO WE BELIEVE THAT LIFE GOES ON?

Martineau said that we do not believe in immortality because we have proved it, but because we are continually trying to prove it. It is almost instinctive. We cannot believe that God is just unless he makes provision for our going on. If sacred values mean anything to God, then life must go on. To think otherwise is to make life a horror and chaos.

My thesis all through has been to show that experience is profounder than argument, as life is deeper than logic.

THE THINGS THAT ALONE COUNT [1]

And when he was come near, he beheld the city, and wept over it, saying, If thou hadst known, even thou, at least in this thy day, the things which belong unto thy peace! but now they are hid from thine eyes. Luke 19: 41, 42.

As the joyful procession swept round the shoulder of a hill, and the fair city gleamed into sight, a hush came over the exulting throng; for the Lord was weeping. He had no bright and futile illusions. A wave of excitement like that which had transported the disciples could not blind him to the actual facts of the case.

I. IF THEY HAD KNOWN?

JESUS knew that the way into that city was the way of the cross. He knew that the city and the nation were doomed. But thronging the streets were the people in gladness rushing to celebrate a great religious festival. They were so busy keeping the religious festival that they did not have time to realize that this was their day of visitation.

Jesus had been teaching them the way of life and pointing out to them the way of peace. But they chose to go their own way, which was the way of destruction. Jesus saw this. He wept. Had they seen this, the story of Israel might have been vastly changed.

II. IF WE KNEW?

We, too, have a day of grace, a day of sweet and helpful visitation. There are things which belong to our peace, and they are the same and eternal things which counted for the Jews in the days of Jesus.

This is a busy day. Everybody is after something, but how often they are not the things which count. Some of the pursuits of life are actually evil. Others are not evil in themselves.

[1] By Hugh Black in "Listening to God." Revell.

But they are just outside of the vital things in life. There are some issues which the world cannot take away. These are the vital issues of life.

We can see this convincingly and clearly if we ask what they will mean for us at the last. The ultimate, the inevitable test of life is death. We may shut our eyes to it; we may act as though it were not and never could be. But that, after all, is the one certainty.

III. IF WE HAD KNOWN?

> "When vain desire at last and vain regret
> Go hand in hand to death and all is vain,
> What shall assuage the unforgotten pain
> And teach the unforgetful to forget?"

What vain regrets many a man has had at the end of life that he has been blind to the things which really count. Many a man has wished that he might live over again, that he might undo the past and let the important things have their proper place in his life. Sometimes the cry is merely one of pain because of his ignorance. Again, it is the cry of despair.

Make a forecast of how you would like to die, with what gains of character and what growth in grace, and what familiarity with the unseen and eternal, what peace of a good conscience, rich with the spoils of life, rich in faith and love and hope. Are the things which belong to your peace the very things which to-day you are neglecting?

THE LORD'S SUPPER [1]

This do in remembrance of me. Luke 22: 19.

The wonderful thing about this institution is that it comes down through the centuries as one of the dearest and sweetest of human experiences. The Master's command, "Do this in remembrance of me," has been the token through all the years of Christian faith and fellowship. In many different ways, sometimes with simplest service, and sometimes with elaborate ceremony, through all the centuries this one bond of union has held and will hold to the end.

I. THREE TRUTHS WHICH COME TO US THROUGH THIS PRECIOUS SERVICE

1. WE have the assurance that our sins have been forgiven through the blood of Jesus Christ. It makes the observance of the Lord's Supper a joy and a strong rock under which we may rest.

2. We have here a custom which brings to us a vision of the earthly life of our Lord. He actually was in the upper room with his disciples. In this busy age we are apt to forget Jesus. But this keeps him in our memories.

3. We have here a bond of brotherhood created by Christ himself. "That they all may be one." The history of Church divisions is a sad one. But here we have a service which is observed by all Christians. And in it is a pledge that eventually all will be one body.

II. INSTRUCTIONS FOR OBSERVANCE OF THE LORD'S SUPPER

1. It must not be neglected. There may be differences of opinion about the frequency of observance. But there must not be forgetfulness.

[1] By Floyd W. Tompkins in "The Master's Memorial," edited by Samuel Blair. Cokesbury Press.

2. We should come to the table with a consciousness of sin. Our very love for Jesus brings us to humility when we enter the Holy of Holies.

3. There should be personal preparation for communion. This may be in the Preparatory Service by private devotions.

4. We should join heartily in both the prayer and praise. This is the privilege of sharing in a service which has an unbroken heritage of nineteen hundred years.

5. Then we should have a vision of the glorious day to come when we shall sit down and eat in the Kingdom of God.

Our life on earth may well be happy and joyous and brave; but after all it is only an experience of education, leading us to look forward to the day when we shall be called to a higher and unending life in the presence of God.

THE WORLD DRAMA [1]

Simon, Simon, behold, Satan asked to have you, that he might sift you as wheat: but I made supplication for thee, that thy faith fail not; and do thou, when once thou hast turned again, stablish thy brethren. Luke 22: 31, 32.

If Jesus had said that Satan had asked to have Peter to sift him as wheat and had left it there, implying that Peter had only his own strength to rely upon in his fight against Satan, there could have been but one end to Peter's story. His life's barque would have sunk like lead in stormy waters. But the picture is this: Satan on the one side trying to take Peter, and on the other Jesus praying for him. . . . The plotting Satan is no match for the praying Jesus.

I. SATAN IS ALWAYS SEEKING TO HAVE US

I HAVE always had difficulty in considering Satan to be purely a mythical figure. If that is true, how will we explain the immoral and hideous thoughts which come to our minds? Satan works on the evil nature within us. We are born with a certain bias of evil. The dice seem loaded against us from the start. Satan takes advantage of this. He works on our passions and he works on our fears.

Satan is amazingly busy in our world. There is no one immune from his wiles and his assaults. He desires to have us all that he may sift us as wheat.

Jesus Christ is also at work. He works by means of the holy influence of the home. He works by means of the teaching and example of godly parents. He works by means of Church and school, by hymn and prayer and the words of the preacher.

[1] By J. D. Jones in "The Inevitable Christ." Richard R. Smith.

185

II. SATAN IS ALSO SEEKING THE CORPORATE LIFE OF THE WORLD

He seeks individuals by stirring up the emotions within them. He seeks the world by stirring up discord and hatreds. He puts class against class. He flames the fires of suspicion and ill will. He sows the seeds of greed, selfishness, and discord among the nation. He sends militarists out to preach, with amazing effrontery, the doctrine that the way to secure peace is to prepare for war.

But Jesus is also busy in the world. He is making supplication for it. Satan does not have the whole field to himself. Jesus works through his Church. He works through the League of Nations. He works upon the minds and consciences of men.

III. THE STRATAGEMS OF SATAN ARE NO MATCH FOR THE PRAYERS OF JESUS

I think of a man once connected with this Church. Satan seemed to have him at one period of his life—for he was profane and drunken and utterly neglectful of religion. But the memories of home and Sunday school never wholly died within him. By these early memories Jesus had been making supplication for him. And at length he "turned again" and spent the rest of his life in stablishing the brethren.

And I dare cherish the same great hope for the world. I do not close my eyes to the evil influences which are at work. I do not shut my ears to the sounds of dissension and strife. But I refuse to believe that the world is racing to destruction—for I see Jesus making supplication for it. . . . The power of evil is limited. The ultimate triumph rests with God.

SOME FRIENDS OF MINE IN PARADISE [1]

And Jesus said unto him, Verily I say unto thee, To-day shalt thou be with me in paradise. Luke 23: 43.

A kind of a river of Life Anthology, I think this study should prove at once strength-giving and inspiring to us all. For while I am speaking of some of my friends in Paradise, you will be saying: "Yes, I, too, have some one just like that Over There." Thus, by playing the chimes of memory in my own soul, I think you will be answering back, peal for peal, chime for chime.

I. MY FIRST FRIEND IN PARADISE IS CHARITY

THIS was her baptismal name and one which also suited her character. Widowed in comparatively young womanhood, she found that the demands of growing children and complex life could only be met in charity. Her children and grandchildren learned to love her as did a multitude of nephews and nieces. With affection for all she could save no little noise and much power. The tearful came to her for consolation and departed tearless. If new arrivals in Heaven should be a bit overcome by the strangeness of it all, Charity would help them adjust themselves.

II. MY SECOND FRIEND I CALL FAIR-MINDEDNESS

She also was widowed. She had been a teacher, and she lived with the great of the ages. Yet when suffering came and affliction in her own household she organized to meet it by preparing her own soul. She possessed that spirit of self-detachment. An enemy might kindle the fires of righteous indignation within her, yet she kept the moral temperature cool enough not to ignore the rights of an enemy. I owe much to fair-mindedness.

[1] By Frederick F. Shannon in "Anglo-American Preaching." Harper.

III. A THIRD FRIEND IS HELPFULNESS

Long before modern people knew about the so-called social gospel she was practicing it. Neither race nor creed nor color could build a fence so high that she could not climb over it on her errand of helpfulness. "Need," she seemed to say, "is my creed." She was especially fond of young people. She understood them. She could pop the best corn, pull the best taffy, and laugh the most contagiously. Of course she had her troubles. Like many another, she gave her own little daughter back to God. Twenty-five years later I saw her making her way to the grave which contained her baby's dust with her arms filled with flowers.

IV. AND MY FOURTH FRIEND IN PARADISE IS LOVELINESS

She must have had her beginnings far back in the mystery of delicate things. She was almost too elusively frail to be caught and crushed in the grip of the coarse and cruel. She was chartless and yet far-sighted, being expert in using the long distance view to correct the aberrations of the near-at-hand. "It is always better farther on," she would say through her tears. "Of course you didn't have time to do it," she would say after one had explained what something had been left undone. Her words uncovered the lie, and only a confession that you could have done it but didn't cleansed the heart. Loveliness made a distinct contribution to Heaven when she entered.

JESUS AND THE INDIVIDUAL [1]

To-day shalt thou be with me. Luke 23 : 43.

JESUS had a supreme interest in the individual. He did not estimate the group the less, but the individual more. Only when he got back to the individual could he hope to see that change of heart and soul so necessary for his kingdom. He never loses sight of the individual who suffers in his eagerness to help the group. His heart went out for Nicodemus of the lonely heart, for the woman of Samaria who thirsted, for Martha who sinned. The gospel of Jesus starts with the individual.

I. THE SUPREME CARE OF JESUS FOR THE INDIVIDUAL IS A REVELATION OF THE HEART OF GOD

Every reader of the Bible is struck with the difference in the attitude of the New Testament from the Old as far as the individual is concerned. It is not that God did not love the individual in the Old Testament, but that man had not learned of that love. There are minds which can deal only with great numbers. A Kepler gazes at the stars. Napoleon plays with the kingdoms of Europe with humans as chessmen. An orchestra director is interested in the harmony of the group. But Jesus was interested in the individual. His happiness concerns him.

II. THE SUPREME CARE OF JESUS IS A REVELATION OF THE VALUE OF HUMAN LIFE

If a man is but a grain of sand upon the desert of time, of what value is life? What is love, or home, or friend, or hope, or common joy? Is it not but an opportunity for pain? What is duty but a sadness, a dreary round we have no heart to fulfill?

[1] W. M. Clow in the "Day of the Cross." Doran.

"No more? A monster then, a dream,
    A discord. Dragons of the prime,
    That tear each other in their slime,
Were mellow music matched with him."
                                    (Tennyson.)

But Jesus never lets man sink to this evaluation. He is the supreme creation. He assures his disciples that, when he leaves them, he is going to prepare a place for them.

III. THE SUPREME CARE OF JESUS FOR THE INDIVIDUAL IS A REVELATION OF THE MOST IMPERATIVE DUTY OF THE INDIVIDUAL SOUL

If God so cares for the individual, if he loves with such a personal care, a great duty is placed upon us to continue that solicitation. The old words, too often sneered at, are true— the first, last, and certain duty of the evangelical preacher is to help the man save his soul.

> One by one we were born, and one by one we die. One by one we must be born again. One by one we must surrender that stubborn selfishness, which is individualism with its motives and purposes unregenerated. One by one we pass into that kingdom of God, which is righteousness and peace and joy.

THE MAN WHO BECAME A ROCK [1]

Thou art Simon the son of Jona: thou shalt be called Cephas, which is by interpretation, A stone. John 1:42.

THE word Jona means literally a dove. There may be in it a reference on the part of Jesus to the softness and weakness which lay beneath Peter's apparent strength.

I. PETER'S NATURAL GIFTS

The three great natural gifts of Peter were: (1) Leadership; (2) Initiative; and (3) Courage.

If you set a dozen men upon a desert island, one is sure to come to the top as a natural-born leader. He commands the others. Such a man was Peter. There was no need for him to seek preëminence as did the mother of Zebedee's children. No one would ever question but that Peter would be at the head in any enterprise he engaged in. He had initiative and was always ready to speak. It was not necessary to urge Peter. He did not hesitate to say: "Thou art the Christ, the Son of the living God." And he had courage to defend himself against great odds—with the sword, if that was necessary.

II. THE DEFECTS OF PETER'S CHARACTER

There were defects in this man which neutralized his natural resources. There were also three of these. They were: (1) Impulsiveness; (2) Inconstancy; and (3) Overweening pride.

Psychologically, impulsiveness is defined as action motived by feeling rather than by reason. This defines the character of Peter. Take the time when he saw Jesus walking on the water. First he cries out with fear, thinking that he is seeing a ghost. Then, when he recognizes that it is the Master, he immediately

[1] By W. Mackintosh Mackay in "The Men Jesus Made." Richard R. Smith.

changes and asks that he be given the gift. Soon again his attitude changes, and he cries: "Lord, save me; I perish." Inconstancy is probably a form of impulsiveness. It followed
Peter through life and caused him trouble. He swayed with
the crowd, and Paul had to withstand him to his face. His
pride is seen in his rebuke to the Master that the cross was not
for him to bear. Those who mount high have far to fall, as
Peter learned at the crowing of the cock.

III. THE ACQUIRED GRACES OF PETER'S CHARACTER

These are qualities which came by grace and sacrifice. They
were, first, a deep sense of sin. This quality seems quite
different from natural Peter. When he cried, "Depart from
me, for I am a sinful man, O Lord," he revealed the sanctified
Peter.

And he also acquired a deep and lasting love for his Master.
Chrysostom rightly said: "If John is the disciple whom Jesus
loved, Peter is the disciple who loved Jesus."

It is a tradition, but it is quite true to the character of Peter,
that when, by fate, he was about to be crucified, he asked that
he might be crucified head down—for he was not worthy to die
in the same posture as his Lord.

THE OPEN DOOR [1]

I am the door; by me if any man enter in, he shall be saved, and shall go in and out, and find pasture. John 10: 9.

THE door is the way of entrance into any structure. It signifies, therefore, the right of admission. But it is also the way of egress. It leads in and it leads out. It is a symbol of liberty. A door through which you can pass only one direction is not a door; it is a trap. Inward and outward—both ways the true door invites us. Christ is the living door through whom those who have entered into peace with God go out into a larger, freer, nobler life.

I. THROUGH CHRIST OUR THOUGHTS GO OUT INTO LIBERTY

It is common to speak of the unbelief which rejects Christ and his teachings as "free thought." No name could be further from the truth. When a man refuses to accept any evidence which he cannot detect with the senses, he is not free.

We come to Christ with our doubts. He tells us of the Father and his love and sends us on our way. He is the door through which we go out in liberty.

Christ is the door of our faith. There is no advance in religious knowledge, except through Him. There is no revision of the creeds save that to which he leads. Without him there may be change. But the only possible improvement is to tune the music of our faith more closely to the keynote of his name. Every forward movement must be through Christ.

II. THROUGH CHRIST OUR AFFECTIONS AND SYMPATHIES GO OUT INTO LIBERTY

The love of Christ is the type of all true and noble love be-

[1] By Henry Van Dyke in "The Open Door." Westminster Press.

cause it does not narrow the heart. The philosophy of the scribes and Pharisees was, "Love thyself." The philosophy of Jesus was, "Love thy neighbor as thyself."

I have no confidence in that kind of Christianity which will not join hands with an honest Hebrew to relieve suffering and enlighten ignorance. I have no confidence in that kind of Protestantism which refuses to take hold of one end of the litter in which a wounded man is lying because a Roman Catholic has hold of the other end. I have no confidence in that kind of a Church which resembles a private religious club, caring only for the comfort and respectability of its members, unreasonably sure of its own salvation, and unreasonably indifferent to the salvation of the world.

III. THROUGH CHRIST OUR BEST ACTIVITIES, OUR NOBLEST POWERS OF EFFORT AND ACHIEVEMENT, GO OUT INTO LIBERTY

We will admit that the Christian life does impose restrictions. It has constraints. It involves sacrifices, resignation, giving up. It cuts off many things: selfish ambition, sensual lust, frivolous dissipation, pursuit of empty pleasures.

But it does something for the man. It gives him a new hope, a new aspiration, a new motive and power of effort, a new force of love and courage.

Christ came into the world to sanctify all forms of honest human toil and all tasks of vital human effort. Christ came into the world not to separate men from life, but to bring true happiness into life. Christ came into the world to consecrate humanity to a holy priesthood, serving God in the ritual of common life.

"Every mason in the quarry, every builder on the shore,
Every woodsman in the forest, every boatman at the oar.

Hewing wood and drawing water, splitting stones and cleaving sod,
All the dusty ranks of labor in the regiment of God.

March together toward his triumph, do the task his hands prepare ;
Honest toil is holy service, faithful work is praise and prayer."

LIFE [1]

I came that they may have life, and may have it abundantly.
John 10: 10.

I. TO EXIST IS ONE THING; TO LIVE IS ANOTHER

I WAS reared in the wide-open country. Most great men have been so reared—and some others. There is plenty of room to expand mental conception there. But more than room is necessary for some folk who have never learned to look beyond the potato patch. In my neighborhood there were two old bachelor brothers living in their old log house where they were born. They worked about twenty acres of ground, and they never went beyond it. The village was only four miles away, but they had never been there. They had never seen a railroad. The church was three miles from their home, and they never attended it. They never visited any one. The preacher sometimes went to see them and talked to them about God, but they did not know what he was talking about. They lived nigh onto eighty years, while this expansive world, with its vast humanity and limitless enterprises, rolled on beyond their ken, while the numberless orbs of the infinite universe whirled over their heads without recognition, and while the omnipotent God signaled them from every material substance and every providence of life in efforts to enlist their attention unto a spiritual concept of himself and his eternal kingdom. They did not live, they simply existed.

II. LIFE IS WHAT MAKES THIS PLANET A WORLD

Life is no small consideration. Think what this planet would be if it had no life on it. Life is what makes it a world. The only thing about it worth consideration is that it is a place to

[1] By E. E. Smith in the *Christian Observer*.

live. You would not give a copper cent for the whole of it, if
you could not live on it. My life is worth more to me than
everything else on earth. Life is our biggest consideration here,
yet it gets the least attention in our scholastic training and in
our world enterprises. We palaver much over our material
sciences which are to this day absolutely ignorant of even what
life is, the only thing that makes any of the rest worth while.
It is time for some one to endow a big university somewhere to
teach our young people nothing else but what life is, and what
it is for, and how to use it for its own development and efficiency. But where would it get its teachers? Our most
reputable teachers are ignoramuses on this subject. They cannot teach us how to make life and how to make it abound
within us. I nominate Jesus Christ to be the head of that university, and I move that everybody in the whole world sit at
his feet to learn about life, the greatest and most momentous
subject in the world, the thing that he came for. While the rest
of the world are wasting their concern on the side issues, he
came into the center, "that they may have life, and have it
abundantly."

III. HOW BIG IS YOUR LIFE?

How big is your life? How much can it take in? What
are its bounds? Are you restricting it to the limits of a
puddle? Binding it to the treadwheel of the mill that
grinds the grits of the glen? Is that all? Then why live?
O friend, life is meant to be something bigger than the hills
and dales, than the mountains and the seas, than the levers
and the wheels. The Son of God did not think it worth
while to come to earth to teach you and me the arts and the
sciences of a comfortable existence, and that existence for
the little space of threescore years. That was too insignificant to draw him hither. He came to throw these lives
of ours into gear with the Omnipotent, the Infinite, the
Eternal, "That they may have life, and have it abundantly."

THE UNFAIR [1]

The Jews took up stones again to stone him. Jesus answered them, Many good works have I showed you from my Father: for which of those works do ye stone me? John 10: 31, 32.

The deed seems but to emphasize the vicious enmity of those who were acting in a cold-blooded, premeditated manner. They knew what they were doing. This was a repeated offense.

I. JESUS DEMANDS A SQUARE DEAL

IT is an easy matter to point the finger of scorn at the Jews and taunt them. But which of us, to-day, are guiltless? They lived in the time, to be sure, but their evidence was not that seasoned evidence of the centuries which we to-day have. It is difficult for us to turn any way without seeing the good works of the Father. If we turn against him, our sin is greater than that of the men who stoned him in his lifetime.

If they by their unfair attitude helped him on his way to the cross on Calvary, do we not by being unfair to him, dishonest in dealing with him, virtually cry aloud, "Crucify him"?

II. WE ARE DEBTORS TO GOD

We enjoy the gifts which God has bestowed upon us. But we forget the giver. We forget the Father's will which is back of the grain, the mill, and the sunshine. In the days of prosperity men are tempted to forget God. They take things for granted. One evening a gentleman attended a conference.

Very early in the deliberations he asked to be excused. Pressed for a reason, he explained that he had to attend a meeting at his church that evening. One of the group in

[1] By Edward L. Keller in "They Crucified and Crucify." Cokesbury Press.

197

utter amazement said: "What! Are you a member of the Church?" If you are a follower of Jesus Christ and your friends do not suspect it, if the world in which you move does not know it, are you not unfair, untrue to him?

III. BUSINESS DEMANDS NO EXCUSE FOR NEGLECTING JESUS

There are many men who expect to do a great deal for Jesus when certain pressing demands on their time are removed. God did not wait for pressing demands to be removed before he came to help you. The idea of some people that God should get the life after it has been drained by other causes is hardly a courteous or sportsmanlike one. The dumb brute will lick the hand of the man who feeds him. Can a man act with less fairness toward the God who has given him so many good things?

You are the judge and the jury. The testimony is before you summed up in these words: "Many good works have I shewed you from my Father." From your decision there is no appeal. The verdict is in your hands. You can send him away to again receive the tantalizing jeers if you wish. You will then be more than an innocent bystander, for you will be giving encouragement to those who lift him up and crucify him. Won't you be honest, fair, and just with Jesus? Won't you give him a square deal by making your decision such as you will not be ashamed of when to-morrow comes or regret a hundred years from to-morrow?

THE QUEST FOR JESUS [1]

We would see Jesus. John 12: 21.

It is almost a commonplace to say that this is what people are saying everywhere to-day. "Sirs, we would see Jesus." Some are saying that discouraging signs abound to-day. I know; I live in the midst of them. But, on the other hand, the age is remarkable in this fact, that everywhere people are saying in effect, "We would see Jesus."

I. THE SEARCH OF THE PEOPLE

EVERYWHERE abound evidences of the search. Religious books, such as Papini's "The Life of Christ," Bruce Barton's "The Man Nobody Knows," and Ludwig's "Life of Jesus" appear among the best sellers. A great motion picture is made on the life which is called "The King of Kings." The search is one.

Humanity is seeking for Jesus as a teacher. They admire his idealism. And his ideals do reach that perfection which is vital. Humanity is seeking Jesus as a comrade. We cannot follow the teachings of Jesus unless some new power is communicated to us. And it is impossible for us to have Jesus as a comrade. The basis of all friendship is unity of interest and outlook, and we lack that.

We cannot have the friendship of Jesus and at the same time the friendship of all that put him on Calvary's cross.

And we want him as a leader. Yes, and they wanted him for a leader when he was on earth. If he had filled men's bellies, they would have been with him. But he would not. So they would have nothing to do with him.

[1] By G. Campbell Morgan in "Great Themes of the Christian Faith," edited by Charles W. Ferguson. Richard R. Smith.

II. THE JESUS MEN ARE CLAMORING FOR IS NOT THE JESUS OF THE BOOK

The Greeks who came asking to see Jesus did not see him. They did see him in a physical sense. But they did not understand him. Even those who were closest to him had not seen him at this time.

"Have I been so long with you, and dost thou not know me, Philip?" (Jesus.)

But a half hour after Pentecost they had seen him and knew him.

Take the trail of the words dealing with *the hour*. Back in Cana he had said to his mother, "Mine hour is not yet come." In the seventh chapter of John we find that they would have laid hands on him, but "his hour was not yet come." In the eighth chapter he taught in the temple and feared no man, because his hour was not yet come. In the twelfth chapter the "hour is come." What hour? You find it in the thirteenth and the seventeenth chapters. You find it in the cross. "Father, save me from this hour."

The Jesus humanity needs is more than a human Idealist, a Man, a human comrade, more than a human Leader. The Jesus humanity needs is the dying, risen, reigning Christ.

HEAVEN [1]

I go to prepare a place for you. John 14: 2.

A little boy's kite was up so high it was out of sight. A gentleman said: "How do you know it is up there? You can't see it." "No," said the little fellow, "but I know it's there, because I can feel the tug."

AND we can feel the tug of heaven. And it makes me believe that it is there. I do not believe that God would put such a universal longing in the human heart without making some provision for its realization.

I. HEAVEN IS A PLACE

"I go to prepare a place."

"Heaven is to be something rather than to go somewhere." (Canon Farrar.)
"Heaven means a state of character rather than a place of residence." (Paterson Smyth.)

Of course the two last statements are true. A man must be prepared in spirit before he can enter heaven. But heaven is more than a mental state. It is a place of residence. When Jesus left the earth he must have gone somewhere. He said, "In my Father's house are many mansions." Those mansions are just as real as the houses we have down here. You can trust God to make good on his promise.

II. HEAVEN IS A PREPARED PLACE

"I go to prepare. . . ."

There are three things about this place I want to point out. First, it is prepared big enough. Merely a look at the solar

[1] By William Edward Biederwolf in "The Adventure of the Hereafter." Richard R. Smith.

system staggers our imagination. There is room enough in heaven. We won't be crowded. Then heaven is full of beauty. We see the outside of heaven. But remember that the inside is more beautiful. And then heaven is a comfortable place.

III. HEAVEN IS A BUSY PLACE

A heaven where we didn't have anything to do but sit by the side of the crystal seas and pearly streams and gaze forever on the eternal beauty and dazzling effulgence about us would be too ghostly. It would be too senseless and insipid. That'll do for some old monk or idle dreamer, but I wouldn't want to go there.

IV. HEAVEN IS A PLACE OF COMMUNION AND SOCIAL ACTIVITY

The people you will enjoy in heaven are the ones the Christian likes to enjoy. There will be no liars, no backbiters, no gossipers, no meddlers. But we shall have there the pure in heart, the noble, and the loving. We shall see there our friends who have gone on before us.

V. HEAVEN IS AN ETERNAL PLACE

Earthly nations and places pass away, but heaven is eternal. It stands forever.

Some one has said that when we get to heaven there will be three surprises. First, to see some people we did not expect to see. Second, not to see some people we did expect to see. And the third, the greatest surprise of all, will be to find ourselves there.

Hobbes, the notorious infidel, said, "I am taking a fearful leap in the dark."

Mirabeau cried: "Give me more laudanum; I don't want to think of eternity."

But the Christian has no fear. He goes to a place—an eternal place—prepared for him.

THE WAY HOME[1]

I am the way: . . . no man cometh unto the Father, but by me.
John 14: 6.

At the bottom of most modern heresies lies the ancient doctrine of work-righteousness. Man, in his pride, wants to build his own ladder by which he may climb into the Father's presence. He substitutes his own moral worth and good deeds for the way of salvation, as it is in Christ Jesus. As a result he fails to find the peace of God which passeth all understanding.

I. THE WAY HOME TO GOD IS A PLAIN WAY

THERE is no excuse for any living man in our land to fail to know the way of life. Churches reach from coast to coast. The name of Jesus is known wherever men meet and talk. Of production of religious books there is no end. The language of the gospel is so simple that a child can understand it. Jonathan Edwards found one four-year-old girl who had experienced conversion.

II. THE WAY HOME IS AN OLD WAY

"We are traveling home to God in the way our fathers trod."

"Abraham rejoiced to see my day: and he saw it, and was glad." (Jesus.)

The way has been so well traveled that a deep groove has been worn into the history and life of our race. The world will never be able to devise a means of salvation which is as satisfying or as joyous. It worked for our fathers, and it will work for us.

III. THE WAY HOME IS A NARROW WAY

"Straight is the gate, and narrow is the way, that leadeth unto life, and few there be that find it." (Jesus.)

[1] By A. W. Smith in the *Christian Herald*.

Since God devised the plan of salvation, we must grant him the privilege of stating the terms under which we shall use it. One of these conditions is that we must confess our sins and forsake them, and rest upon Christ alone for salvation. We must come in the appointed way or be rejected. There is no alternative.

IV. THE WAY HOME IS A BROAD WAY

"Whosoever will, let him take the water of life freely." (Jesus.)

The word "whosoever" is world-wide in its scope. It takes in every individual, regardless of sex, race, nation, color, or station in life.

> There was a sailor who, far out at sea, felt an awakened conscience. He was in great distress, as he had lived a wicked life. There was no one on board to tell him what to do. While reading his Bible one night, he came across John 3: 16, and he put his finger on the word "whosoever." Then he said: "Whosoever, that means anybody, that means everybody, that means me."

V. THE WAY HOME IS A SAFE WAY

There are no wrecks along the Jesus way of life.
"He shall give his angels charge over thee, to keep thee in all thy ways."

> An old soldier of the Civil War, of my acquaintance, set out for the front with a Bible in his knapsack, which his mother had given him. She asked him to read daily the ninety-first Psalm. He survived the war, with its perils and temptations, and died at a ripe old age as an honorable citizen. During the perils of war and the years of a long life he had always found the Jesus way of life a safe way.

FRIENDS OF GOD [1]

Ye are my friends. John 15: 14.

Friends! Here is a magic word. At the sound of it faces come trooping out of the shadows and pass in review before the inward eye—comrades of the way who daily walk beside us; absent friends, living and laboring in distant places; dear friends of other years who have sailed beyond the sunset. He who has one true and understanding friend knows what Jesus meant when he said, "Ye are my friends." Religion, he tells us in his own incomparable way, is a glorified friendship between a believing man and the eternal God.

THERE are three laws of friendship which, when applied to the believer's relation to God, make religion a glowing experience.

I. THE FIRST REQUISITE OF THIS ASSOCIATION OF HEARTS IS THAT TWO PERSONS SHALL BELIEVE IN EACH OTHER

A friendship that is worthy of the name can no more grow in the atmosphere of distrust and suspicion than roses can bloom in Arctic snows. The soul of religion is simple confidence in Almighty God. Is he not good and true, and will not the Judge of all the earth do right? As soon as the heart begins to trust the goodness and wisdom of God the divine friendship has begun. In the formal language of creed and pulpit we call this faith. But James, exceedingly human in his approach to religion, speaks of the soul's assurance of God in more informal language: "Abraham believed in God, and he was called the friend of God."

II. FRIENDSHIP GROWS THROUGH FELLOWSHIP

The old friends—friends who have been with us through storm and sunshine—these are the best. A golden wedding,

[1] By Costen J. Harrell in "Friends of God." Cokesbury Press.

205

happy anniversary of half a century of comradeship, is lovelier
than plighted troths and wedding bells. How inseparably two
lives are intertwined through fifty years of fellowship in the
holiest of all human bonds! After the same principle the divine
friendship ripens through long fellowship with God. By the
holy intimacies of closet and trysting place, by labors with him
in the vineyards of the world, by walking with him in duty's
path and standing with him in the battle front—so through the
joys and testings of the years are our hearts established in the
love of God. Our books on theology call this "sanctification"
and "growth in grace." Paul writes in simpler phrases: "I am
persuaded that neither death, nor life, . . . nor things present,
nor things to come, . . . shall be able to separate us from the
love of God, which is in Christ Jesus our Lord" (Romans 8:
38, 39).

III. WE BECOME LIKE OUR FRIENDS

What great love is bestowed upon us that we should be called
the friends of God! "And it doth not yet appear what we
shall be: but we know that, when he shall appear, we shall be
like him" (1 John 3: 2).

Friendship is the union of hearts in thought and purpose,
a joyful interchange of life, an affinity of soul that flour-
ishes amid the trials of time and survives the shock of
death. The religion of Jesus Christ is like that, and the
gospel is nothing less than his open invitation for us to
enter into the circle of God's friends.

No task is too hard, no way is lonely, and the future is bright
with promise when the heart serenely sings:

> "I have a Friend, O such a Friend,
>   He sought me ere I knew him;
> He drew me with the cords of love,
>   And thus he bound me to him."

THE LAWS OF LIFE [1]

Henceforth I call you not servants; for the servant knoweth not what his lord doeth: but I have called you friends; for all things that I have heard of my Father I have made known unto you. John 15: 15.

OUR Lord calls us his friends, not because we love him, but because we know him. As we grow in wisdom and knowledge of God, understanding him, we become entitled to this term.

I. THE REVELATION OF NATURAL LAWS

Isaac Newton is the man who cut the man of the present from the man of the past. He took the law of the falling apple and generalized it so that it applied to all the universe. First men saw only harshness in these laws of nature. He felt like rebelling. But later he realized that this is a lawful world —that if, instead of always obeying the same laws there would be a change with each event, it would be a difficult place in which to live.

The scientist, with that humility which belongs to those who love the truth, is very "agnostic" in laying down the law, is very doubtful whether any law has been finally stated: but the thing of which he is certain and of which he has made us certain is that "the world is lawful to the core."

Once we spoke of the aviator as defying the law of gravitation. Now we know that he is using the law. If nature should be merely a matter of caprice, little could be accomplished in the world.

II. THE REVELATION OF SPIRITUAL LAWS

But surely if God is thus God of the physical world, he cannot be an altogether different God in the spiritual world.

[1] By Maude Royden in "The Friendship of God." G. P. Putnam's Sons.

Why dare we not assume of him that stability that we find in the world he made?

The spiritual is not opposed to the physical. Both of these must be in harmony, and both are under the power of the God who made and controls them.

All about us there are spiritual laws operating. All the time we see people transformed by love, healed by faith, restored by hope, corrupted by hate, destroyed by cruelty. There must be laws which control these things as law controls the flowing of the river and the tides of the sea.

Unless we understand the spiritual laws, the physical ones which we do understand may prove our destruction. The meaning of life is too severe for us unless we know the spiritual laws. Economic misery, industrial struggle, international strife made life seem hopeless. We cannot live without God. And we can only have friendship with him by knowing of him and his laws.

We shall apply ourselves to the understanding of that law with the same courage, the same confidence, the same certainty in the unfailing operation of God's love, as became us when we studied the laws of science.

"I DO NOT ASK TO SEE THE DISTANT SCENE" [1]

I have yet many things to say unto you, but ye cannot bear them now. John 16: 12.

Growth is the law of everything that lives. There is nothing that has not come up from simpler conditions—music, painting, architecture, art, science, trade, economics. Ours is a moving world, and it is impossible to keep things stationary in a moving world. Nothing comes into life full-grown. Everything develops. It is "first the blade, then the ear, then the full corn in the ear." Once we were offered evolution or Christianity; but, lo and behold, as somebody puts it, "we decided to take both." As old Dr. McCosh used to say, "Evolution is nothing in the world but organized causation."

I. GROWTH IS THE LAW IN THE FIELD OF EDUCATION

You cannot hurry the education of a child. He must have the first lessons first. No teacher starts a six-year-old child with the mysteries of quadratics. You do not give a little child a razor. You do not talk to him about psychology. The education of the race is like that.

In his "Up from Slavery," Booker Washington tells of an old colored man during the days of slavery who wanted to learn to play the guitar. In his desire he applied to one of his young masters to teach him. The young man replied: "All right, Uncle Jake, I will give you lessons, but I am going to charge you for them. I will charge you a dollar for the first lesson, fifty cents for the second, and twenty-five for the third." To which Uncle Jake replied: "All right, Boss, I'se agreed, only I wants you to give me that las' lesson first." So many of God's children would learn the last lesson first.

[1] By Malcolm James MacLeod in "When the Morning Wakens." Doran.

God's way is line upon line, precept upon precept. Gradually his laws are revealed. Until the time of the New Testament the only method known of reprisal was "an eye for an eye." We hear many ask questions as to why the Master did not tell us certain things.

It is enough that he did not. There are many things which are not made plain in the Scriptures. But he has probably revealed to us as much as we are capable of understanding. There will be more made known later.

II. THE SAME LAW HOLDS IN THE EDUCATION OF THE RACE

The revelation of God to the race is a gradual one. He waits his appointed time. Columbus landed in the West Indies in 1492. A few years later Ponce de Leon landed on the shores of Florida. John Cabot came out in 1497. Then Sir Francis Drake made a flying trip. But one hundred and twenty-eight years passed before the Mayflower touched the New England shore. It took time for God's revelation.

As when an ocean liner is sailing out of the harbor she must creep slowly to avoid collision, so when a new truth is launched there are many obstacles in its path, and it must content itself with very tardy progress until it reaches the open sea. The morality of the Pentateuch is the morality of the primer. As the nation advanced more light was given.

God permitted many things because he was educating the race. Polygamy was a part of the Mosaic law as was slavery. But what an injustice to judge Abraham and David by twentieth-century standards. There has been a constant move from the morality of Moses to the morality of Jesus.

"The morality of a progressive dispensation is not the morality from which it starts, but the morality with which it ends." (Canon Mozley.)

WHEN THE SPIRIT IS COME [1]

Howbeit when he, the Spirit of truth, is come, . . . he shall glorify me. John 16: 13, 14.

THE ministry of John the Baptist looked toward the coming of Jesus. The ministry of Jesus looked toward the coming of the Spirit. It was expedient for them that he go away; but he did not want to leave without telling them to wait, preparing while they waited for the coming of the Holy Spirit.

I. WHEN THE SPIRIT CAME THE DISCIPLES THOUGHT MORE, NOT LESS, ABOUT THE CHRIST

They understood and loved him more under the ministry of the Spirit than they did when they had personal contact. Under the new inspiration they went forth as fiery heralds to spread his truth, ready to pay the price, even to bonds and imprisonment and death. That same test would seem to hold to-day. The individual who is touched by the Holy Spirit exalts Christ. The Church which is touched by the Holy Spirit exalts Christ. More of the Spirit, more of Christ.

II. WHEN THE SPIRIT COMES HE SPIRITUALIZES BELIEVERS

We cannot dispense with reason in religion, but we will do well to remind ourselves that we need something more. We need the spirit of God. We need that which enlightens the heart. The greater part of our religious differences, the meagerness of our fruitage, and our regrettable failures result from the head process in a realm where the heart should have been preëminent.

III. WHEN THE SPIRIT IS COME HE WILL CHRISTIANIZE OUR RELIGION

Religion and Christianity have not always been synonymous. Orthodox Christian zeal has often led to most unchristian ac-

[1] By William Edward Snyder in "Sermons of Power." Cokesbury Press.

tions. One has but to recall the rack and thumbscrew to realize the truthfulness of this statement. In the "Bonnie Brier Bush" we have the pathetic portrayal of a man, old Lachlan Campbell, who was most rigid in orthodox honesty, but he erased the name of his daughter from the Church roll when she took her first wayward step. There was rigid and honest religion, but it had been untouched by the Spirit.

IV. WHEN THE SPIRIT CAME IT DEMONSTRATED HOW MUCH COULD BE DONE WITHOUT A MAN-DEVISED PROGRAM

Just a short time before the disciples were talking organization. One of their number, Judas, had deserted them, and they must find somebody to take his place. But when the Spirit came there was a mighty power which gripped them, which made their whole human program seem insignificant. When there is a wearisomeness of goals, then we need the power of the Holy Spirit.

> "With all thy quickening powers
> Kindle a flame of secret love
> In these cold hearts of ours."

"IF I STILL HOLD CLOSELY TO HIM" [1]

Ye shall be sorrowful, but your sorrow shall be turned into joy.
John 16: 20.

Sorrow is not physical; it is mental. It is the pain of the mind. When we speak of suffering, we usually mean physical suffering, but there is a suffering far deeper and keener and sharper than anything the body knows. It is the suffering of the mind, of conscience, of heart, and this alone is real sorrow.

BUT how shall we meet sorrow? There are a number of ways.

I. FORGETFULNESS

Strive as you may to forget your trouble, they tell us. Anything which will drug the memory is considered wise and prudent. The mourner who would follow this rushes into society. Travel and change will make her forget. But there are nobler souls who prefer to remember, even though remembering brings pain. Consolation by forgetfulness brings fearful consequences. Families drift apart by this method.

II. WORK

Yes, work is a blessing, and we may lose our bitterness in applying ourselves to it. It will be remembered that this was what saved John Bright in an hour of despair. Work is not a curse; it is a blessing. Many bitter things can be forgotten by whole-hearted application to noble work.

III. MINISTERING TO OTHERS

Often one's trouble is largely self-pity. Nothing cures this like helping others in distress. Many times their distress is greater than yours.

[1] By Malcolm James MacLeod in "When the Morning Wakens." Doran.

"Go out, my dear woman, into the world and find a home where there is less sorrow than yours and then come back and repeat your request." (Answer of a saint to praying woman in poem by Sir Edwin Arnold, "The Light of Asia.")

IV. RESIGNATION

"Well, I suppose that I must be resigned. I suppose I shall have to grin and bear it. Looks, after all, as if that's the only thing to do."

But this is not the Christian way. Jesus taught his disciples to say, "Thy will be done," not "Thy will be endured."

V. TRANSFORMATION

The transformation of sorrow into something beautiful and holy is the Christian way to meet it. We must become poets of life. Wordsworth made beautiful verses from the common things of life. Burns found beauty in an old bridge, a mare, a field mouse, and a daisy. Barrie takes the village of Thrums and transforms it into a thing of beauty. This we must do with sorrow.

"Reverend sir, I have not found it a vale of tears. It has treated me well. It has been a garden of happiness with a love lane in it. These bottles are a symbol. To you they may smell of ether, to me they smell of roses. To your eyes things may look blue. To mine it serves for 'the old June weather, blue above land and wall.'" (A character in "Confessions," by Robert Browning.)

God often leads his children into dark places in order to see the stars. We learn after a while that it is really possible to see in the dark.

LOVE'S DRAUGHT [1]

The cup which my Father hath given me, shall I not drink it?
John 18: 11.

The expression "cup" is commonly used throughout the
Old Testament to denote some experience of life in relation to God. For instance, the Psalmist says, "The Lord
is the portion of my inheritance and of my cup"; and again,
"My cup runneth over"; and yet again, "I will take the cup
of salvation." Christ thus takes a well-understood figure
and applies it to himself, and his words are invested with
a deep and tender meaning by the fact that he himself had
given a cup to his disciples, in the drinking of which for all
time they should commemorate his dying love.

I. A PROGRESSIVE SUBMISSION IS SEEN IN THE BIBLE STATEMENTS

THERE are two prayers and a question which show how the
conviction grew upon Jesus that he must drink of this cup the
Father had given him.

"If it be possible, let this cup pass from me."
"If this cup may not pass except I drink it, thy will be
done."
"Shall I not drink it?"

This decision is a glorious triumph of love and loyalty. He has
already drunk much, but not one drop is to be spilled.

> "Death and curse were in the cup,
>   O Christ, 'twas full of thee;
> But thou hast drained the last dark drop,
>   'Tis empty now for me.
> That bitter cup, love drank it up,
>   Now blessing's draught for me."

II. THE APPLICATION OF THESE WORDS TO THE DISCIPLES

He still asks, as he asked the first disciples, "Can ye drink
of the cup that I drink of?"

[1] By J. Stuart Holden in "Redeeming Vision." Revell.

Sometimes we think that the cup we have is more bitter than we can bear. But it is well to remember that all our experiences are limited and of fixed duration. They do not last forever. The Father has not put in any cup a greater measure than can be borne. He is not indifferent to our pain or our weakness. He knows, also, what is needed to strengthen our lives. The cup not alone burdens; it heals. It only harms him who is unwilling to partake of it.

III. IT IS THE CUP OF VICARIOUS SUFFERING

Christ drank of his cup for others. His followers must do likewise. To save others became the passion of Christ, and it must also become our passion. "Without the shedding of blood there is no remission of sin." Death must work in us before life can work in others.

Only he whose heart has been broken can touch the broken heart of another without causing pain; only he who himself has known loss and impoverishment can encourage the one from whom all things seem to be slipping away; only the one who has known the smart of sorrow and the sting of pain can help some burdened, sorrowing, stricken heart to sing songs in the night.

The ATONEMENT FROM CHRIST'S POINT OF VIEW [1]

The cup which my Father hath given me, shall I not drink it?
John 18: 11.

St. Paul interpreted the atonement in the words, "He loved me, and gave himself for me." But the view of Jesus is shown in the text of this sermon. We will notice the following things regarding his point of view.

I. CHRIST DID NOT DENY THE REALITY OF PAIN

He knew that he was to suffer shame and pain. There would be the bitterness of a false accusation. There would be early death and association with sin. But to the cross he went. We are again hearing about the cross of Jesus Christ.

"So the thought came to our Lord. Why, the whole thing's at stake. If you are really the Christ, you had better come down out of that if you expect us or anybody else ever to believe in you. If the temptation of the pinnacle of the temple was great, what shall we say of the temptation on the pinnacle of the cross? To take the pain out of life and the sting out of sin, would not that be a sure way to the hearts of men? But he who hung there and suffered there was as though he heard them not." (Hubert L. Simpson, in "The Intention of His Soul.")

Pain does exist. It had a part in the suffering of Christ. One who deals with sickness as I do has little patience with those who say that pain does not exist.

II. JESUS SAW THAT HIS PAIN WAS NOT BROUGHT ABOUT BY SECONDARY CAUSES

It would have been easy to attribute his death to secondary

[1] By Arthur F. Winnington-Ingram (Bishop of London) in "Good News from God." Longmans.

causes. There was the ambition of Caiaphas, the treachery of Judas, the worldliness of Herod, the cowardice of Pilate, the fickleness of the populace. It is true that all these took a part in the crucifixion. But Jesus looked upon all these things and said: "The cup which my Father hath given me, shall I not drink it?"

Remember that it is God's only Son who drinks. You have your cup, of course. But can you say that God does not love you because of it? In his plan he permits his own Son to drink.

III. CHRIST DRAINED THE CUP TO THE DREGS

The result was a peace and joy, broken for a time by the pain on the cross, but coming back with even greater strength. Is there not a lesson for us when the cup is pressed to our lips?

We may legitimately ask that the cup be removed. We can take any available methods to remove it. But if it proves to be the Father's will that we drink it, let us do it in the right spirit. Thousands who have drank in that spirit have found that Jesus is with them, and what may have looked like a bitter experience becomes a sweet one. Saints have been made by suffering.

THEN JESUS CAME [1]

Then the same day at evening, being the first day of the week, when the doors were shut where the disciples were assembled for fear of the Jews, came Jesus and stood in the midst, and saith unto them, Peace be unto you. John 20: 19.

It is true that Jerusalem was filled with rumors that the Crucified had in some mysterious way broken out of the tomb and had been seen alive. But the tidings had seemed but mockery to them. They had seen the last of him. No doubt of that. "As for me, I'm going fishing," said Peter. "That's all I am good for now." "As for me," said Thomas, "except I shall put my finger in the print of the nails and my hand into his side, I will not believe." Such was the state of mind of all of them.

AND then Jesus came.

I. HE COMES IN A TIME OF CRISIS

When Rome was corrupt to the very core and thoughtful men were in despair, then Jesus came as the babe of Bethlehem. When John the Baptist was shut in Herod's prison, then Jesus came into Galilee. When he was needed the most sorely, then he comes.

Things have come to a crisis in our own day. These days of transition are difficult ones. We hear on every side the cry, "Jesus, come back." And he is coming back. We can look for him in days such as this when he is most needed.

II. HE COMES IN UNEXPECTED WAYS AND AT UNLIKELY TIMES

The disciples were not looking for him, nor was anybody else. Mary Magdalene was eager to find his body. She did not dream of finding him. She saw the angels, but did not recognize the Master when he spoke to her.

[1] Dr. Henry Alford Porter in "What We Preach." Judson.

That is the way Jesus comes—unexpectedly. Wilfred Grenfell, Oxford student, was not converted by the culture of Henry Drummond. But Moody reached his heart. It was one of the unexpected things in the kingdom. He moves in mysterious ways. We should always be listening for the coming of his feet.

III. HE COMES THROUGH CLOSED DOORS

It is impossible for any man to shut Christ entirely out of his life. He is a dividing line in personal as well as human history. There is a line in every man's life which divides two great dates for him—one is B.C., the other is A.D. To some he comes as he came to Pilate. There was no advance warning. But Pilate had to decide between Jesus and the mob.

He breaks through the cold and brings peace to the troubled heart.

Are there not times when the heart goes out in a passionate desire for a deeper peace than you have ever known? It is told how Dante, wandering one day over the mountains, drew near to a secluded monastery. He knocked at the gate. It was opened by a monk. "What do you seek here?" And with a gesture of despair, the poet replied, "Peace." Ah, that is the old craving and the same old search in our day not less than in the centuries gone by.

CHRIST AMONG THE COMMON THINGS OF LIFE [1]

As soon as they were come to land, they saw a fire of coals there, and fish laid thereon, and bread. . . . Jesus saith unto them, Come and dine. John 21: 9, 12.

HERE Christ stands among the common things of life; the fire, the fish, the bread—all common things; a group of tired, hungry fishers—all common men.

I. JESUS STOOD ON THE SHORE, BUT THE DISCIPLES KNEW NOT THAT IT WAS JESUS

That seems strange. Why did they not recognize him? Perhaps they looked for a glorified Lord who would come in the clouds of heaven. Or he might appear in the sacred precincts of the upper room where they had met for prayer. So if they were looking for Christ at all that morning, it would hardly be by the seashore. And this man was cooking a meal. They thought only of a fellow fisherman.

II. THE ENTIRE EARTHLY LIFE OF CHRIST WAS LINKED WITH THE COMMON—EVEN THE COMMONEST THINGS OF LIFE

You and I would hardly have picked out his life training for one who was to be the Messiah. There are two reasons.

1. With most of us dignity is synonymous with some kind of separation from common life. It dwells in palaces, not cottages. We have yet to learn that true indignity is sin, meanness, malevolence, small-heartedness.

2. We have not learned to look for Christ in the common things of life.

III. JESUS SAID, "CAST THE NET ON THE RIGHT SIDE OF THE SHIP AND YE SHALL FIND"

They cast and did find. This is a funny thing. Christ knew

[1] By William J. Dawson in "The World's Great Sermons," Volume X. Funk and Wagnalls.

more about the management of their fishing than they did. We, too, must learn that Christ knows more about the proper management for our lives than we know ourselves.

And what a lesson for any Church! There are the souls to be reached. Christ has a way for getting them. Do we insist on letting down the net on the wrong side—the side which is not his?

IV. JESUS SAID UNTO THEM, "COME AND DINE"

Dine on what? Not on the fishes they had caught, though they were many. The fire was started before they drew in their nets. Christ had prepared the feast. It is ever thus. It is true with the Church to-day. The feast is ready. We must accept the invitation. Come and dine. There must have flashed in the eyes of these men that scene a few months before when five thousand sat before him and feasted on the loaves and fishes.

V. THEN JESUS TAKETH BREAD AND GIVETH THEM, AND FISH LIKE-WISE

There is no mistaking this one thing. This was more than a breakfast. It was a sacrament. Here on the lakeshore, without a church or an altar, the true feast of the Lord was observed.

Bread and wine, the commonest of all foods to the Oriental, are elements indeed, because they are necessary to the most elementary form of physical life, things used daily in the humble home. By linking himself imperishably with these commonest elements of life, Christ makes it impossible to forget him. Once more the thought shines clear, Jesus among the common things of life.

SELF-EXAMINATION [1]

Simon, son of Jonas, lovest thou me? John 21: 16.

Of course Jesus knew whether Simon Peter loved him. He did not ask the question three times to get information. He did not tell Simon that he did or did not love Him as he might have done. He gave the question to Simon to work out for himself.

I. A MATTER OF PERSONAL INVENTORY

WHEN Adam and Eve sinned in the garden, God came to them with questions. They were not for information, but for their self-probing. In the wrestling at the Brook Jabbok, God asked Jacob what his name was. It was to call Jacob's attention to the fact that his name indicated that he was a supplanter, a cheater. God asked Elijah at Horeb what he was doing there. The question was to make him take stock of himself. God sent the wise men to Herod with a question, "Where is he that is born King of the Jews?" The question went home to Herod, as it was intended. We are told to examine ourselves whether we be of the faith; and before we partake of the sacrament of the Lord's Supper we are exhorted not to think of ourselves more highly than we ought to think, but to think soberly. In other words, God puts up to us the hard job of self-analysis.

II. A TEST OF MOTIVE

For a sample case let us here and now bring ourselves individually to the witness stand. Let us put the probing question, "Lovest thou me?" Let us each ask himself the following cross-questions on that: What is my motive in professing Christ and joining the Church? Why did I become a minister or a Church worker? Why do I pray? Why do I teach a Sabbath school class? Why do I contribute of my means to the Church

[1] By E. B. Smith in the *Christian Observer.*

and its missionary enterprises? Am I trying to feed Christ's lambs and sheep because I love him? Or is it because I want to show how well I can do it, and win popularity? Do I preach because I like to orate, or teach because I like to instruct, or hold office in the Church to be looked up to as a leader? If I were to be crucified for doing these things, would I do them? Would I be a Christian if I knew I would be persecuted for it; if my business would become bankrupt for lack of patronage; if I and my family would be ostracized socially; if it were a public disgrace to be known as a Christian? Or am I a member of the Church, enlisted in the cause of Christ, reading my Bible, saying my prayers, teaching, preaching, contributing, attending the worship of the Church, any or all of these things, and more, because I want to escape hell and go to heaven when I die? That is, am I doing it all for my own welfare here and hereafter? Is the prime motive self? Let us each candidly and alone look inside of himself for the answer to these questions, then come to the question, "Lovest thou me?"

III. A TEST OF LOVE

Do you and I love God? Honestly, do we? Or are we simply trying to placate him that we may get something out of him? You have perhaps heard of the man who said, "I would hate God if I were not afraid to." You and I cannot love God by simply making up our minds to do it. We may turn our steps because we think we ought for some reason, but we cannot turn our hearts that way. Many a man turns his steps unto Church activities and moral precepts, while his heart goes on in its old way. He does what he thinks is to his advantage, though he does not love to do it.

We cannot love God by simply resolving to do it. It requires a miracle, a new heart, and God alone can do it for us. The object of self-examination is to drive us to God for rescue from ourselves and a kindling of our love for him. We must come to him for the love motive for service. O friend, the big need of to-day is the love motive. Have you got it?

WAIT [1]

Being assembled together with them, he charged them not to depart from Jerusalem, but to wait. Acts 1: 4.

THE disciples were ready to go. Jesus said, "Wait, you had better wait." This was not the warning of expediency, but a warning lest their message become shallow, thin, and ineffective. One can spoil a cause, an undertaking, a message, spoil almost anything by haste. The larger the task the more fitted must a man be for it. One cannot build a towering skyscraper on sand. A spiritual message demands a spiritual experience.

I. THERE ARE TIMES WHEN IT WOULD BE SPIRITUALLY SUICIDAL TO WAIT

At such a time the only honorable way out is through the deed. Once face to face with a man's stark need one cannot wait, he must act or lose his chance forever. The Good Samaritan cannot wait to find out the details of the man's life. In making the supreme choices of life, after one has thoughtfully considered the matter, one must dare to choose, leaving the issue with God. Likewise in the region of faith man cannot wait till the Judgment Day to ascertain whether life is worth living; he must adventure in the spirit of heroes, and God will do the rest.

II. BUT THERE ARE TIMES WHEN "TO WAIT" IS THE HIGHEST WISDOM AND THE NOBLEST ACTIVITY

It was Milton, one of the loftiest poets of the Anglo-Saxon race, who said, "They also serve who only stand and wait." Serve by their unconquerable faith that somehow God will achieve order out of chaos, light out of darkness, joy out of pain. To wait courageously in the light of tragic circumstances is to have achieved the mastership of life. Wait, without bitterness, without rancor, without hate!

[1] By Victor F. Scalise in *Church Management*.

225

III. THE MAN CAN AFFORD TO WAIT IF HE HAS DONE HIS WORK WELL

He need not waste his energies going about here and there telling the world how good his work is. Let him work with a will, put his heart in his task, be true to the inner vision, and give expression to his nature.

When a man is tempted to be discouraged because he does not see the light of dawn upon his days, he need not worry, let him wait. To the waiting mind, life ultimately speaks. If man can take a beating standing up and wait for the turn of the tide, his spirit has triumphed over hell and despair. Failure cannot vanquish him. When Disraeli was laughed at when he made his first speech in the House of Commons he said, "Wait, you will hear from me." They did.

> "With aching hands and bleeding feet
>   We dig and heap, lay stone on stone;
> We bear the burden and the heat
>   Of the long day, and wish 'twere done.
> Not till the hours of light return
> All we have built do we discern."

IV. THEY THAT WAIT FOR JEHOVAH SHALL RENEW THEIR STRENGTH

The spiritual life is deepened when in quietness and peace we can hear the whisper of God.

When Wilson lay dying, Baker spoke of the uncertain future of the League of Nations. With the purposes of God shining in his eyes Wilson said, "Baker, they can't stop God." The mills of God grind slowly, but they grind exceeding small.

Waiting is not wasting time; it is an occasion for drawing power, vision, light, strength for the task. God works slowly, but to no uncertain end. Wait, and when the Spirit of God shall have come upon you, then you may go to the ends of the earth making God the partner of your life.

FORBIDDEN KNOWLEDGE [1]

It is not for you to know the times or the seasons which the Father hath put in his own power. Acts 1:7.

Probably the last man to live on earth who knew everything was Lord Bacon. John A. Broadus used to lament the fact that he could not read all the books in the world. It would take a man over three hundred years to read all the titles, and after reading more than ten thousand years he would only have started to read all the books that have been published.

I. WE DO NOT KNOW ALL THAT WE COULD KNOW

LAZINESS and torpor have stagnated inquiry. Poverty has held many in the bondage of ignorance. Conceit and false pride have acted as opiates. False notions of knowledge have prejudiced the pious. This has gone so far with some that they insist that an education is contrary to the Scripture.

One of the very first commands to man was that he should have mastery over things of the earth, the sky, and the sea. Man has a capacity to know, and from this we can reason that he ought to know. God would not give the capacity unless it were for some use.

Faith and knowledge are close kin. No science is possible without faith, and faith rests on the highest knowledge, a scientific plus a spiritual knowledge. An erroneous view of nature does not contribute to the knowledge of God or soundness of faith.

"The lips of the priest guard knowledge, and men seek instruction from his mouth, for he is the messenger of the Lord of hosts."

[1] By J. M. Dawson in "The Light That Grows." Sunday School Board of the Southern Baptist Convention.

II. NOT ALL FACTS HAVE THE SAME VALUE

Some knowledge is essential, some is only useful, some is needless, while some is positively harmful.

The knowledge denied our first parents was the knowledge of the forbidden fruit. It was an experimental knowledge of evil, of disobedience, which is punished with suffering. There are some things it is better not to know. It is better not to know the taste of intoxicating liquor, the zest for gambling, the madness of vice, the license of anarchy.

On the other hand, there is some knowledge which is as a pearl of great price. It is called the excellency of the knowledge of Christ Jesus, our Lord and Saviour, whom to know is life eternal. We may not be able to comprehend Jesus, but we can apprehend him. We cannot account for him, but we can come into spiritual relations with him. And our knowledge of him grows more and more.

III. THERE ARE SOME THINGS WE DO NOT NEED TO KNOW

They would be as worthless to us as junk. There are even some things in the Book of God we do not need to know. It is not necessary for us to know the color of Jezebel's eyes, or who Melchizedek was, or the identity of some of the apocalyptic symbols.

We do not need to know what the morrow holds in store for us. That is in our Father's hands. We are not left to blind fate. There is a dynamic in the universe which drives us on.

"Out of the light that covers me,
    Bright as the sun from pole to pole,
I thank the God I know to be,
    For Christ, the Conqueror of my soul."

A SOUL-WINNING CHURCH [1]

But ye shall receive power, after that the Holy Ghost is come upon you: and ye shall be witnesses unto me both in Jerusalem, and in all Judæa, and in Samaria, and unto the uttermost part of the earth. Acts 1: 8.

Every Church ought to be a soul-winning Church. That is the great purpose for which the Church was founded. If it fails in this, no matter what else it may do, it has failed in the very thing for which it exists. Statistics lead us to believe that there must be a great many Churches that are not soul-winning Churches. Whole denominations are actually decreasing in membership. . . . The only explanation is that many individual Churches are not winning souls for Christ. Individual Churches fail to be soul-winning Churches because the individual members of the Churches are not soul-winning Christians.

WHAT is the program for soul-winning?

I. THE PERSON

The early soul - winners were just plain, ordinary people. There was not a university graduate among them. But they did have several qualifications very essential for soul-winning. They knew Jesus Christ. That is the first and most important thing. Then they lived lives in keeping with that knowledge. One cannot be a soul-winner unless his life measures up to his confession. The spotless character of a professing Christian will win the skeptical to Jesus when books of theology will fail.

II. THE PLACE

There is one good place to start your work of evangelism. It is where the disciples started. You start right where you are. It isn't necessary to move to the next town. The Christian can

[1] By Walter L. Lingle in "The Southern Presbyterian Pulpit." Revell.

start in his own home, the teacher in her own class. It doesn't mean that you are to stop where you start. But there is always a place close at hand for beginning.

Some one has said that the light that shines farthest shines brightest at home. Jesus does not want us to be content until the gospel has been preached to every creature. He laid upon his Church the greatest task that was ever laid upon any group of mortal men. Our marching orders are to go and disciple all nations. . . . The angels in heaven might be amazed at such a task.

III. THE POWER

The person: It is you. The place: It starts right where you are. The power: That is beyond human strength. It comes from God. It is the Holy Ghost.

Back in the days of the Great War a train on which I was traveling stopped away out in the open field one evening and remained there for what seemed an interminable length of time. After a while I got up and walked toward the engine to inquire what was the matter. The first man I met was the fireman, and I asked him if the train had broken down. He replied: "No, the engine has gone dead." When I asked him what he meant he replied: "In these war days the coal is so poor it will not burn. The fire has gone out, and there is not one ounce of steam in the chest."

What could human ingenuity do? The best engineer cannot make a locomotive self-propelling if it has no power. So it is with many a Church. After all the organization has been accomplished, there is still one essential thing lacking. There must be power. It must come from God.

THE DAY OF PENTECOST [1]

This is that. Acts 2: 16.

The Day of Pentecost has been described as, in a sense, His birthday—*dies natalis*. His mission was to constitute the Church, as the body of Christ, to rule and guide it, to add to it those who were being saved, and to reveal to them things the eye hath not seen, nor ear heard, nor the heart of man conceived, but which are made known to the Spirit-led.

I. THIS IS THAT

THE Day of Pentecost was *this*. For ten days one hundred and twenty loyal souls had been waiting for the gift of the Spirit. Then it came. *That* was the prophecy of the prophet Joel which foretold that the day would come when men-servants and maid-servants would break forth into prophecy. The Day of Pentecost was the fulfillment of that prophecy.

II. THIS IS NOT THAT

We must confess that to-day "This is not that." The professing Church is far removed from its Pentecostal prototype. *That* was united. *This* is divided. *That* was full of triumphant joy. *This* must pay choirs and choristers to sing for it. *That* made little of material wealth. *This* courts it. *That* was characterized by simplicity of methods. *This* must have paid agents and evangelists. *That* was a commonwealth of mutual helpfulness. *This* permits class distinctions.

III. THIS MIGHT BE THAT

The apostle did not say that Joel's prophecy was completely fulfilled on the Day of Pentecost. That was but the first in-

---

[1] By F. B. Meyer in "Five Musts of the Christian Life." Bible Institute Colportage Association.

stallment. The Spirit was to live on through the life of the
Church. The Spirit is alive to-day and is asking an opportunity to work. Noble are the instances in which the Spirit was
allowed its way. When the Spirit was permitted to use W. C.
Burns, he won Kilsyth, then Scotland, then Inland China.
When it touched and used Dwight L. Moody, he moved the
world. When John Wesley permitted the Spirit to use him,
it led to a mighty movement.

IV. THIS SHALL BE THAT

Andrew Murray gives the following five steps for the acquiring of the Holy Spirit:

1. I believe there is a Pentecostal blessing to be received—the anointing of the Holy Spirit and the enduement with power.
2. I believe that it is for me.
3. I have never received it; or if I received it once, I
lost it.
4. I long and desire to secure it at all cost; and am prepared to surrender whatever hinders.
5. I do now humbly and thankfully open my heart to receive all that I believe my Saviour is waiting to give; and
even if there be no resulting emotion, I will still believe
that I have received according to Mark 11: 24.

When Christians are anxious to receive the Holy Spirit, *This*
may be *That*.

THE INEVITABLE RESURRECTION [1]

Whom God hath raised up, having loosed the pains of death: because it was not possible that he should be holden of it. Acts 2:24.

He (Paul) does not represent the great fact of Christ's resurrection as incredible and impossible, "as the manner of some is." On the contrary, he asserts that, following the death of the Redeemer, his resurrection was inevitable. And so, indeed, it was. It was not thus by a necessity of inflexible fatalism, but by the inevitable outcome of divine purpose of eternal love moving through Creation, Providence, and Redemption to the ultimate consummation and the glory of the kingdom of God.

I. AT HIS CREATION MAN WAS DESIGNED TO ATTAIN THE SPIRITUALIZATION AND DEATHLESSNESS OF HIS SPIRITUAL NATURE

SIN arrested and forestalled this transforming exaltation of man and brought him under the dominion of carnal-mindedness and death. But the purpose of God's love persevered. The incarnation of the Son was promised, as a pledge of a Messianic Redeemer who could overcome death brought by the sin of woman. This promise lighted the flames of faith, and they always glowed in the Hebrew nation. In confidence Abel offered a more excellent sacrifice than Cain. By it Enoch walked with God. By the light of the promise Abraham set out for a strange land. It was the source of hope and the inspiration of the holy books of Israel.

This hope of a Messiah was closely tied with the hope of bodily resurrection.

"These are the words which I spake unto you, while I was yet with you, that all things might be fulfilled which were written in the law of Moses, and in the prophets, and in the Psalms concerning me." (Jesus.)

[1] By Warren Akin Candler in "Easter Meditations." Cokesbury Press.

II. THE APOSTLES RECOGNIZED THAT THE RESURRECTION OF JESUS WAS THE FULFILLMENT OF THIS HOPE

Jesus had instructed the apostles that their great task was to be his witnesses, and they understood that the major fact of their witness was to be concerning the resurrection. The central note of Peter's great Pentecost sermon was of the resurrection. When the lame man was healed in the temple, Peter again used the opportunity to speak of the resurrection of Jesus.

This was the staple and substance of their message, whether they preached in the synagogues of the Jews or in the market places of the gentiles. They knew nothing of a Messiah over whom death could prevail and the grave triumph.

III. THE CONSEQUENCES OF THE RESURRECTION FOR MANKIND

If Christ did not rise, the divine purpose of the creation of man is frustrated. The heavenly Fatherhood is reduced to impotence. The everlasting God is defeated by the powers of evil. The incarnation of Christ is made a transient and brief episode. The only sinless man who ever walked the earth falls before death. The possibilities of human righteousness are submerged in the waves of sin. The fairest hope that ever filled the hearts of seers with joy changes to darkness and despair. The holy expectations which flowed through Israel are disappointed. The apostles of Christ are found false witnesses. Human sin is left without possibility of pardon and cleansing. The holiest who have died have perished with sinners.

It cannot be so.

"Now is Christ risen from the dead, and become the first fruits of them that slept." (1 Cor. 15: 20.) "If we believe that Jesus died and rose again, even so them also which sleep in Jesus will God bring with him." (1 Thess. 4: 14.)

THE TRIUMPHANT TREE [1]

Whom ye slew and hanged on a tree. Acts 5: 30.
Cursed is every one that hangeth on a tree. Galatians 3: 13.
God forbid that I should glory, save in the cross. Galatians
6: 14.

> "There was a bright and happy tree;
>   The wind with music laced its boughs,
> Thither across the houseless sea
>   Came singing birds to house.
>
> Men grudged the tree its happy eves,
>   Its happy dawns of eager sound;
> So all that crown and tower of leaves
>   They leveled with the ground.
>
> They made an upright of the stem,
>   A crosspiece of a bough they made;
> No shadow of their deed on them
>   The fallen branches laid.
>
> But blithely, since the year was young
>   When they a fitting hill did find,
> There on the happy tree they hung
>   The Saviour of mankind."
>
> (Gerald Gould.)

I. THE CROSS TEACHES THE TRANSFORMATION OF UGLINESS INTO BEAUTY

The angular form of the cross is at war with every principle of beauty. Yet no other tree has been so immortalized in art, architecture, and literature. Built into a cross, the tree of degradation has become the inspiring theme of the artists of the world.

Similarly the cross has revealed to Christians the value and meaning of suffering. It has literally turned mourning into joy.

II. BUT THE CROSS WAS NOT CHANGED FROM A CURSE TO A GLORY UNTIL JESUS DIED ON IT

Victor Hugo said: "The first tree of liberty was planted by

[1] Samuel Judson Porter in "Lamps of Gold." Richard R. Smith.

God, himself, on Golgotha. The first tree of liberty was that cross on which Jesus Christ was offered, a sacrifice for the liberty, equality, and fraternity of the human race."

"It expelled cruelty; it curbed passion; it punished and repressed an execrable infanticide; it drove the shameless impurities of heathendom into a congenial darkness. There was hardly a class whose wrongs it did not remedy. It rescued the gladiator; it freed the slave; it protected the captive; it nursed the sick; it sheltered the orphan; it elevated the woman; it shrouded as with a halo of sacred innocence the tender years of the child. In every region of life its ameliorating influence was felt. It changed pity from a vice into a virtue. It elevated poverty from a curse into a beatitude. It ennobled labor from a vulgarity into a dignity and a duty. It sanctified marriage from little more than a burdensome convention into little less than a blessed sacrament. It revealed for the first time the angelic beauty of a purity of which men had despaired and of a meekness at which they had utterly scoffed. It created the very conception of charity and broadened the limits of its obligation from the narrow circle of a neighborhood to the widest horizons of the race." (Frederick William Farrar.)

There is little question but that the death of Jesus on the cross gave not alone to the tree, but to the whole human race, the most beautiful and potent force of all time.

TOLERANCE [1]

Refrain from these men, and let them alone: for if this counsel or this work be of men, it will be overthrown: but if it is of God, ye will not be able to overthrow them; lest haply ye be found even to be fighting against God. Acts 5: 38, 39.

Two characteristics honor Gamaliel. The first is generosity, and the second is common sense. For, if truth is ultimately to prevail, there must be a sifting of ideas to that end. There must be tolerance.

I. ETHICAL REASONS OF TOLERANCE

In our present stage of intellectual and spiritual development, varieties of beliefs and opinions are inevitable. We must have respect for the opinions of others, subject to three conditions:

1. Opinions held must be honest. No one can ask for respect of sham opinions. But tolerance is a duty when opinions are honestly and enthusiastically held.

2. The one who expresses his views must take them seriously. When I run across those who are of a different faith I do not question them on their belief, but on their sincerity and loyalty.

3. Then there is another condition. That is that those who expect tolerance from us also extend it to us. One idea absolutely intolerable is that force should be used, by either Church or State, to compel folks to our way of thinking.

II. INTELLECTUAL REASONS FOR TOLERANCE

It may be just as well not to try and determine just what intellectual reasons actuated Gamaliel. But there are, in gen-

[1] By Russell Henry Stafford in "Christian Humanism." Willett, Clark, and Colby.

eral, three different motives which produce this attitude which we call tolerance.

1. Indifference. Tolerance purchased at the cost of convictions is costly indeed. One of the sad things of our day is that so much of the tolerance abroad in the land seems to be born in a kind of kind-hearted agnosticism which thinks that no truth can be found.

2. Condescension. This is infuriating. How would you like to be told that you are a Congregationalist because you do not know any better? Or apply it to a Roman Catholic or Christian Scientist.

3. The third and only right motive of an intellectual order for tolerance is an admission, in all humility, that our minds have limitations and probably do not grasp the truth with perfect clearness in its entirety. That does not mean that we will compromise our convictions. But it does admit human limitation and the possibility of others seeing things different from ourselves. Humility is back of real tolerance.

We can afford to be patient and brotherly amid the dissensions which mark this stage of religious progress, as the like of them have marked all stages hitherto; and we must seek, in constant expression of this attitude, to replace vain controversies with understanding and mutual esteem among the parties to them.

TOLLGATES ON THE ROAD TO HEAVEN [1]

*Many of them also which used curious arts brought their books
together, and burned them before all men.* Acts 19: 19.

TOLLGATES have pretty well passed out in America, but we
must still pay for the cost of roads. Likewise the road to
heaven has its costs. Salvation may be free, but those who
travel the salvation road must be prepared to pay the toll. And
what are the tolls we pay?

I. FIRST WE MUST LET GO BAD HABITS

The Ephesians mentioned in the text found this was the first
tollgate. Bad habits—in this instance, bad books—must be
given up. When old John Vassar became convinced that his
brewery was a pesthouse, he turned the key and locked it
against the world. It was a toll he must pay to pass along the
road to heaven.

II. THEN WE MUST YIELD UP INDIVIDUALISM FOR THE COMMON GOOD

Our first religious experiences may be personal. But if we
grow in grace our experiences will become social. An automobile driver tried to escape his toll one night by turning off the
lights and gliding noiselessly through the gates. But he met
another car without lights coming in the other direction. We
seldom have the whole road to ourselves in this world.

III. THE NEXT TOLLGATE DEMANDS OF THE CHRISTIAN THAT HE FORSAKE THE IDEAL OF AVERAGE DECENCY AND ASPIRE TO SOMETHING BETTER

Average decency does not get one into heaven. Business is
full of practices which will not stand the Book. Individuals are
crafty in hiding their real earnings from the government. There
is a roguery carried on behind the scenes of so-called Christian

[1] By J. B. Baker in "American Lutheran Preaching." Harper.

business which one cannot square with Christ. The toll demands that these be cast out for something better.

IV. NEXT COMES LEGALISM

The legalist gives as much as the law allows. The Christian gives in love. How our Church people reveal their legalism when it comes to giving! If there are five hundred members and a five-hundred-dollar deficit, many are ready to give their share—one dollar—but no more. If the benevolent quota is four-fifty per member, they feel they have done their duty when they give four-fifty. If the law demands a mile, they go a mile—no farther.

V. THE FINAL TOLL IS THAT OF THE PHYSICAL LIFE ITSELF

The soul crosses by paying with the material body.

When Emperor Franz Joseph of Austria was buried, his body was carried in great pomp to the royal mausoleum. Before it went a courier who was halted by a black-robed figure symbolizing death. "Who comes here?" said the keeper of the gate. "Emperor Franz Joseph of Austria," said the courier. "I know him not," said the keeper. "But," said the courier, "he is the Head of the Holy Apostolic Church." Again the black-robed figure said, "I know him not." Then the courier, abandoning his flourish, said, "This is Franz Joseph of Austria, a poor sinner who begs for admittance." "Let him enter," was the reply.

THE ALTAR IN NATURE [1]

The whole creation groaneth and travaileth. Romans 8: 22.

THE altar is the oldest piece of church furniture in the world. In London the other day archæologists found beneath the crypt of one of the old churches a Roman altar to Jove. Dig beneath Roman culture, and you will find an altar to Zeus. Deeper than Grecian culture you will find an altar to the Cretan Minos. And you can keep digging until you find beneath all civilizations the altars of primitive men to gods they did not know, but whose existence they suspected.

I. THE IDEA THE ALTAR STANDS FOR IS SACRIFICE

And that is evidently one reason why Protestantism is afraid of the altar. The center of interest in a Protestant church is not its altar, but the pulpit. The vestigial remains of the altar will be found in the communion table in front and beneath the pulpit. The reason is historically clear. Born in the midst of theological controversy, these Protestant Churches feared the masses. They revolted against a gross and carnal idea of human sacrifice. They feel that the altar is a relic of those bad days of superstition when men still believed in human sacrifices.

The altar stands for more than worship, for something more definite, more poignant, more tragic, more mysterious, and more vital than that.

II. THE ALTAR STANDS FOR SUFFERING

It means a suffering victim and a suffering worshiper, too. The worshiper identifies himself with his oblation and offers both to God. As far back as you find altars you find a worshiper tormented with the idea that there is something wrong

[1] By George Craig Stewart in "Six Altars." Morehouse.

with himself. **We call it a** sense of sin. He has it because he is a man.

"The animals do not lie awake and sweat for their sins." (Walt Whitman.)

"Were our ears sharp enough, we should hear in nature, thousands of times a minute, sighs and groans of pain like those heard by Dante at the gate of hell." (Huxley.)

In nature itself there is the principle of suffering.

The sun burns itself up and ripens our harvest.

The mountains strip themselves to pour their rich mineral foods into the valleys.

The corals die that an island of their bones may lift its fronds above the waves.

The mineral gives itself up to a higher order of life, a plant.

The plant is torn from the roots to give itself to the higher life of the beast.

III. COME HIGHER

Homer gives his eyes to produce the "Iliad."

Milton loses his sight to regain for us a "Paradise."

Mothers and fathers with joy lay down their lives for their children.

The law is evident: No sacrifice, no leadership; no suffering, no progress; no pain, no character; no blood poured out, no redemption.

IV. COME TO THE HIGHEST

If at the heart of the nature of things we find suffering, sacrificial suffering for a higher end; if we find it rising in clarity and beauty from mineral to vegetable, from animal to man, we may expect to find this sacrificial principle in God himself.

And then we turn to Jesus, where God and man meet, and find the central fact is the Cross.

APOSTOLIC OPTIMISM [1]

Rejoicing in hope. Romans 12: 12.

This apostolic optimism was not born of sluggish thinking or of idle and shallow observation. I am very grateful that the counsel of my text lifts its chaste and cheery flame in the twelfth chapter of an epistle of which the first chapter contains as dark and searching indictment of our nature as the mind of man has ever drawn. . . . I say it is not the buoyancy of ignorance. It is not the flippant, light-hearted expectancy of a man who knows nothing about the secret places of the night; the counselor who has steadily gazed at light at its worst, who has digged through the outer walls of convention and respectability and pushed his way into the secret chambers and closets of life.

I. IT IS AN OPTIMISM BASED UPON THE REALITY OF THE REDEMP-TIVE WORK OF CHRIST

TURN where you will in your study of Paul, and you will find that the redemptive work of Christ is the base and groundwork of his life. The earlier pages of this epistle are concerned with the great arguments for redemption. But with Paul it does not end there. It diffuses itself through all his writings. Even when he is discussing the eating of meats, the great doctrine reappears and interposes its solemn yet elevating principle: "Destroy not him with thy meat for whom Christ died."

The sources of this redemption for Paul lay back in eternity. He emerges with expressions such as these: "Foreknew," "foreordained," "chosen in him before the foundation of the world," "eternal life promised before times eternal," etc.

[1] By John Henry Jowett in "The World's Great Sermons," Volume X. Funk and Wagnalls.

II. IT IS AN OPTIMISM BASED UPON A SENSE OF REALITY AND GREATNESS OF HIS PRESENT RESOURCES

"By Christ redeemed," "in Christ restored"; such are dynamics of the present. In almost every sentence Paul gives a present dynamic which he can count upon as his friend. In the apostle's thought dispositions are powers. They are forces vitalizing and energizing the common life of men.

Are we bold enough in our thinking regarding the present spiritual realities? We do not associate with every mood the mighty energy of God. We oust from our thought some of the mightiest and most aggressive allies of saintly life. To Paul love was more than a relationship, faith was more than an attitude, hope was more than a posture.

III. IT IS AN OPTIMISM BASED UPON THE REALITY OF FUTURE GLORY

He looked forward to the day when Christ should be manifested—"the glory that shall be revealed." He pondered the thought of death as gain. He thought of the time when he would be at home with the Lord.

This is a reality of Christian faith. Men have revolted against effeminate contemplation in favor of active philanthropy. "But, my brethren, pulling a plant up is not the only way to keep it from going to seed." Richard Baxter's labors were not thinned because of his contemplation, "The Saints' Everlasting Rest."

Go up beforehand and see your lodging. Look through all your father's rooms in heaven. Men take a sight of the lands ere they buy them. I know that Christ hath made the bargain already; but be kind to the house ye are going to and see it often.

GOD AND COMPANY, BUILDERS [1]

We are laborers together with God. 1 Corinthians 3: 9.

Men and God are partners.

Partnership is the secret of success. Nations formulate treaties and act in concert with one another. Families form matrimonial alliances, and so increase their wealth and strengthen their social position. But the greatest partnership is that established between God and man.

I. GOD—THE MASTER BUILDER

"It is fascinating to watch God build. He has so many ways of doing things. Sometimes he builds as an artist paints pictures; sometimes as a weaver threads beautiful dreams; sometimes as a mason builds arches and cathedrals. Ever watch God transforming dust and moisture and sunlight into a glorious sunset? What a delight to follow him as he transforms a dirty bulb into a beautiful, fragrant hyacinth or a proud, spotless lily. In these spring days he is running the sap up the arteries of the trees and fashioning buds and fluting the leaves on the lilac bush. You can almost see them grow."

You cannot think of God without thinking of growth and building. From the beginning of time he has been shaping the universe and humanity for his purposes. He has placed the blue prints on the trestle board. Then he calls for his partner to help him.

II. THE FELLOW CRAFTSMAN

No task is obscure that has God for a partner. Ninety-nine per cent of life is God's handiwork. The other one per cent is man's. The herdsman Moses, the tentmaker Paul, the fisher-

[1] By Samuel W. Purvis in "The God of the Lucky." National Publishing Company.

man Peter, the missionary Livingstone—these are all fellow craftsmen. They work with God.

Whatever these and other men have done they have accomplished with the help of God. He has a hand in the building of cities, the widening of rivers, the digging of ores, the manufacture of machines. Man has the resources of the infinite. Earth is not his goal. It is his starting place. When Victor Hugo lay dying he said: "I know that I am the chrysalis of an archangel."

III. THE ENTERED APPRENTICE

Man, the most capable in the animal kingdom, is born the most helpless.

But he learns quickly. He saw logs floating, and built himself a boat. He harnessed the wind, and learned to guide his craft by the stars. He has even chained the lightning to make it do his will. This "learner" man is the entered apprentice. God takes him and calls him to life. He makes his work a sacred calling. He teaches him that he has a great partner who can be depended upon to help him with his task. No matter what his calling may be, he can be a builder with God.

> Happy that man who says: "I am going out to-day to do my work for God—I am building for time and eternity— my firm's name is God and Company, Builders."

THE MAN OF THE DECORATION [1]

This is my body, which is broken for you. 1 Corinthians 11: 24.

You remember the title of a popular book a few years back, "The Lady of the Decoration." Certainly Christ was decorated as man never before or since. Decorated? Yes, by the crown of thorns and the wound prints in his hands and feet. Decorated? Yes, by the sword thrust of the Roman soldier. Decorated? Yes, by the malice of his enemies and the accusations they flung like mad against his white life. Decorated? Yes, by the scarlet robe and the mocking wand of authority thrust upon him by Herod's soldiers. But above all he was decorated by the cross.

I. "THIS IS MY BODY"—INCARNATION

INCARNATION simply means putting flesh on something—giving it a body or a house. Every building is the incarnation of some architect's dream. Every invention is the incarnation of some inventor's dream. The incarnation of Jesus Christ means that God was clothed in a body. Here is where Christmas and Good Friday come close together. Christmas means that God took for himself a body. Calvary means that men stole that body from him and nailed it to a cross.

II. THE BODY OF CHRIST WAS BROKEN—CRUCIFIXION

The broken Christ never appeals to some people. They do not care for broken things. Charles Lamb, in "The South Sea House," tells of John Tipp, who was endowed by nature "with a sufficient measure of the principle of self-preservation." He never mounted the box of a stagecoach or leaned against the rail of a balcony or looked down a precipice or let off a gun or went upon a water party. His motto was "Safety first." But

[1] By Herbert Booth Smith in "The Master's Memorial," edited by Samuel Blair. Cokesbury Press.

the world has been made by the folks who have put something worth while ahead of safety. The man who gives of his
money to God can say: "This is my wealth which was broken
for you." The parents who give a child for the mission field
can say: "This is our family which was broken for you." So
every tired worker in the kingdom can say when he reflects
upon his broken and sick body: "This is my body which was
broken for you." The crucifixion of Christ was a real and
genuine sacrifice. As he looks over our world he can say:
"This is my body which was broken for you."

III. CHRIST'S BODY WAS BROKEN FOR YOU—APPROPRIATION

Professor Royce, the New England philosopher, who might
not have been expected to make such an answer, said, when
asked what is vital in Christianity: "What is most vital in
Christianity is contained in whatever is essential and permanent
in the doctrines of the Incarnation and the Atonement." "This
is my body," is the fact of the incarnation. "Which is broken
for you," is the fact of the atonement.

This is the wonderful thing about the death of Jesus:
that it concerns me. The death of Savonarola doesn't concern me. He died for his boldly asserted opinions. He
didn't die for me. The death of Cæsar doesn't concern me.
He died from Pompey's thrust, but not for me. The death
of Scott, the explorer, doesn't concern me. He died amid
the Arctic snows, paying the price for his bold adventure
into the far north. . . . Paul died as a martyr; died because
he was bold enough to preach a Christian gospel in a pagan
world. He died for Christ, but not for me. But Jesus
died—not as a hero or a martyr, but for me; and if I don't
get hold of these two words, I don't understand Calvary.

THE INTERPRETER [1]

Wherefore let him that speaketh in a tongue pray that he may interpret. 1 Corinthians 14: 13.

PAUL was speaking, in this text, of that "speaking in tongues" which was apparently common in the Corinthian Church. This phenomenon was probably similar to some exercises one may witness even to this day. In Nashville a few years ago I attended a religious meeting of negroes. The worshipers were stirred to a frenzy and leaped from their seats, shouting in strange language. This was probably "speaking in tongues." The early Christian Church was full of this sort of thing. What St. Paul is saying is that it may be all right, but the man who speaks "in tongues" should also be able to interpret.

"If, then, I am worthy to be an interpreter at all, we three, you, my neighbor, whose mind I would fain interpret, you my kind listener, to whom I address my interpretation—we three constitute a community. . . . Let us call it a Community of Interpretation." (Josiah Royce.)

I. THE INTERPRETER

The mother is the first and greatest of interpreters. It is hers to explain the world to the baby; to teach him the meaning and the nature of things. Was there ever a parent who did not wish he knew a million things more, that he might answer the questions of his two-year-old?

And father and Sunday school teachers—they are interpreters. It is theirs to unfold the world to eager eyes and ears. Yes, all of us are interpreters.

II. THE THING TO BE INTERPRETED

Take the four great words which Dr. Cabot gives us as the

[1] By Washington Gladden in "The Interpreter." Pilgrim Press.

things men live by. They are Work, Play, Love, Worship. What a mission it is to interpret these things to boys and girls—and to men and women.

To interpret worship—to open young eyes to the wonder and the greatness of the things unseen and eternal, the things of the spirit, the nearness and the reality of the influences which surround us, that press on our thought and kindle our emotion—if we can only so interpret to them the nearness of this spiritual realm in the midst of which we are always living, and the infinite resources which are always within the reach of our wishes, then, indeed, the gateways of wisdom and paths of peace will open to them.

And there are other words, as Citizenship. How this needs to be interpreted.

III. THE PEOPLE TO WHOM THE INTERPRETATION IS TO BE GIVEN

To all people, Christianity.

To both native and foreign-born Americans, citizenship. It would be a mistake to suppose that only the foreign-born need to know the first principles of American citizenship.

The one thing needful is that we should be freed from this primal conception of society as a chartered struggle of interests and get possession of the true idea of society as a coöperation of harmonious and common interests—as a Commonwealth, in which the welfare of each is promoted by the good will of all.

To employers we need to interpret the hopes and needs of labor. To those who toil we need to interpret the purposes and burden of capital.

But not only do people need to be explained to each other; all of us are in constant need of having truth and life and duty interpreted to us.

COMPLEMENT [1]

He was buried. 1 Corinthians 15: 4.
He rose again. 1 Corinthians 15: 4.

I. HE IS DEAD

"There came a day, a dread day, when the sun went down at noonday behind a blood-splotched wooden cross on the hill that was, in shape, like a skull.

"And remembering how the black night came at midday, all said, 'He is dead.' "

THE curious crowd, unconscious of spiritual values, said it. Pilate said it. The elders said it. The centurion who supervised the crucifixion said it. The Sadducees said it. The Pharisees said it. Caiaphas said it. The people, who hoped it might be him who redeemed Israel, said it. The women who followed afar off said it. The disciples, disappointed in him and disappointed in themselves, said it. Joseph of Arimathea not alone said it, but he took the body and buried it in his own tomb.

The hopes of the followers crashed with that death. A huge chasm arose between them and their fondest hopes. His royal robes became a shroud. His only crown had been one of thorns. His coronation acclaim, spit from sneering lips. His throne was a blood-splotched cross. His only glory—shame. His inaugural speech, a lonely cry. His coronation companions were two thieves.

He died and they mourned.

II. HE ROSE AGAIN

There came a day when he resumed his power, recovered his challenged rights, regained his waning influence,

[1] By Robert G. Lee in "Beds of Pearls." Sunday School Board of the Southern Baptist Convention.

reasserted his sacred grandeur. In the midst of malignant enemies he arose, confounding their counsels, thwarting their efforts, laughing to scorn their malice.

The victory of Jesus over death is the best-established fact in human history. Upon this resurrection the apostles founded their message and their work. Christ's death was purposed from the beginning of eternity. It was prophesied through the ages. It was peered into by angels. But it found its complement in the empty tomb. When he arose as a victor from the grave, he established Christian history.

No risen Christ, a tomb as worthless as any tomb—a cross no more than a martyr's cross. No risen Christ, a king of terror with no rival, a black shadow which no sun ever penetrates. No risen Christ, no trumpet to sound through death's dreary dominions to awake the dead from eternal sleep. No risen Christ, death mocks our hopes like a coarse comedian or a heartless satirist. . . . No risen Christ, the whole history of Christianity and its existence is unintelligible. . . . No risen Christ, the whole earth in deepest mourning dressed, will, like Rachel of old, go down to judgment weeping for her children, finding no comfort.

CALVARY [1]

Christ arose. 1 Corinthians 15: 4.
And when they were come to the place, which is called Calvary, there they crucified him. Luke 23: 33.

ABOVE all the mountains of human history stands Calvary. Grand Horeb, Hor, lofty Pisgah, Ebal, Gerizim, Carmel, Tabor, Moriah, Hermon, and Olivet, of sweet memories, have a place in the history of redemption; but Calvary stands higher and nobler.

I. THERE IN BLOODY GARMENTS GOD COURTED OUR LOVE

There, at the interlocking of the ages, Christ put away sin by sacrifice of himself, redeeming man from death unto life, canceling man's debt of judicial obligation by an equivalent which afforded legal satisfaction—voluntarily passing under death's dreadful shadow, though owing the law no debt.

At Calvary God permitted his Son to suffer and die. He who feeds the ravens permitted the agony of the cross. No wonder the clouds were black on that day, and the sun withdrew its light. No wonder the rocks were rent. Earth has no darker sin, history no blacker page, humanity no fouler spot than Calvary.

II. THE SADDEST STORY OF GOD IS CALVARY

The saddest story of man is Eden. The saddest story of God is Calvary.

It is a far cry from the Garden of Eden to Calvary, but they have very intimate relations. The tragedy of one is the reason for the tragedy of the other. In Eden we see the beginning of the tragedy which is to end on

[1] By Robert G. Lee in "Beds of Pearls." Sunday School Board of the Southern Baptist Convention.

Calvary, and the agony of the atonement for sin which we see on Calvary has to do with the tragedy of sin which we learn in the Garden of Eden.

From Calvary go the rays of light which reveal and brighten all human history. It reaches in the past to the mount of transfiguration, back to the day of the paschal lamb. The shadow of the cross rests on everything in the Bible. You see it in Bethlehem's manger. In the workshop of Nazareth it appeared. It was seen on the waters of Galilee. The cross was there when Judas gave Jesus the kiss of betrayal. The shadow hung over Caiaphas and Pilate.

III. IN CALVARY WE SEE THE SUPREME INTERPRETATION OF GOD

We have seen that the agony of God over sin is eternal. It existed from the end of time.

> "His holy fingers formed the bough
> Where grew the thorns that crowned his brow;
> The nails that pierced the hands were mined
> In secret places he designed.
>
> He made the forests whence there sprung
> The tree on which his body hung;
> He died upon a cross of wood,
> Yet made the hill on which it stood.
>
> The spear that spilt the precious blood
> Was tempered in the fires of God.
> The grave in which his form was laid
> Was hewn in rocks his hands had made."

It is impossible to find words adequately to express the divine plan. God, loving man and agonizing sin, plans for his own death to redeem the world. But that is the theology of Calvary. There Christ died and the world found life.

DEATH TO BE DESTROYED [1]

The last enemy that shall be destroyed is death. **1** Corinthians
15:26.

IT is well to talk of good news from God, but in and through
all our human activities stalks death. And it is good news to
know that this enemy shall eventually be destroyed.

I. DEATH IS AN ENEMY

Death is an enemy of human happiness. It comes to a home
where harmony and joy prevail, and leaves grief and bitterness.

"Men fear death as children fear the dark." (Bacon.)

II. THE GOOD NEWS FROM GOD ABOUT DEATH

1. Death is going to be destroyed. The enemy shall not go
on forever. "He that believeth in me, though he were dead,
yet shall he live." As the children said in the play, "The Blue
Bird," by Maurice Maeterlinck, "There is no death." There is
no part of the Easter preface more beautiful than those words,
"Who, by his death, hath destroyed death."

2. Death is not as bad as he looks. I have been present at
hundreds of deathbeds and have seldom found a person who has
actually feared death as it finally comes to him. Once I found
a girl who was facing death who was afraid. "Would you
trust me to carry you into the next room?" I asked. "Yes,"
I would," she replied. "Then trust Christ, who is stronger
than I, to carry you over," I urged.

3. Those who have crossed over are still in touch with you
who love them. I am sure of this. "God is not a God of the

---

[1] By Arthur F. Winnington-Ingram (Bishop of London) in "Good
News from God." Longmans.

dead, but of the living." I have a letter here from a woman who has lost her mother, but she has had an experience which teaches her that her mother is close to her. And here is the instance of a mother who lost her son in the war. He came into the room and kissed her and then vanished.

If you ask me whether these things actually took place, I could not say; but I do believe this, that there are certain times when God does give some special vision when he sees that there is a need for it.

III. HOW SHOULD THIS PROMISE AFFECT US?

First of all, it should have an uplifting and ennobling effect upon our lives. When we think that we are living in the presence of those who are with God, we should shape our lives accordingly. When we come to the communion, they are gathered here with us.

Are you really living like those who may be called, even this year, or in ten or twenty years' time, to join the communion of saints in the other world?

THE PERILS OF MIDDLE LIFE [1]

Quit you like men, be strong. 1 Corinthians 16: 13.

Moses is forty when he is first moved by the great impulse to deliver his people. Joshua is forty when he brings back the report which makes him a marked man for life. Luther began the period of his greatest usefulness at forty, and the same is true of Wesley. Chaucer began to write "Canterbury Tales" when he was in his forties, and Walter Scott was forty-three when he began to publish the "Waverley Novels." "Paradise Lost" was published when Milton was fifty, and Bunyan wrote the "Pilgrim's Progress" when he was about the same age. Pitt is Prime Minister at forty-eight, Webster is forty-eight when he makes his reply to Hayne, and Clay is forty-four when he makes his great speeches on the Missouri Compromise. Wellington is forty-six at Waterloo, and Cæsar forty-two when he crosses the Rubicon.

I. IT IS IN THESE YEARS THAT THE WORLD IS STAGGERED BY FALLS OF MEN IN THE LIMELIGHT

WHAT a record there is of men in these critical years failing in the trust reposed in them: Samson—Saul—David—Judas—Ananias—Demas—Benedict Arnold—Aaron Burr—Tweed.

II. MIDDLE AGE IS THE TIME OF GREAT TEMPTATIONS

It is in the years of maturity that temptations assail the strongest. The animal propensities are at their greatest strength. The blood is hot and rushes like a torrent to the finger tips. Maturity is headstrong and dominant.

"He who warms both hands at the fires of life must take heed that they are not burned."

[1] By Charles L. Goodell in "Life Reveries." Revell.

III. IT IS IN MIDDLE LIFE THAT THE INNER LIGHT OFTEN FAILS

"Heaven lies about us in our infancy!
Shades of the prison-house begin to close
  Upon the growing boy;
But he beholds the light, and whence it flows,
  He sees it in his joy;
The Youth, who daily farther from the east
Must travel, still is nature's priest
  And by the vision splendid
  Is on his way attended.
At length the Man perceives it die away,
And fade into the light of common day."

                        (Wordsworth.)

IV. MATURITY IS THE PERIOD OF GREATEST RESPONSIBILITY

Youth is the age of preparation; old age is the time of rest. Maturity is the time of production. The conflict of life is strenuous in this period. Romance loses its glitter; social amenities are a burden. Responsibility crowds the soul. And in this time of responsibility men are often made bitter and disappointed. That is the tragedy. Perhaps there are enough things to make one bitter. Yet it is a tragedy when it happens.

"Take time—even if you have to take it by violence— take time to be quiet."

V. MIDDLE AGE SHOULD BRING A KINDLINESS

Middle age should have learned the lesson of tolerance.

"Listen, be silent, pray; because your time is shorter than it was twenty years ago, it is all the more necessary that you direct it rightly now. Life and death are to you greater adventures than when you were young. You had more time then to make mistakes. Now you have less time, more knowledge. Go directly into your path and remember that death is not the end; it is only the beginning of something better."

FOREWARNED, FOREARMED [1]

We are not ignorant of his devices. 2 Corinthians 2: 11.

As is shown by a reading of this chapter, Paul was speaking of the devil. He does not tell us what the devices of Satan are, but they have probably been the same from the beginning of time. And these characterizations which he has to-day would also fit the days of Paul.

I. HE LABELS EVIL THINGS WITH PLEASANT NAMES

When Prince George of Greece went over to Crete he was received with great enthusiasm as the new governor. He was carried through crowded streets lined with festoons and banners. But back of the decorations smoldering fires revealed the tragedy of rioting which was being kept from him. Satan is like that. He covers filthy things with nice names. Who but Satan called the world of self and pleasure a gay world? who called the business man whose transactions bordered on the shady a smart man? Who smiled and said the profligate was only fast?

II. HE MAKES HIS ONSET ON OUR STRONGEST SIDE

Our characters are complex things. Weakness and strength are strangely mixed. Men take us at our worst side; God is always on our best side. And Satan, strange to say, assails that side too. Moses was a meek man, yet in passion he brake the tables of stone. Abraham was called father of the faithful, yet his worst sin was because of the lack of faith. The patient Job sinned through impatience. Tolerant John sinned through intolerance.

[1] By G. H. Morrison in "Flood-Tide." Hodder and Stoughton.

III. HE USES TOOLS

He uses the right instruments to do his work. He is a clever administrator and picks his agents skillfully. Take the experience of Jesus. When he was in the desert, Satan came in person and tempted him. But failing that time, the next opportunity he used Peter as his agent. It was a master stroke of genius, but Jesus saw through it. "Get thee behind me, Satan."

The same methods are used by Satan to-day.

It is not the men who hate us, and it is not the men and women we despise who tempt us most. It is those we trust and those who love us best who often prove hell's aptest members.

IV. HE SHAMS DEFEAT

While the battle rages a man is strong. But when the enemy is apparently defeated, men relax and morale falls. Satan shams defeat to bring about this state of relaxation. Then he strikes. Many a soul has been lost because it won in the first encounter.

V. HE LAYS EMPHASIS ON THE MORROW

Now is the accepted time with God. But we are prone to think that to-morrow is just as well. This is the archdevice of the archtempter. It is for breaking with sin—to-morrow. It is for starting on a higher level to-morrow. But God says, "To-day, to-night."

And God, who says it, is here to give the power that now can save, and now can cleanse, and now can send you home, with old things passed away and all things new in Jesus Christ.

DIVINE PHOTOGRAPHY [1]

But we all, with open face beholding as in a glass the glory of the Lord, are changed into the same image from glory to glory, even as by the Spirit of the Lord. 2 Corinthians 3: 18.

The one thing of supreme value for time and eternity is character. "For we brought nothing into this world, and it is certain that we can carry nothing out"—except character. This character must not measure up merely to human standards, but it must resemble the character of Christ, for "we are to be like him."

I. TAKING A PICTURE

THE text suggests the photographic process. You place the camera before the object, focus it, then open the shutter to let in the rays of light which pencil the photograph on the plate. The physical eye is a camera. The light comes through the pupil. The spiritual eye is a camera by means of which the divine likeness is photographed on the heart.

In photography there must be the exposure. So in the spiritual photography. That which covers the eyes of the soul must be withdrawn. The eyes of understanding must be enlightened. The veil of sin must be removed. Unbelief must be taken away. Then adjustment is necessary. The camera must be in the right position. Jesus must have our whole attention. This kind of photography requires a time exposure.

II. THE OBJECT

The object to be photographed is the "glory of God." It was photographed through Jesus Christ, and men saw it on his face. If we are photographing God, we will let the world know it through our lives. They will see the glory to which we have been exposed.

[1] By Horace S. Smith in the *Homiletic Review* (July, 1930).

You can focus your camera on a landscape or a mountain and take a picture of them on a plate no larger than your hand. Ten thousand rays of light from stars billions of miles away and millions of miles apart will stream through the small opening of your eye and image the vast canopy of the sky on the retina. That is wonderful, but think of carrying the image of the great God who inhabiteth eternity on the tablet of your heart.

III. THE PROCESS AND THE METHOD

It is a progressive process. It goes from glory to glory. Hawthorne's story of "The Great Stone Face" is a good illustration of the process. God's Spirit will work the transformation as the sunlight pencils the photograph on the plate in the camera.

Not by beholding, but while beholding, is the miracle worked.

"The State and the Church are languishing for leadership. The objects for which they contended in the late war have not been secured. The love of many grows cold; faith wanes on all sides. But there is a sure remedy for these backslidden conditions. It is found in the lives of those who live in the Master's spirit and serve their fellows for his dear sake." (S. Parkes Cadman.)

REAL LIFE [1]

Nevertheless I live; yet not I, but Christ liveth in me: and the life which I now live in the flesh I live by the faith of the Son of God, who loved me, and gave himself for me. Galatians 2: 20.

Life, as we see it with our outward eyes, is a play, an illusion, a masquerade. Men and women are going to and fro on the earth, busy with many tasks, pursuing many pleasures. . . . It is like an immense and unending dance. The figures are curiously arranged, intricate, forever changing—now peaceful, now warlike—but always the dance goes on, tracing strange patterns and evolving new combinations.

I. THERE ARE TWO GREAT MYSTERIES GOING ON HERE

1. UNDER this masquerade there are dying souls. The process of death is a constant one. At birth we are given a reservoir of energy. We use it day after day until we have exhausted the supply. It is not the last trip which wore out the steamship. The first voyage took its toll. Each one has added to it. So it is with man. When you wind a new watch, you begin to use it up.

To have our affection set on earthly things alone is to go the way of death. Infidelity is practical faith in things seen and unfaith in things unseen.

2. Life and peace—peace in life, and life in peace—that is the other great reality. Paul is telling of this reality. In this dying he has found real life. The satisfaction of the finding the answer to the longing for eternity is his secret. The sacred book of the Egyptians was called the "Book of the Dead." Our Scriptures should be called the "Book of Life." Out-

[1] By Henry Van Dyke in "The Open Door." Westminster Press.

wardly men and women are daily perishing. But inwardly they are being renewed. Surely this is a mystery.

II. THERE ARE TWO THINGS REVEALED IN THE TEXT WHICH ARE ALWAYS REPEATED IN HIGHEST CHRISTIAN EXPERIENCE

1. There is nothing so life-giving as the knowledge that we are loved. Even in our human relationships when this knowledge comes, it lifts us out of the dust and thrills us with vital power. And when that love takes the form of a sacrifice and suffers for our sake, then its power to move and quicken us is deepened a hundredfold.

2. But think what it means to know that this love, which has done so much for us, is the love of the Son of God. It sets the seal of eternity upon it. It lifts the sacrifice of Jesus and lifts us with it, up into the very heart of God. To believe that this love of Christ, from which none can separate us, is none other than Divine Love, the same that created us, is faith deep and mighty.

Come, then, and let us testify to this hidden life, and renew it and refresh it, in communion with Christ. In this world we must be either dying daily, or living daily in immortality; withering away in dreams or awakening to glorious realities; perishing with the sensual or surviving with the spiritual; vanquished or victorious.

"Far and wide, though all unknowing,
  Pants for thee each human breast;
Human tears for thee are flowing,
  Human hearts in thee would rest."

THE RAISED VALUES [1]

Together with Christ he raised and seated us within the heaven-ly sphere in Christ Jesus, to display throughout the ages to come his surpassing wealth of grace and goodness toward us in Christ Jesus. Ephesians 2: 6, 7 (Moffatt).

The affirmation to be explored is that the Christian view of God, man, and the universe, confirmed by living Christian experience, has broadened, deepened, and intensified life whenever and by whomsoever it has been or is whole-heartedly proceeded upon. This is not to say that there have not been interpretations of the Christian scheme of things in terms of dogma which have definitely narrowed and shadowed life. Some of these have been accepted and dominated over periods of Christian history. But they have been perversions or distortions. With every revival and spring-tide of vital Christian faith and experience, with every recovered contact with the springs of life in Jesus Christ, there has come every time the same exultant sense of a mighty quickening of the powers of personality and the enrichment of the values of life.

I. THIS CLAIM IS MADE FOR CHRISTIANITY ON THE GROUND OF ITS RANGE

TAKE the Christian view of God. It has three great affirmations. God is light. God is love. God is a spirit. There is not a word here beyond a child's uttering. Yet every thought is deep down where all our thoughts are drowned.

Take the Christian view of man. Where will you find a nobler conception of man? See the emphasis Christianity gives to his origin, his personality.

Take the Christian view of the universe. "We now know too much of matter to be materialists," said the Earl of Balfour. The words marked an epoch of thinking in life.

[1] By Thomas Yates in "British Preachers, Third Series," edited by Sir James Marchant. Revell.

II. THIS CLAIM IS MADE FOR CHRISTIANITY ON THE GROUND OF ITS REALISM

There is one reality which much of our present-day realism evades. Take contemporary fiction. We have a whole range of it steeped in decadent perversity. It is sodden with disbelief in the higher aspects of human nature. It rejects the possibility or even the desirability of self-reverence or self-control in either sex. But with all its boast of realism one of the greatest of life's realities it evades. That is sin.

Christianity speaks it. It faces up to it. It brings it within the shadow of the Cross of Christ.

III. THIS CLAIM IS MADE FOR CHRISTIANITY BECAUSE OF ITS RADIANCE

God has made everything beautiful in its time, but has made nothing as beautiful as his evangel in Christ Jesus. Christianity knows of the lighted life. It knows of conversion which is the unceasing romance of religion. It speaks of love which lamps the thousand lights of life. It tightens human responsibility when it speaks of service.

An old sculptor whose fame stands secure in the history of art was once blazing at a block of untouched marble in silent contemplation. He was seeking with his artist soul the possibilities lying in it. He was heard to say in a whisper which was half a sigh and half an impatience, "what Godlike beauties thou hidest."

So Christianity speaks to man.

THE CHURCH OF GOD [1]

Christ also loved the church, and gave himself for it. Ephesians
5:25.

I AM speaking particularly to you young people who have
just been received with open arms into the fellowship of this
Church.

I. THE CHURCH IS THE MEDIUM THROUGH WHICH THE CREATOR ASSERTS HIS SOVEREIGN MAJESTY TO MAN

There are no accidents in God's universe of worlds. Everything is ordained with precision. Harmony is the rhythm of his
innumerable systems. Therefore the Church is no accident,
as some cynics would have us believe. The story of the Church
is written all through the Old and New Testaments. Roving
shepherds became social builders, and the temple of the Lord
was builded.

And so it was to these imperfect children of the morning that God whispered his secrets and sealed the sacred
covenant with the promise of world redemption through
sacrificial ransom of his only Son.

II. JESUS LOVED THE CHURCH AND GAVE HIS LIFE FOR ITS PERFECTION

He was himself a devoted participant in the synagogue worship. He knew every phase of the Church activities. He knew
the double-minded men who occupy the front seats and sometimes preach from the pulpit. He knew the imperfections of
the Church. The greatest parables he gave were directed toward
the Church: The sower; the mustard seed; the tares; the great
supper; the dragnet; the vineyard workers; the vine and its
branches.

[1] By S. R. Bratcher, in "Advertising Jesus." Cokesbury Press.

III. THE BEST PEOPLE IN THE WORLD ARE AFFILIATED WITH THE CHURCH

This is a broad affirmation and is made advisedly. I know that many good people do not belong. But their neutrality has curbed their usefulness in the world. Ninety per cent of the nation's Presidents have been Church members, and the biographers of some of the rest, such as Jackson, Lincoln, and Jefferson, apologize for their nonmembership. The friendly sympathizers, who for some pretense or other are living without a Church, remind one of the lone disciple, whom John saw, who was going alone in his own way.

IV. THE CHURCH IS THE UNLIMITED SOURCE OF LIFE'S GREATEST ASSET—SERVICE

The Church is the university for the training of the world's leadership. Jesus put great emphasis on deeds. "If any one among you would become great, let him be the servant of all." The Church believes in deeds. It believes in preparing people to perform deeds. There are no easy Christian tasks. But Christianity has the faculty of getting people great enough for heavy tasks. If you were to make a list of the names of those who have best served the world, you would find that it was a list of those who were also loyal to the Church.

V. THE CHURCH OF GOD IS THE ONLY GREAT OUTSTANDING INSTITUTION IN THE WORLD

It is the mother of many great institutions. But there is no substitute for the Church. Some would place fraternal orders first. But the Church existed before any of our fraternal orders. What is good in them was taken from the Church. Thus Masonry has its story of the building of the temple. The Odd Fellows have their story of Jonathan and David. But they got their stories from the Church.

LOYALTY [1]

One thing I do. Philippians 3: 13.

PAUL had a very complex career. He was a theologian, preacher, general superintendent, executive, traveler, and writer. It is quite certain that we cannot take this text as meaning that he was a man of but one type of activity.

I. THERE WAS A UNIFYING PURPOSE THROUGH ALL OF HIS ACTIVITIES

It is this purpose running through the plans of a man which makes it possible for him to build. I have in mind a man I knew at two different periods separated by a period of years. When I first knew him he was a wastrel, amiable and attractive, but weak, foul of habit, and undependable as to his intentions. When I next met him he had changed beyond recognition. He was clear-cut, clean, competent, and straight. There was a mark of dollars upon him. The reason: He had made the one great passion of his life the making of money.

II. ST. PAUL'S LOYALTY WAS TO AN ALTRUISTIC PROGRAM

There is no need to specify that it was not himself whom St. Paul sought to serve when he yielded his life to one dominant purpose. The apostle to the gentiles stands in history as the type of man who subordinates self to the loftier and temporally more enduring object of his devotion.

But when, in expression of our love, we put forth the energies of our being in a concentrated profusion of generous and sacrificial service, so that our deeds translate our thoughts into reality, then the best of English words to describe this mood, at once more practical and more honorable, is "loyalty."

[1] By Russell Henry Stafford in "Christian Humanism." Willett, Clark, and Colby.

The range of objects for loyalty is very wide. Most conspicuous is the one we know as principle. But principle is harsh and hard and lacks the warmth and emotional appeal of loyalty to some unselfish purpose. Altruistic loyalty translated to the Church and to nations is the redeeming force of future society.

III. ST. PAUL'S SUPREME LOYALTY WAS TO JESUS CHRIST

But we have not told the whole story by showing St. Paul's loyalty to an altruistic purpose. There is something finer and greater than this. That was his devotion to Jesus Christ. He cared greatly for the redemption of the world; the gospel was his great cause; his principles were righteousness and truth. But all of these were subordinated to his loyalty to his Lord.

I doubt whether humanitarian zeal could long be maintained against the discouragements of actual human degeneracy and obliquity if it were not grounded generally in loyalty to Jesus.

THE RESURRECTION LIFE [1]

If ye then be risen with Christ, seek those things which are above, where Christ sitteth on the right hand of God. Set your affection on things above, not on things on the earth. For ye are dead, and your life is hid with Christ in God. When Christ, who is our life, shall appear, then shall ye also appear with him in glory. Colossians 3: 1-4.

Just as in his first letter to the Church at Corinth he (Paul) assumed that no Corinthian Christian would deny the fact of Christ's bodily resurrection, and from that fact made his overwhelming argument for the resurrection of the dead, so in this epistle to the Colossians he assumes that no one among them would doubt the existence of the resurrection of life in their souls, or would hesitate to conform their faith and conduct to its heavenly type and requirements.

i. THE RESURRECTION LIFE IS THAT WHICH ANIMATES THE SOULS OF ALL WHO TRULY LOVE AND SERVE THE GLORIFIED CHRIST

CHRISTIAN experience is a living reality. Every Christian, however humble, knows what it means to live in the spirit of the resurrection. To the Christians at Rome Paul wrote that, "like Christ was raised from the dead by the glory of the Father, even so we also should walk in newness of life." To the Philippians he wrote giving his own aspiration that he might know "the power of Christ's resurrection." And he told them that they looked for a heavenly city with the glorified body. Peter writes in his epistle to the strangers throughout Pontus, Galatia, Cappadocia, Asia, Bithynia, telling them of the living hope of the resurrection. John writes in the book of Revelation (1: 5) of the time when the Christian shall have the glorified body of his Lord.

[1] By Warren Akin Candler in "Easter Meditations." Cokesbury Press.

II. THE FAITH IN THE RESURRECTION IS THE SECRET OF APOSTOLIC POWER

How else can you explain the aspirations and achievements of the early Christians? By what law of materialism can you account for the wonderful accomplishments of that little band of apostles?

The heavenly life cannot spring from earthly sources. The new birth is too great to result from accidents of heredity and environment, and, even if it were possible to derive spiritual life from such things, the life thus brought into being would be a precarious sort wholly conditioned upon external circumstances for continued existence; it would be utterly incapable of triumphing over the vicissitudes of time, to say nothing of winning the victory over death and the grave.

No purely material force can explain the change which comes in life through regeneration. John calls it a passage from death to life. Paul refers to it as a new creation and "deliverance from the power of darkness and translation into the kingdom of his dear Son."

III. THE CHRISTIAN LIFE IS NOT SO MUCH A COPYING OF THE CONDUCT OF OUR LORD'S COURSE IN THE FLESH AS IT IS A PARTICIPATION IN HIS SUPERNAL NATURE IN THE HEAVENLIES

It is a life "hid with Christ in God."

The resurrection-life in a redeemed soul is so identified with the life of its risen Lord that he feels assured that when Christ shall appear he also shall appear with him in glory.

> "O what a blessed hope is ours!
>   While here on earth we stay,
> We more than taste the heavenly powers,
>   And antedate that day.
> We feel the resurrection near,
>   Our life in Christ concealed,
> And with his glorious presence here
>   Our earthen vessels filled."

PAUL'S COMFORTERS [1]

Men that have been a comfort to me. Colossians 4: 11.

SOMEHOW we always think of the apostle Paul as a strong man, mentally and spiritually, whatever he may have been physically. We think of him as the helper and comforter of others. Our text reminds us of a truth we are inclined to forget—that even the strongest and greatest are helped by human comfort of the right sort. Let me introduce you to some of Paul's comforters.

I. ANANIAS

Ananias comes first. After Paul's conversion he found himself in a difficult position. He could have no communion with the Christians at Damascus, for they had been terrified at the news of his approach. It is also certain that the unconverted Jews could have no true sympathy with his state of mind. He fasted and prayed in silence. As he thus waited on God, a vision was granted to him. One came and restored his sight.

We know very little about Ananias, except that he was a converted Jew. He is never mentioned by Paul in his letters, but when Paul told the story of his life, he always told of his Damascus experience and of the man who came to him and said: "Brother Saul, the Lord, even Jesus, that appeared to thee in the way as thou camest, hath sent me, that thou mightest receive thy sight, and be filled with the Holy Ghost."

These words were followed by a dissipation of the darkness. Luke says there fell from his eyes as it had been scales. That is a medical man's description. Paul's own expression is, "And in that very hour I looked up into his face."

[1] By J. E. Williamson in *Church Management.*

273

It was a face he had never seen before, but the sympathetic voice and the expression of Christian love assured him of reconciliation with God, and he learned that the God of his fathers had chosen him to do his will, and his soul was comforted and made strong to suffer great things for the name of Jesus, and to bear that name "before the Gentiles, and kings, and the children of Israel." So I put Ananias first because he befriended Paul at the outset of his Christian experience, when he was sorely in need of a friend.

II. BARNABAS

Barnabas stands second. When Paul had to leave Damascus because the Jews had determined to kill him, he went to Jerusalem, and would have joined himself to the disciples there, but they were afraid of him. His hasty escape from Damascus would hardly permit letters of commendation, and again he needed a friend. It was then that Barnabas, already known as a generous contributor of his wealth to the poor, came forward as the "Son of Consolation."

He "took him by the hand" and brought him to the apostles. Whether they had met before we do no know. We know that Barnabas told them the wonderful story of Paul's conversion, and how he had preached Christ so boldly at Damascus, and the apostles welcomed Paul as a friend and a brother, more than forgiven—for Christ's sake and for the sake of Barnabas also. When Paul set out on his first missionary journey Barnabas accompanied him. I rather think that he was responsible for the financial side of the trip, too. Surely he deserves a foremost place in the ranks of Paul's comforters.

III. OTHERS

Luke, the physician-evangelist, with skillful fingers, sympathetic heart, and cultured mind, truly a beloved physician, was a comforter to the very last. Mark was profitable for ministering, Timothy was his son in the faith, and Onesiphorus often refreshed him. Truly, Paul had his comforters.

THE TWO AND THEIR MONEY [1]

The love of money is the root of all evil. 1 Timothy 6: 10.

WE could paraphrase this text to-day and say that money is an easy source of family dissension and misunderstanding. There is apt to be a constant bickering over money matters unless some principle is accepted in the beginning. There is a principle—the Christian one—which should be considered.

Money is to be kept as the servant, never allowed to become the master. It is to be a servant to the major purposes for which life exists, and in order to insure this the Christian religion lays down the general idea of stewardship. Its background is as follows: God is the owner and giver of all things. We, his children, handle our money as we do our time and strength, as stewards to whom he has intrusted these things during our lifetime. In recognition of this relationship, some proportion of what is received is to be, first of all, set aside as especially sacred to him. This proportionate amount is then administered for his kingdom. Further, the balance of the income is to be used, not selfishly, but in the same spirit in which a steward would naturally act.

I. THIS PLAN DEMANDS AN ACCOUNTING OF WHAT IS RECEIVED

If a person sets out to budget his income for God, he soon finds that it is convenient to budget it to cover other items. This attitude of budgeting is one of the keys to successful home management. In adopting it a family often saves more money than the giving costs them.

II. THIS PLAN MAKES SAFER WHATEVER MONEY WE DO HAVE

Money is only good for things which it can buy. If used

[1] By Albert W. Beaven in "Fireside Talks for the Family Circle." Judson.

foolishly, it can become a source of weakness and folly. But when a portion of the income is expended wisely, it tends to insure that the rest will be expended wisely.

III. THIS PLAN WOULD GUIDE HUSBAND AND WIFE TO THE FINER THINGS OF LIFE

It would introduce the study of Christian principles into home affairs which would be helpful. When the time came to expend the money which had been set aside for God, it would inevitably bring the home makers into contact with other young people of noble and high ideals. It would put them in touch with the Church and social institutions which are laboring for the advancement of mankind.

IV. THIS PLAN BRINGS HUSBAND AND WIFE INTO THE PRESENCE OF CHRIST

It is difficult to find Christ when the family is divided. In the old-fashioned home, where the husband was boss and handled money matters, money problems were not discussed. In the home based on Christian stewardship husband and wife start with an agreement on money. There is unity of thought.

An agreement on the use of money eliminates that creator of family discord—"trying to keep up with the Joneses." When a home is running into debt there is danger ahead.

"Twenty dollars a week income and twenty-one dollars a week expenditure is hell, whereas twenty dollars a week income and nineteen dollars a week expenditure is heaven."

The spirit of unselfish fair play induced by a genuinely religious attitude is to money matters what oil is to the engine. It is worth more than any lubricant as an aid toward the solution of problems which surround the discussion of money.

DOES YOUR ANCHOR HOLD? [1]

Which hope we have as an anchor of the soul, both sure and steadfast, and which entereth into that which is within the veil. Hebrews 6: 19.

I remember one night, when unable to go to sleep, going out in the fog and darkness, and hearing the captains shout to one another, "Does your anchor drag?" And every time the ship swung far around in the awful wind, every time the seething white sea determined to eat the very timbers of the ship, you would hear the shout, "Does your anchor drag?"

I. SOULS ADRIFT

How sorry the plight of the man who has no hope; no hope for the future, no hope of employment, no hope of increase in the comforts of life, no hope of a wider friendship, no hope of God, no hope of eternal life. He has lost his anchor.

Did you ever have an anchor, Mr. Man? Was your faith once anchored in God? Or did you never have one? Do you have one which does not stand firm but drifts? If it drags, it will beat you upon some other ship until you are crashed.

It is dangerous for you to get anywhere away from the anchor of God. It is dangerous to play with any anchor which is less firm.

II. WHY ANCHORS DRAG

Perhaps you have drifted because men have persecuted you. You have been injured and feel that there is no justice in God's world. But beware. Let no man's persecution shake you of your trust in God.

Perhaps you have been betrayed by some one who loved you. Did you put your whole faith in some man and then have him

[1] By Russell H. Conwell in "Borrowed Axes." Judson.

violate that faith? Then, because of this, you decided that you would cut away and expose yourself to the winds and storms. Beware. Why do you allow yourself to be destroyed? Keep your faith in God. Don't let the anchor drag.

Perhaps you have been in want. You are hungry. Perhaps you did not come to Church because you had no clothes to wear. You thought God had forgotten you. Then you said, "All right, I will live as I want to, then." But you must not commit suicide because of this. Beware. Do not let your anchor drift.

III. A SURE ANCHORAGE

There is an anchor which holds. Have you trusted some Christian man high in his Church and then found him false? It would be unusual if we did not find some such man in the course of a lifetime. You are not responsible for his anchor. But you are responsible for your own. Don't let it drag.

Have you faced great sorrow? Perhaps your little one was taken away from you. This is a test on weak anchors. But there is a strong and mighty one which holds even in a time like this.

Perhaps you have been to the gates of death yourself. There are rocks there. But there is an anchor which holds. During the storm which I used as an illustration one of the men called back: "Don't be alarmed; my anchor holds."

Can you, when death comes, and when your friends are gathered around, just look up and say: "My anchor holds?" If you cannot, prepare yourself for it now.

THE ALTAR IN THE LIFE [1]

Lo, I come to do thy will, O God. Hebrews 10: 9.

THERE is in the church the lectern (originally meaning a Roman couch), and on it what we call a holy book. The lectern is a symbol of the flaming message communicated by God to the inward ear of the lawgiver and the prophet, the psalmist and the evangelist. And by the lectern is the altar, where

> "Heaven comes down, our souls to meet,
> While glory crowns the mercy seat."

But it would not be there were it not first here within the human heart.

I. EACH MAN'S LIFE IS LIKE THE CHURCH

It has its outer court where any one may enter and feel at home. It is open to all. A man has but to say to one of us, "How do you do?" and he enters the outer court. Then there is within a holy place, where but a few enter—relatives and intimate friends. And then there is the holy of holies, where a curtain hangs, through which no one enters—no one except the soul itself.

In many a life, if we should enter the holy of holies, we should be smitten with horror at the altar and its God.

II. PICTURES OF THE ALTARS OF THE HEART

1. The secret chamber of a bad man's mind. There are men and women who have but one altar in their lives, the altar of the worldly, sensual, devilish. They are the ones who say, "Eat, drink, and be merry; for to-morrow we die."

2. The altar to Mammon. Watts painted it. Chesterton in-

---

[1] By George Craig Stewart in "Six Altars." Morehouse.

terpreted the painting. Above that altar arises a throned figure with the face of a blind beast, an imperial thing with closed eyes, and fat, sightless face. He lets his hands and feet fall upon the Godlike figures of the young. There is but one word which interprets this figure. It is self, self, self.

3. The Christian altar in the heart. There is the man who goes across the country to redeem the sins of his wayward son. He wounds himself for the boy's transgressions. There is the child dying from diphtheria. But before the doctor can come the mother sucks away the deadly phlegm with her own mouth. She dies, but the child lives. There is Rupert Brooke, dying and gladly giving his life for his country. There is Titus Oates, companion of Captain Scott, who, when food was low, simply said good-by and walked out never to return. It is seen in Major Ross, who spent two years in Indian swamps to find the mosquito that carries yellow fever, and in the case of Major Walter Reed, who took up the work when death took Ross.

And life goes on. It leads to the very cross of Jesus.

"There is an altar I must build,
  Strong and foursquare of rough-hewn stone,
With bitter labor shaped and laid,
  And I must build it all alone.

No other hand but mine must rear
  That altar in the secret place,
Remote, untrod, where even now
  God waits to meet me face to face.

There is no back but mine must bear
  The fagot up the long incline;
The wood of kindling must be laid
  In order by no hand but mine."

FAITH [1]

Faith is the substance of things hoped for, the evidence of things not seen. Hebrews 11: 1.

I propose to give here a nontheological discussion of a theological term, the word "faith." The word is largely a theological one, but the thing itself is not merely theological. In fact, the reason I feel less incompetent to discuss this subject than most others in theology is that in my daily work I walk by faith and not by sight. My tools and materials are atoms and molecules, things no one has ever seen, and no one can see. Every act is carried on in obedience to natural laws, for which I know no reason; but if I should lose faith in them, it would be at the risk of my life. In this, however, I am doing no more and no less than every one else. Every one who lives must put constant faith in the laws of nature. Unwavering, unquestioning faith, for nobody knows much about the natural forces which he nevertheless is compelled to put faith in.

I. THE DISTINCTION BETWEEN FAITH AND BELIEF

BELIEF is purely an intellectual process. Faith involves action. The scientist must put faith in many things he does not believe. He does not believe that two parallel lines meet. He does not believe that a circle is made up of a lot of straight lines. He does not believe in the square root of minus one. He does not believe that ether is harder than steel and softer than air. But he has faith in these because, by using them, he is able to carry his calculations to correct conclusions.

The chemist believes that one hundred years ago Faraday discovered benzene. But suppose that this is not actually true. It would make little difference as far as chemistry is concerned; for we have benzene, and it is rendering a service to life. Faith

[1] By Edwin E. Slosson in "Sermons of a Chemist." Harcourt, Brace.

in its use is quite separate from the belief in the act of the discoverer. On the other hand, if a chemist thinks he can make a new compound out of benzene by adding something to it, that is faith. It can hardly be belief, for it has not actually happened. But he has faith in the unseen venture.

II. FAITH IN GOD

Faith in God runs parallel to faith in natural laws. We may believe many things about God. But when we walk, we walk by faith.

"Faith is the courage of the spirit which projects itself forward, sure of finding the truth." (Thomas Aquinas.)

Our social life is a commentary on faith. It would be as impossible to live with men without faith as it would be impossible to breath if one did not have faith in the air.

Our national life is a commentary on faith.

By faith Columbus set out in an open boat to go around the unknown world.

By faith the Pilgrim Fathers dared the Atlantic.

By faith Washington took up arms against a great empire.

By faith Jefferson bought land where millions now live.

By faith Christian missionaries went to the cannibal islands and gave us Hawaii.

What is there that cannot be accomplished by faith? The Bible says, Nothing.

THE OLD-TIME RELIGION [1]

By faith Abraham went forth, although he did not know where he was to go. Hebrews 11: 8 (Moffatt).
Let my people go. Exodus 5: 1.

THE man who clamors for the old-time religion is asking for something which is not as old as he thinks it is. He usually refers to a type of faith which does not go back of 1850. With this type of people the sighing for the old-time religion is a *delusion*. If he means the belief in verbal inspiration of the Scriptures, he is really asking for a newfangled idea. The attitude of mind is somewhat like that of the old lady who protested against the use of stained glass windows because she preferred the glass just as God made it.

Then that cry is usually an *invasion*. Folks seeking to invade the searching inquiries of the modern social interpretation of the old gospel, cry for the old-time religion which did not interfere with business. But real religion always did. But the greatest charge that one can bring against this cry is that it is a *repression of to-day's new insight*.

It has been pointed out by George Adam Smith that the kingdom of God is not obstructed by being blown up, but by being sat upon. The most effective way of sitting upon the kingdom of God to-day is to begin to sing about the old-time religion.

I. THE OLD-TIME RELIGION IS THE RELIGION OF ABRAHAM—A RELIGION OF INTELLECTUAL AND SPIRITUAL DARING

The old-time religion of his day was not good enough for Abraham. He traveled far away from his homeland to find one good enough. Abraham was one of these adventurers who make

[1] By Halford E. Luccock in "The Haunted House and Other Sermons." Copyright, 1923. Used by permission of the Abingdon Press.

history. Without such men and women there would be no history at all. These men have not been satisfied with the past. Jesus was the most reckless innovator of them all. "Ye have heard it said of old, ... but I say unto you."

"Humanity has struck its tents and is on the march." (General Smuts.)

"The dogmas of the quiet past are inadequate to the stormy present. The occasion is piled high with difficulty and we must rise to the occasion. As our case is new, so we must think anew and act anew." (Abraham Lincoln.)

II. THE OLD-TIME RELIGION WAS THE RELIGION OF MOSES—A RELIGION OF SOCIAL REVOLUTION

"Revolution" is a strong word. But it is required to explain the religion of Moses. After the vision in the wilderness Moses was not satisfied with conventional things in religion. He learned that the will of God meant the release from bondage for millions of toilers.

"The old-time religion." Let us have it. Let us put it in industry. It will sound like the crack of doom to certain industrialists and profiteers. Let the old-time religion—the religion of Moses—say what it has to say about social injustices. Then we shall know the power of religion in the world. The real old-time religion ends at the feet of Jesus. It is the religion of active, sacrificing love.

JESUS THE PIONEER [1]

Looking unto Jesus the Pioneer. Hebrews 12: 2.

THE text is from the Moffatt translation. The word "pioneer" makes us think at once of the restlessness of the Christian spirit. The Christians in the best sense are pilgrims. They are always looking for fairer cities ahead. Neither the City of Destruction nor the City of Vanity Fair can stop them.

> "One army of the living God,
>   To his command we bow;
> Part of his host have crossed the flood,
>   And part are crossing now."

I. JESUS WAS A PIONEER OF PURE LIFE

Jesus lived a sinless life. Now we are talking about sin, and I know that some people think it is old-fashioned. There is a philosophy abroad to-day that we are animals and might as well recognize it and cater to the animal qualities. It isn't new. Ever since there have been men there have been recurrent periods of animality. But the contemporaries of Jesus, at least some of them, were much more successful than we are to-day. They murdered better than we do. We cannot equal the general callousness of the Romans of the period of Jesus.

These people of the olden days surpassed us. We cannot recover that unashamed animality. And we cannot simply because Jesus was a pioneer of a pure life.

II. JESUS WAS A PIONEER OF AN ENDURING LIFE

"I have meat that ye know naught of," he told his disciples. He had the ability to keep his mind on spiritual issues.

"Steadily endured" is a phrase which characterizes Chris-

[1] By Umphrey Lee in "Jesus the Pioneer." Cokesbury Press.

tians. It tells a story of those who had the secret of spiritual life.

An old chronicler tells of a girdle-maker and a shoe-maker who were burned at Salzburg. "They lived long," he writes, "and cried so unceasingly to God that it was pitiful to hear." But they didn't recant, mind you. They never took anything back. They endured. . . . That is what faith is, the conviction of an unseen world, of unprovable values, of a future so wonderful that for it one can endure the lesser afflictions of the moment.

III. JESUS WAS THE PIONEER OF OUR SALVATION

Men have always tried to explain what Jesus meant to the world in his deepest significance, and they have always used the terms of their own times. They have talked about punishment and pardon, when punishment and pardon are much in the minds of men. They have talked about the majesty of God's moral government, when governmental problems were to the fore. But always men have been trying to account for a conviction that somehow Jesus has broken a way through to a freer, more abundant life, and has made for us an entrance into the Eternal City whose builder and maker is God.

Jesus is the pioneer. After him we must come in a small way. But as his followers we will try and walk these paths he has opened. There is the pathway of the pure life, the pathway of enduring life, and the pathway of salvation. And these we will open to others.

THE CITY TO COME [1]

For here have we no continuing city, but we seek one to come.
Hebrews 13: 14.

THE dream of the perfect city has long rested with seers and saints. To the modern practical-minded man it seems impossible, perhaps. It is because it finds it hard to build a city, even of dreams, with unseen realities.

There are always two things which enter into this city of dreams. The first is, of course, the hope of immortality. As long as men continue to grow old they will dream of the city of immortality where their youth may be renewed. The second is the return of Jesus. In its cruder form the expectation is for bodily return. But in the higher form it is the expectation for the city built on the ideas of Jesus.

I. IN THIS CITY THERE IS THE CHRISTIAN SCHEME OF VALUES

There will be neither bond nor free. The early Christians knew no social distinctions. In their groups there were rich and poor, bond and free. While they knew nothing of social problems which worry us to-day, they did bequeath to us a respect for the social principles upon which our Christian city is to be established.

In that city the beatitudes of our Lord will be realized, and the gentle-hearted and peacemakers and steadfast of soul, who are here persecuted for righteousness' sake, will come to their own.

II. THERE WILL BE A FIDELITY OF MORAL DISTINCTIONS

The good and bad are to be separated, for the New Jerusalem is to be also the Judgment Seat. What this means practically

[1] By Umphrey Lee in "Jesus the Pioneer." Cokesbury Press.

may be realized by the student of religious history. Professor Glover, for instance, points out that the old Scottish Christianity owed much of its ruggedness of character to the prominence of this doctrine.

The doctrine of the judgment is a great adventure in faith. It is a venture in faith of the morality of the universe. Christianity affirms that the good will be separated from the bad, that the beggar of to-day may be with his Lord to-morrow. It affirms that other distinctions—tongues, knowledge, beauty, and power—may pass away, but justice remains.

III. IT WILL BE A CITY OF PROFOUND OPTIMISM

This spiritual optimism, for some reason, has been able to survive all of the periods of despondency and depression. Things have never been so dark but that the Christian has looked forward to the New Jerusalem. The dream is not one of building a city by social forces. It is to be built by the power of God.

"If God be for us, who can be against us?"

"Men were not to imagine that they were left to themselves to plan out a better world and forward it as best they might. They were to think of themselves as working toward a fulfillment of what God had ordained. They were to answer every call to noble endeavor with the uplifting sense that the power which directs all things is on their side." (E. F. Scott.)

"O sweet and blessed country, the home of God's elect!
O sweet and blessed country that eager hearts expect!
Jesus, in mercy bring us to that dear land of rest;
Who art, with God the Father, and Spirit, ever blest."

WHO ARE THE BLESSED?[1]

Behold, we count them blessed that endure. James 5: 11.

We have been thinking of our own personal complaints. There is something in our lives which chaffs and frets, and we are confident that we could live better if only we could be delivered from it.

I. ALL OUR HEROES AND HEROINES HAVE BEEN ENDURERS

THERE are other folks whom we have called "lucky." But we have not made these the idols of our lives. They have seemed more like marionettes moved by hidden forces. We have envied the rich rather than admired them. They also are but chessmen upon the board. But there are some we remember. They were the heroes of our childhood books. What book hero ever lived life from a soft chair? The very romance of the story was that which told of his enduring to the end. And then a little later we had our heroes of school athletics. They were not the boys who were afraid of the knocks. They were the sturdy ones who could endure to the end. And now we are grown up. We still have our heroes in business, social, and public life. We follow the reasoning of our childhood days. Our heroes are still those who endure.

II. WE AND THEY

Yes, this applies to ourselves as well as to others. Most of us are better judges of others than we are of ourselves. How true this is in spiritual qualities. We count "them blessed that endure." Shall we not as well count ourselves blessed as we endure?

[1] By Frank W. Norwood in "The Gospel of the Larger World." Doran.

We admire endurance when we see it in others; let us emulate it for ourselves. We admire unselfishness when we see it in another, but in ourselves we are prone to be selfish.

We do not know, we cannot realize, how the battle honestly fought in secret, how the burden firmly borne where no eye seemed to see, gives a tone and quality to life and to influence which nothing else can give.

III. HE COUNTS THEM BLESSED THAT ENDURE

This is another pronoun. And a great one. If you read the thirty-seventh Psalm, you will note how it is suggested that the good will always be delivered and the bad punished. (Dr. Norwood read this Psalm for the Scripture lesson.) It is a very fundamental idea, but naïve. It doesn't always work out that way in life. There is a difference between the kind of blessedness of the Old Testament, that kind where a man is always expected to win in the end, and the beatitudes of Jesus.

Personally, I have always wished that the closing words of the book of Job had been lost. I am very glad that the patriarch got his camels and sheep; he deserved to have them better than most people I have read of. But to balance his great spiritual experience by a stockyard has something tragic in it.

God counts you blessed now that you are enduring. And his verdict coincides with my own most manly conviction. We also hold those blessed that endure.

FIVE WRONG IDEAS ABOUT GOD [1]

The God and Father of our Lord Jesus Christ. 1 Peter 1: 3.

THERE are some people who do not like to think about God. But Jesus did. He was ever thinking and talking about him. Those who do not like to think about him usually have a wrong idea about him. Those who learn Jesus' idea of God will like to keep him constantly in mind. Let us see what some of the wrong conceptions folks have are.

I. IT IS WRONG TO THINK OF HIM AS AN ABSENT GOD

Jesus did his best to help people to see that God is very near. He has been in the world ever since he made it. He did not go away. He dwells in the heart of every one of his children. It is never necessary to tell him anything in order to inform him, because he knows it all before one can speak.

II. IT IS WRONG TO THINK OF HIM AS AN UNKNOWABLE GOD

It is true that men have invented many long and un-understandable terms for God. But Jesus threw all these aside and called him "Father." And he told men that, when they spoke or prayed to him, they should call him Father. Every one knows what a father is like. A father is interested in his children. He feeds and clothes them and protects them. Jesus said that God was just like a father in these respects.

III. IT IS WRONG TO THINK OF GOD AS A SOLEMN GOD

In olden days, before Jesus, many made this mistake. They thought of God as a stern lawgiver who demanded justice and was peeved if men did not respect him. One draws away from such a man. But Jesus gave a different picture. He liked to

---

[1] By Charles E. Jefferson in "Under Seventeen." Revell.

think about God's love and kindness. He thought of the sunshine and the showers, and knew that God was good because he
sent these. He thought of his kindness to the birds. He even
said that not a single sparrow could fall without God knowing
it.

IV. IT IS WRONG TO THINK OF GOD AS BEING TOO BUSY TO THINK ABOUT COMMON PEOPLE

There are so many people that some men cannot see how God
can care for each one. Of course, they thought, he might be
interested in the great men. But could he be bothered with the
common people? But Jesus was sure that God cares for each
person. To show how he did care he told the story of the lost
sheep. The shepherd was not satisfied until he brought the lost
sheep back to the fold.

V. IT IS WRONG TO THINK OF GOD AS A VENGEFUL GOD

Some even went so far as to show that God got pleasure out
of making men suffer for their sins. But Jesus did not tell of
that kind of God. He told of a God who holds no grudges. He
thought of one who loves to forgive when the sinner really
seeks forgiveness. Certainly God will go farther than a shepherd in recovering his sheep. For this noblest conception of
God take the story that Jesus told of the prodigal son.

THE CHRISTIAN BROTHERHOOD [1]

Love the brotherhood. 1 Peter 2: 17.

In his sermon at Athens, Paul declared that God "hath made of one blood all nations of men for to dwell on all the face of the earth." Although there are many superficial differences, and some differences which are not superficial, there is a common substratum of humanity that makes the whole world kin.

"There is nothing of concern to humanity that is not also a concern to me." (Terence.)

THE two great social doctrines of Christianity are the Fatherhood of God and the Brotherhood of Man.

I. LOVE IN THE BROTHERHOOD IS TO BE INTENSIVE THAT IT MAY BECOME EXTENSIVE

One on reading this text may feel, at first, that Peter is dealing with small things when he should be concerned with great things. Instead of talking of the brotherhood of man, he is concerned with a narrow group. But for the realization of brotherhood a quality greater than human love is required. It takes redeeming love. It is a little too much to ask that all society at this stage of human experience possess redeeming love. But it is practicable that in the Brotherhood itself this love exist.

The New Testament contains two Greek words which show this.

II. PHILANTHROPIA

This is made up of two words meaning "love" and "man." Our word "philanthropy" is derived from it. *Philanthropia* is

[1] By Gilbert T. Rowe in "The Southern Methodist Pulpit." Cokesbury Press.

a widespread affection. It is the impulse which prompts one person to supply another with a match or to give a traveler needed information. The Chinese possess this quality to a marked degree. Philanthropia is genial. It is the common politeness which makes human associations smooth. When the village mill owner, who has grown rich with custom, decides to pave the streets of his village to enrich the lives of his employees, it is *philanthropia*. But if the people misinterpret his motives and accuse him of trying to blind their eyes that they may not see his stealing, he is apt to forget his good intentions and declare that, since he is not appreciated, he will not do this thing.

III. PHILADELPHIA

This word is also made from two Greek words. One means "love" and the other "brother." *Philadelphia* has an intensity which *philanthropia* does not possess. It believeth all things, hopeth all things, endureth all things.

Such is the love which should reign in the heart of the Church. Yet it does not always reign in the Church. The tie which should bind all Christians together has been weakened by unbrotherly conduct. This is one of the tragedies of organized Christianity. Trying to found the brotherhood on *philanthropia* is not successful. It must have redeeming, sacrificial love.

THE ONLY PERMANENCE [1]

He that doeth the will of God abideth forever. 1 John 2: 17.

The Christian life is not merely meditative or contemplative, but active. Christ did not lay stress on mere believing of truth, except as the necessary foundation for the building of character. Deeds rather than creeds are to express the faith of those who follow him, and it is by misplaced emphasis on the latter that the Church has weakened her witness, often to the point of discredit.

I. THERE ARE EXTERNAL POSSIBILITIES FOR GOOD IN EVERY LIFE

You have seen a stone dropped into the quiet waters of a lake. Little ripples circle from the center. That is a very feeble presentation of our actions in God's eternity. Even when the workers rest from their tasks, their works do follow them. It is not difficult to find illustrations of those in humble circumstances who have realized great possibilities of good. There was a young man in a Chicago shoe store. But he caught a vision of life. As a result the name of Dwight L. Moody is to-day known around the world.

We are training now for unending obedience, and our present energies are but creating and developing those qualities and capacities which shall fit us to take share in Heaven's service.

II. DAILY LIVING DEMANDS A WHOLE-HEARTED SURRENDER TO GOD

No matter what his position in life, one does not do his part of the work of the Kingdom unless he gives himself wholeheartedly to the task.

"This one thing I do."

[1] By J. Stuart Holden in "Redeeming Vision." Revell.

His will is imperious in its demands, and his love will brook no rival. In the constitutional government of our country, while the king is nominally supreme, many of the acts of government are really due to the Prime Minister. And it is often so in individual lives. We call Christ "Lord," but at the same time seek to be our own Prime Ministers, merely submitting our plans to him for approval and often not waiting sufficiently long for him to express disapproval. . . . "No man can serve two masters," even though the second one is self. Concentration is the expression of consecration, and is a large part of the determination of all spiritual success.

III. WILLINGNESS TO DO GOD'S WILL MEANS A CONSECRATED EFFORT TO LEARN THE WILL OF GOD

No earthly parent would make his wishes obscure and at the same time expect his child to carry them out. Human affection is but a reflection of the love of God. An absolute obedience to God means enlightened vision and empowered action.

"Whatsoever He saith unto you, do it."

> "The strong man's strength to toil for Christ,
>   The fervent preacher's skill,
> I sometimes wished; but better far
>   To be just what God will.
>
> I know not how this languid life
>   May life's vast aims fulfill;
> He knows! and that life is not lost
>   That answers best his will.
>
> No service in itself is small,
>   None great, though earth it fill;
> But that is small that seeks its own,
>   That great that seeks God's will.
>
> Then hold my hand, most blessed Lord,
>   Guide all my goings still,
> And let this be my life's one aim:
>   To do, or bear, thy will."

THE BATTLE OF LIFE [1]

To him that overcometh will I grant to sit with me in my throne.
Revelation 3: 21.

Life in its essence means striving, struggle, and in the end either victory or defeat.

I. THE BATTLE FOR PHYSICAL EXISTENCE

IT begins with the first days of life with the child. One disease after another crowds and seeks to crush the little life. And it ends only when finally death has been made the victor. Sometimes we see it in the life of the young man as he fights the disease settling upon him. Again we see it in middle life, the most dangerous of all physical ages. And then again it is in the life of the aged.

II. THE BATTLE FOR FAME

The annals of political history are full of these struggles. Burr comes within one vote of defeating Jefferson for the Presidency, but that one vote seals his career. James G. Blaine misses the goal of a lifetime's strenuous activity as the result of a chance remark of an obscure clergyman. From the past we learn that this struggle has always interested men. Their names may be forgotten, but their ambition for fame controlled their lives.

III. THE BATTLE FOR HEROISM

This takes us to a higher sphere. The true hero is not concerned for his fame. He is mightily concerned that the principle for which he stands shall triumph. Said Savonarola when he was told that the order of the Pope separated him from the Church militant and triumphant: "From the Church triumphant, no! For the other I do not care."

[1] By Frederick D. Kershner in "Sermons for Special Days." Doran.

IV. THE BATTLE FOR INDIVIDUAL CHARACTER

Every man and woman is engaged, day by day, in a ceaseless battle to perpetuate the moral life. The supreme teachers of life have always emphasized that life is a struggle. They have taught that purity and nobility are qualities which are won by a struggle. Only the superficial and shallow interpreters of reality speak of the easy road to virtue.

V. THE FATE OF THE SLACKER

In the battle for character, victory is always possible. In the external world it is sometimes true that circumstances over which we have no control prevent us from achieving success. But in the world of character we occasionally find that men and women are not fighting. They think that it is not worth while. There is but one unpardonable sin in the world, and that is the sin of ceasing to want to be better than you are. The slacker will suffer and feel the biting lash of sin.

VI. THE LESSON FOR THE NEW YEAR

Robert Browning, in his somewhat difficult and yet fascinatingly vivid interpretation of "Childe Roland to the Dark Tower Came," has taught the significance of courage and fidelity even under the most unfavorable circumstances.

> "Heaven is not reached at a single bound,
> But we build the ladder by which we rise
> From the lowly earth to the vaulted skies
> And we mount to its summit round by round."

LIFE'S LIBRARY [1]

And the books were opened. Revelation 20: 12.

My childish daydream was to be a writer broadcasting truth to the uttermost fringe of the earth. I earnestly coveted the prerogatives of authorship and longed for the opportunities which never came. I fancied that the only class of people capable of making and leaving impressions were gifted writers and eloquent speakers—a kind of super-race of celebrities, few and intermittent.

I. WE ARE ALL WRITING BOOKS

I HAVE written forty of them. Every word, thought, and action is recorded in this biography. And as much as I might wish it, not a line can be blotted out. Others are doing and have done the same. There are all kinds of books on many subjects. Reviewing them pays. Go over these books which record the past and see what they picture in advice for to-day. Most of them tell of failures to come to that glory we desired.

"I came to my teacher with a quivering lip,
My task undone;
'Master, give me another sheet,
I have spoiled this one.'

In place of the old sheet stained and blotted,
He gave me a new one, clean, unspotted,
And into my glad face smiled:
Do better next time, my child.'

I went to the Throne with a quivering heart,
The Old Year done;
'Father, hast thou another chance for me?
I have lost this one.'

He took the Old Year stained and blotted,
And gave me a New one clean, unspotted,
Then down into my sad heart smiled,
'Do better next time, my child.' "

II. WE ARE THE EPISTLES OF GOD

"Ye are our epistles, written in our hearts, known and read of all men." Thus, St. Paul wrote to the Church at Corinth.

[1] By S. R. Bratcher in "Advertising Jesus." Cokesbury Press.

He meant that as we walk down the street, drive along the high-way, write at our desk, sing in the choir, or even read or pray, folks are reading us. We are the books.

"For wealth and wisdom look within." (Portia, in "Merchant of Venice.")

This is true in life's library. Many cheap books are bound in expensive covers. On the other hand, some most valuable books have cheap covers. The analogy should be clear. The clothes do not make the man.

> "He wrote no words save on the sand
>   Long centuries ago,
> And one would think that what he said
>   Like sand would drift and blow;
> But he knew well the surest way:
>   He made his love a pen
> And wrote his message ever more
>   Upon the hearts of men."
>
> (A. W. Peak.)

III. THE BOOKS ARE TO BE OPENED

We are not alone living epistles, but our eternal reward will depend upon what the books reveal when they are opened. The New Testament warns us that every word and every thought will come to judgment. If our sins still live in the pages of these biographies, we shall be condemned. But if they have been blotted out, we shall live.

At the beginning of a new year is the time to plan to make the new book clean. Let our failures rest in the past, but resolve that the new volume is one which we may bring with joy to our makers.

THE APOSTLES' CREED [1]

I believe

BACK of us—not very far back, perhaps—lies a period in which Christians commonly knew what they believed. They placed that belief in a creed which probably was as good a statement of the common belief as it was possible to make. It is known as the Apostles' Creed. There is still a very great need for belief and a vital living out of the beliefs. In some ways, we think that we have outgrown the creed. Perhaps we feel that with some of its affirmations we are out of sympathy. But its great affirmations still represent about the best statement of Christian faith for every body of believers. We use this creed in our services. Let us see what it signifies.

I. THE USE OF THE CREED IS AN ACT OF WORSHIP

Some are under the delusion that in joining in the creed they are submitting to some theological test. That is far from the truth. It is contrary to the very spirit of Protestantism to lay close-fitting formulas for her people to walk in.

There are some, perhaps, who ought not to repeat the creed. If they have thought out their own faith, and it runs contrary to the words, it is well that they keep silent. But because, somewhere, incidental phrases or words or ideas appear in the creed which are not a part of his personal faith, the rejection of the whole is senseless. The creed should be recited with the same freedom with which the hymns are sung. One does not ordinarily refuse to sing a verse with which he is theologically unsympathetic. Nor does he hesitate to read a Psalm which con-

[1] By William P. Merrill in "The Common Creed of Christians." Revell.

flicts with some of his ideas. The Creed, like the Hymn and the Psalm, is a part of worship.

II. THE CREED EXPRESSES THE GREAT UNITIES OF THE FAITH

Probably the creed is not what you would write to-day if you were to express the beliefs of Christian people. That Jesus was born of a certain woman, whose name is given, and was put to death by a Roman governor, whose name is also given, seemed important to those who formed the creed, and it is important for us also. It is putting emphasis on the personality of this Jesus. "Who was," "He descended," "He shall come"—these statements are the emphasis on the person. And there are the mighty affirmations: "I believe in the Holy Ghost, the holy catholic Church."

> Taken with the freedom with which the Christian has the right and duty to take all things, "the freedom with which Christ has made us free," this ancient creed is a great, strong, noble expression of vital truths on which the whole structure of Christianity and the Christian Church rests, the best, the only practical statement of common faith. . . . One has a defective Christian experience who does not believe, definitely, strongly, really, in God our Father, in Christ our Lord, in the Holy Spirit, in the one Christian Church, in the forgiveness of sins, and in life eternal. It is good for the Church, as a body, to rise and say, "This is what we stand for."

MY GOSPEL [1]

According to my gospel. A frequent saying of St. Paul's.

There is all the difference in the world between a religion and a gospel. Religions are as thick as autumn leaves. Almost every man is compelled to shape one for himself, in which traditional and personal elements may be strangely mingled. But not every religion could be called a gospel. Indeed, broadly speaking, that title is reserved for the Christian faith.

I. CHRISTIANITY DID NOT APPEAR TO THE WORLD AS A NEW RELIGION, BUT AS "GLAD TIDINGS"

In no particular did Jesus break with the ancient faith of the Jews. He kept the Sabbath, worshiped in the synagogues, and in every particular observed the law. But he had a message which far transcended Judaism. To keep the gospel within the historic faith of his fathers was like keeping new wine in old bottles. The good news cannot be confined to sectarianism or nationalism.

Life is always changing. There is human sorrow to-day as in the days of Jesus. We have all the creeds we need. But there is a vital need for a reinterpretation of the creeds to give place to the gospel. Good will is needed. Men need to know that God loves them.

II. THE STORY OF THE GOOD NEWS

It is the long story of how God loved man and sought after him. He watched mankind grow to consciousness—when he could discern between good and evil. Then man dreamed of God's help. He discovers that help comes from within. God

[1] By Frank W. Norwood in "If I Had But One Sermon to Preach." Harper.

is within rather than without. Man finds his greatest help, outside of the God within himself, in spirit-filled men.

Then God sends his prophets. The purer the prophet, the more help he can be to man. So he finally sends the purest and best of the prophets. We know him as Jesus. He was the world's true saint. He was so holy and pure that he said that he was one with God. And knowing his character, we believe him.

But what happened?

This! The age-long conflict is precipitated. Evil comes to a maximum of badness. Good comes to its supreme demonstration as a spiritual force. Evil clenches its fist and smites at the face of God in him. The Spirit of God is triumphant in the dark hour.

> "O love of God, O sin of man,
> In this dread hour thy strength was tried.
> And victory remains with love!
> Jesus, our Lord, was crucified."

It is the atonement, the at-one-ment.

The old folk-word called the Gospel, "God's spell." That is what it really is: God's spell over man.

LIFE'S TWILIGHT PERIOD [1]

Bible Basis is the story of Naomi

There have been a thousand sermons preached for the guidance of youth, for every one directed to the needs of old age, while middle age is scarcely recognizable as a distinct region in homiletic literature. No doubt it is a territory somewhat hard to define. Speaking arithmetically, I suppose it ought to be about the age of thirty-five, but he would be socially impertinent who assumed that by merely halving the figure seventy the territory of middle age was placed beyond dispute. . . . Many practical as well as sentimental considerations dispose us to advance the line nearer to the setting sun.

I. MIDDLE AGE IS THAT PERIOD IN LIFE WHEN FAILURE, SHOULD IT COME, SEEMS ABSOLUTE

For this reason it seems to be the most critical period of life. At thirty-five recovery is possible; at fifty-five, or a little later, resignation begins to be appropriate; but somewhere between these two lines it is too early to fail, but too late to recover.

Youth has its hopes, old age its memories, but middle age is life's twilight period when hopes remain, but are not enough to see by, and memories are too recent and acute to induce repose.

II. FOR NAOMI THE PERIOD WAS ONE WITHOUT HOPE

When she returned to Bethlehem, even her friends looked at her carefully to make sure it was she. Had she been young, there would have been hope. Had she been aged, she would have had reverence and remembrance. But in the twilight of life what was there?

[1] By Frank W. Norwood in "The Gospel of the Larger World." Doran.

Had she gone back in prosperity, they would have rejoiced to have remembered her. In her pain she preferred to be forgotten. Her own words reveal the thought of her heart. "Call me not Naomi [pleasant], call me Mara [bitter]; for the Almighty hath dealt very bitterly with me. I went out full, and the Lord hath brought me home again empty: why then call ye me Naomi?"

III. THE MIDDLE YEARS ARE THE YEARS OF SELF-REVELATION

Youth was too busy to take notice. Age will be too kindly to remember. But life's interpreter is near the middle of the journey. Youth can recover. Age can forget. The meaning of life lies halfway. Youth lives with the future. Age lives with the past. Middle ages face the reality of the present.

I have watched life with observant eyes, and I am no longer surprised when men and women suddenly break midway through life. The neighbors say: "Is this So-and-So? We had thought he was settled in his ways, staid and respectable, and lo, he has suddenly succumbed."

IV. YET NAOMI WAS WRONG

To have brought back from Moab a spirit such as hers was greater than to have brought back a fortune. It is not failure to lose a fortune if one keeps his soul. It is not failure to see a gossamer faith fail, but one based on rugged realities to take its place.

To have gone out full, and to have returned empty, may set the neighbors gossiping, but to have kept one's soul and to have kept one's God is to have lost only the emptiness and to have kept the fullness of life.

And later:

"There is a son born to Naomi."

"And they called his name Obed: he is the father of Jesse, the father of David."

THE SKEPTICISM OF JESUS [1]

THE word "skeptic" in its original meaning is a noble word. It comes from the Greek *skeptikos,* which means a thoughtful, reflective person. Its verbal form is *skeptesthai,* which means "To look carefully, to look about, to view, to consider."

I. JESUS AS AN OBSERVER

Jesus was a close observer of human life. His words show us a very keen insight into the humanity of his day. He explored the recesses of heart and mind. He saw the jobless man in the market place, the children playing in the street, the Pharisee who paraded his virtues in public, the woman who lost a coin, and other intimate things.

He was a close observer of nature in field, sky, and sea. He saw the raven and the eagle, the shining fish in the sea. He watched the sower as he toiled and drew a parable from nature. He knew that foxes had holes and the birds had nests.

He was a close student of literature. He did not have access to great libraries, but he knew the rabbinical works. He quotes from the Old Testament accurately, showing a knowledge of the Bible.

Surely, if skepticism means looking around, considering, Jesus was a skeptic.

II. THE SKEPTICISM OF JESUS EXPRESSED

These quotations show how he questioned the conventional thinking of his day:

"Why are ye so anxious about to-morrow?"
"Why do ye see so clearly the sins of your brethren, but fail to see your own?"

[1] By Frank W. Norwood in "The Gospel for a Larger World." Doran.

"Why do you make the Sabbath a day of gloom instead of a day of rejoicing?"

"Why do ye call upon men to fast when the bridegroom is nigh?"

"Why do ye make the market place a place of parade for the sanctities of the soul?"

"Why do ye think it is pious to dress in somber robes and wear long hair?"

"Why do ye dare supplant the word of Moses with your own traditions?"

"Why do you go about to kill me when I only tell the truth?"

"My God, my God, why hast thou forsaken me?"

III. THE SKEPTICISM OF JESUS WAS THE SKEPTICISM OF A GREAT BELIEVER

The real believer should be a real skeptic. In order to know whereof he believes he must know whereof he disapproves and disbelieves in the opposites of his religion. No man can be strong in the faith until he is strong in his unbeliefs.

The questions which Jesus asked in his day are the questions which we cannot get rid of. They still persist. They startle in New York and London as they did in Jerusalem.

THE PRAYER HABITS OF JESUS [1]

It is interesting to study the prayer habits of Jesus. In the Gospels we find recorded fifteen instances of his praying, several of them quoted by more than one writer. Given chronologically they are as follows: Luke 3: 21; Mark 1: 35; Luke 5: 16; 6: 12; Matthew 14: 23 (Mark 6: 46); Luke 9: 18; 9: 28, 29; 10: 21; 11: 1; John 18: 41, 42; 12: 27, 28; Luke 22: 41, 42; John 17; Matthew 26: 39, 44 (Mark 14: 39); Matthew 27: 46 (Mark 15: 34; Luke 24: 46).

I. HOW HE PRAYED

1. *Usually alone.* "And he withdrew himself into the wilderness, and there prayed." (Luke 5: 16.)

"And when he had sent the multitudes away, he went up into a mountain apart to pray: and when evening was come, he was there alone." (Matt. 14: 23.)

"And it came to pass, as he was alone praying." (Luke 9: 18.)

"And he was withdrawn from them about a stone's cast, and kneeled down, and prayed." (Luke 22: 41.)

2. *With others.* "And it came to pass about an eight days after these sayings, he took Peter and John and James, and went up into a mountain to pray." (Luke 9: 28.)

"In that hour Jesus rejoiced in spirit, and said, I thank thee, O Father, Lord of heaven and earth, that thou hast hid these things from the wise and prudent, and hast revealed them unto babes; even so, Father; for so it seemed good in thy sight." (Luke 10: 21.)

"And it came to pass, that, as he was praying in a certain place, when he ceased, one of his disciples said unto him, Lord, teach us to pray, as John also taught his disciples." (Luke 11: 1.)

[1] By E. P. Lanahan in *Moody Bible Institute Monthly.*

II. WHEN HE PRAYED

1. *In the early morning.* "And in the morning, rising up a great while before day, he went out, and departed into a solitary place, and there prayed." (Mark 1: 35.)

2. *All night.* "And it came to pass in those days, that he went out into a mountain to pray, and continued all night in prayer to God." (Luke 6: 12.)

3. *In great crises:* (a) *At his baptism.* "Now when all the people were baptized, it came to pass, that Jesus also being baptized and praying, the heaven was opened." (Luke 3: 21.)

(b) *At the raising of Lazarus.* "Then they took the stone from the place where the dead was laid. And Jesus lifted up his eyes, and said, Father, I thank thee that thou hast heard me. And I knew that thou hearest me always: but because of the people which stand by I said it, that they may believe that thou hast sent me." (John 11: 41, 42.)

(c) *In the garden.* "And he went a little farther, and fell on his face, and prayed, saying, O my Father, if it be possible, let this cup pass from me: nevertheless not as I will, but as thou wilt." (Matt. 26: 39.)

"He went away again the second time, and prayed, saying, O my Father, if this cup may not pass away from me, except I drink it, thy will be done." (Matt. 26: 42.)

"And he left them, and went away again, and prayed the third time, saying the same words." (Matt. 26: 44.)

(d) *On the cross.* "And about the ninth hour Jesus cried with a loud voice, Eli, Eli, lama sabachthani? that is to say, My God, my God, why hast thou forsaken me?" (Matt 27: 46.)

III. WHERE HE PRAYED

We learn from the records that he prayed most often at a great distance from everybody, choosing nearly always a quiet spot. His favorite places of prayer were the hilltops back of Nazareth, the slopes of Olivet, and the hillsides overlooking the Lake of Galilee.

WHAT IS RIGHT IN BUSINESS [1]

The habit of directing large affairs generates a nobility of thought in every mind of average ability. For affairs themselves show the way in which they should be handled, and a good head soon grows wise and does not govern too much. Emerson.

You may compare automobiles to-day with those of 1905. Then make a comparison of business. You will find that the comparisons show a striking parallel. The drivers of the automobiles of those days were men of daring and courage, but they were not very considerate of buggies and wagons. But motor cars have improved. Likewise business.

Of course business is not 100 per cent right. But business has been improving in the past twenty-five years. Our greatest difficulties of to-day are those of adjustment.

I. THE DIFFICULTY OF APPLYING RIGHT PRINCIPLES TO INCREASINGLY COMPLICATED SITUATIONS

It is not easy to determine what is right and what is wrong. Take the discount rate of the Federal Reserve Bank of New York. You may question, first, what this has to do with morality, but it has a great deal to do with it. The thing bristles with moral complications. It is not that men will act in bad faith, but that they will fail in applying the principle in a complicated situation.

When I was in Germany serving on the Dawes committee, I asked the labor leaders what we could do for them. To my surprise they suggested the stabilizing of currency. It was the paramount great moral principle.

II. WHAT IS RIGHT IN BUSINESS REQUIRES THAT THE GOLDEN RULE BE APPLIED BY MEN OF UNDERSTANDING AND KNOWLEDGE AS WELL AS CONSCIENCE

I want you to get into your mind right now, once and

[1] By Owen D. Young in "The Pew Preaches." Cokesbury Press.

SERMON HEARTS

for all, that when you discuss what is right in business the difficulty lies not in determining what is right in principle. It is rather in the application of the principle to the vast, complex problems of modern business life. If you ask me what is right in principle, I will answer that the Golden Rule supplies all in principle that business man needs; yet if you ask me to apply the Golden Rule to a bank rate, I find it exceedingly difficult to do.

There must be technicians who are able to take the Golden Rule and apply it to the complicated affairs of business. It is not the crook we have to fear. Big business does not lend itself to crooks. Instead the danger lies in the honest man who does not know.

III. THE RESPONSIBILITY OF THE MANAGERS

Once the manager was required to get results for the owners. He could do this honestly if he could; dishonestly if he had to. But he must get results. But gradually there has come the conviction that the manager is a trustee of an institution with a responsibility for administering the institution as a public utility.

He has a responsibility toward the owners, toward the employees, and toward the public he serves. For the owners he will want to so manage the business that he can get the best discount rates; for the employees he will want to so manage the business that they will think that it is a good place to work; for the public he will want to so manage the business that it will have confidence in his products. He is no longer a lawyer to defend the rights of the owners, but a trustee for an institution.

THE LAW OF RETURNS [1]

Two and two make four. Book of Numbers

Two and two make four. Never by any sort of bad luck
or ill chance only three and a half; never by any amount of
coaxing or stretching four and a half; but always and
everywhere just four and no more! It is a definite, absolute statement of fact. It always has been so and always
will be so. No one can imagine a world where two and
two will not make four.

Occasionally men may find a four-leaf clover, but the
clover which makes the grass green, feeds the cows, supplies
the bees with honey, and fills the haymow is the three-leaf
clover.

I. TWO AND TWO MAKE FOUR IN THE REALM OF PHYSICAL HEALTH

EVERY individual owes it to himself and the world to keep
his body in good health. No man can do the most in his profession or calling unless his body is strong. Some are born
with a good physique. But the sustaining of health is a matter
of the right intention and sound practice. The fellow who
drinks coffee by the quart until his skin is yellow cannot build
good health. Physical efficiency cannot be bought by the bottle
at the drug store. It is a matter of two by two. Good food,
but not too much. Exercise, but exercise which meets the
need. Regular hours for labor and play. These things count.

II. TWO AND TWO MAKE FOUR IN THE MENTAL REALM

It is not genius which makes men great. Real geniuses are as
scarce as four-leaf clovers. And most men of genius attribute
their success to constant plugging.

[1] By Charles Reynolds Brown in "The Cap and Gown." **Pilgrim
Press.**

"I seem to have formed the habit of observing more close-ly than many of my associates." (Agassiz.)

Darwin collected notes for twenty-two years before he pub-lished his "Origin of Species." Knowledge is power, but not that kind of knowledge which is merely a mass of information. The knowledge which is power means insight, grasp, discrimi-nation, productiveness. It is not the sole return of genius, but rather the natural return of a long life of consistent, intellectual effort.

III. TWO AND TWO MAKE FOUR IN THE MORAL REALM

Continuity counts in the moral realm as in the others. There is no justification in this for the idea often expressed that a young man can sow his wild oats and then by a mere sudden spasm begin anew as a fine and moral man. There are no short cuts to spiritual soundness. There is a penalty for planting and hoeing corn on Sunday. But it shows in the men, not the corn.

There is no shuffling or chance in the moral world. Im-pulses lead to choices; choices become habits; habits harden speedily into character, and character determines destiny. Two and two make four all the way up, all the way down, and all the way in.

INDEX OF SERMONS ANALYZED—BY AUTHORS

INDEX OF SERMON TITLES

320 SERMON HEARTS